Beyond the Royal Gaze

Beyond the Royal Gaze

CLANSHIP AND
PUBLIC HEALING
IN BUGANDA

NEIL KODESH

UNIVERSITY OF VIRGINIA PRESS *Charlottesville and London*

University of Virginia Press

© 2010 by the Rector and Visitors of the University of Virginia

All rights reserved

Printed in the United States of America on acid-free paper

First published 2010

9 8 7 6 5 4 3 2 1

Library of Congress Cataloging-in-Publication Data

Kodesh, Neil, 1974–

    Beyond the royal gaze : clanship and public healing in Buganda / Neil
Kodesh.

       p.   cm.

    Includes bibliographical references and index.

    ISBN 978-0-8139-2927-9 (cloth : alk. paper) —
ISBN 978-0-8139-2970-5 (e-book)

    1. Clans—Uganda—Buganda—History. 2. Healing—Social aspects—
Uganda—Buganda—History. 3. Healing—Political aspects—Uganda—
Buganda—History. 4. Ganda (African people)—Social life and customs.
5. Buganda—Social life and customs. 6. Buganda—Politics and
government. 7. Buganda—History—Sources. 8. Buganda—Antiquities.
9. Historical linguistics—Uganda—Buganda. 10. Ethnology—Uganda—
Buganda. I. Title.

    GN659.U3K63 2010

    967.61′01—dc22   2009035116

For Shanee

contents

ILLUSTRATIONS

acknowLeDGments

The difficult work of building communities, and the benefits derived from participating in such endeavors, lies at the heart of this book. Baganda long ago recognized the relationship between individual and community well-being, and like the actors in this story I have benefited tremendously from the support of several overlapping communities.

Sid Lemelle introduced me to African history as an intellectual pursuit at Pomona College, and the energy and excitement he generated in the classroom propelled me to graduate school at Northwestern University. In a stroke of good fortune, my interest in early Ganda history coincided with David Schoenbrun's arrival at Northwestern. I could not have asked for a better adviser, mentor, and now friend. David has a remarkable knack for striking the appropriate balance between guidance, critique, and encouragement. He managed to point the way forward whenever I thought I had reached a dead end, and he continues to serve as a model for how to combine intellectual rigor with a grounded sense of perspective. For this, and so much more, I owe him a tremendous debt of gratitude. At Northwestern I would also like to thank Jon Glassman for his continued support and keen analytical eye, as well as Karen Tranberg Hansen and Bill Hanks for introducing me to the world of anthropology.

I am grateful to the Uganda National Council for Science and Technology for permission to conduct research in Uganda and to the Makerere Institute of Social Research for providing institutional affiliation. Funding for research in Uganda was provided by the Social Science Research Council, the International Institute of Education, the Academy for Educational Development, and the Graduate School at the University of Wisconsin–Madison. Dissertation write-up funds were provided by the Graduate School at Northwestern University and the Woodrow Wilson National Fellowship Foundation. The Institute for Research in the Humanities at the University of Wisconsin–Madison provided release from teaching in spring 2008 so that I could work on revisions of the book manuscript.

I am indebted to countless people in Uganda for both facilitating my research and extending the sort of hospitality that made my stays there such a wonderful experience. At Bulange, I would like to thank D. L. Serunyiga Kasolo and John Sserwanga for enduring my constant visits and continuous pestering. Too many people to acknowledge took too much of their time to discuss the histories of their clans, accompany me to clan estates and other significant sites, and teach me about Ganda healing practices. I am particularly grateful, however, to George William Kalule, Kawooya Bakazirwendo, Peter Lukoma, Lukoda Wamala Kaggwa, and Walusimbi Benedicto for their generosity in this respect. Medi Mayanja and Hakim Mayanja provided much needed assistance at the front and back ends of my research period in Uganda. None of the research that informs this book, however, would have been possible without the support of Musa Lwanga Mayanja. I will always cherish the many, many hours we spent learning from each other as we learned about Buganda. His companionship, intellectual instincts, and superb translation skills proved invaluable throughout my stay in Uganda. I am grateful to Wasswa Ddamulira for introducing me to both the Luganda language and Hamidah Ddamulira, who from the moment we met her proved a true friend. I would also like to express thanks to Jag and Smita Joshi for their hospitality and to Agnes Lupo and Lawrence Okwong, who never failed to make us laugh and ensured that the time we spent in Uganda, and in particular at Plot 90 Kira Road, was more enjoyable than I could ever have imagined.

I owe a debt of gratitude to colleagues who have read and commented on various parts of the manuscript: Florence Bernault, Kate de Luna, Shane Doyle, Jon Glassman, Holly Hanson, Fran Hirsch, Kairn Klieman, David McDonald, Tony Michels, David Newbury, Jennifer Ratner-Rosenhagen, David Schoenbrun, Ed Steinhart, Rhiannon Stephens, Jim Sweet, and the participants in the University of Wisconsin–Madison/Northwestern University African History Workshops. I am particularly grateful to Tom Spear and Jan Vansina for their careful reading of my dissertation and their suggestions for transforming it into a book manuscript. John Rowe and Henri Médard generously provided copies of invaluable sources. I thank the staff at the University of Virginia, particularly Dick Holway, Raennah Mitchell, and Mark Mones, for their assistance throughout the publication process, and I thank Joanne Allen for her valuable editorial support. I am grateful to Tanya Buckingam, at the Cartography Lab at the University of Wisconsin–Madison, for creating the maps that appear in this book. Parts of chapter 2 appeared in "History from the Healer's Shrine: Genre, Historical Imagination, and Early Ganda History," *Comparative Studies in Society and History* 49 (July 2007): 527–52, and parts of chapter 3 appeared in "Networks of Knowledge: Clanship and Collective Well-Being in Buganda," *Journal of African History* 49 (July

2008): 197–216; these are reprinted with the permission of Cambridge University Press.

Finally, this book could not have been completed without the continuing support of my family. I thank my parents for providing me with a world of opportunities and my brothers for offering the sort of unquestioned assurance and encouragement one always hopes to receive from siblings. Most important of all has been Shanee. It is common for scholars of seemingly faraway places to thank loved ones for enduring long periods of separation during the research process. Such was never the case for us. We have been together every step of the way, and I honestly could not have imagined it otherwise. Life without her is simply unthinkable. And with the recent arrival of little Morris, the future seems more exciting than ever. For everything, I dedicate this book to her.

a note on Ganda names

Most full Ganda names usually include a Christian or Muslim name, a clan name, and a family name. These names are preceded, when appropriate, by an honorific title such as Nnalongo (Mother of Twins), Ssalongo (Father of Twins), or Hajji (a title bestowed upon Muslim men who have made the pilgrimage to Mecca). The order in which Baganda presented these names to me, as well as the names people included when introducing themselves, varied from person to person. When referencing these conversations, I have therefore cited names in the form in which they were presented to me by each person.

One additional point about names deserves mention. Doubled consonants have a heavy sound in Luganda, in contrast to single consonants, which have a soft sound. While this distinction is often significant, early writers tended to ignore it. For example, the well-known Ganda prime minister Apolo Kaggwa, who is mentioned frequently throughout this book, spelled his name Kagwa. While I retain this spelling in citations and in the bibliographic entries, I use the now widely accepted form Kaggwa in the text.

Beyond the Royal Gaze

1

"That is where we gather to beat the drums and call the spirits," explained Ssalongo Benedicto Walusimbi, a healer and prominent member of the Civet Cat clan, referring to the sacred site, or *kiggwa* (pl. *biggwa*), located on the clan's principal estate. "The existence of a *kiggwa* is very important in Buganda," he continued, "because it is where people who believe in their totems [clans] meet." He then elaborated by describing how clan members gather at the *kiggwa* to "talk about the past" and to "feast, drink, beat drums, and sing and dance in order to praise the spirits for having kept us alive." In the past, many *biggwa* included a large conical shrine that housed a clan's most prominent spirits for similar public gatherings, during which clan members engaged in ceremonies designed to ensure their collective well-being and provide relief from collective problems such as famine, epidemics, and warfare. Yet these days—and most likely in the past as well, judging from early twentieth-century ethnographies—*biggwa* also function as places where individuals seek cures for conditions such as madness, epilepsy, and infertility, all of which, according to Walusimbi, are "usually linked to the spirits of your clan."[1]

A series of shrines located on secondary clan estates and individual homesteads provide the links connecting individual searches for treatment and the collective endeavors undertaken at *biggwa* situated on primary clan estates. Individuals who fall sick or experience difficulties in their personal relationships might first approach a shrine for relief. If these efforts prove unsuccessful, however, they then visit the *kiggwa* to determine the cause of their problems. According to Walusimbi,

> The difference between a shrine and a *kiggwa* is the scale of operation. A shrine is operated by a single person like me to act as a place of healing. A *kiggwa* brings together many people, similar to a big hospital like

Mulago. When the shrine fails, a person is referred to the kiggwa. The kiggwa acts like a headquarters because you find very many people there from all different levels of the clan—household, lineage, patrilineage—all connecting to the kiggwa. The person who heads the shrine is appointed by the ancestral ghosts of the ancestors who operated at the shrine previously. But a person cannot operate from a shrine that does not belong to his or her clan. You construct it on your own but it has to be connected to the clan. For example, a person from the Civet Cat clan cannot operate from a shrine that belongs to the Bushbuck clan. For a person to construct a shrine he has to seek permission from the head of the kiggwa because the shrine belongs to the clan.[2]

My conversations with healers about Buganda's past revealed how the underlying logic informing individual pursuits of treatment and collective clan endeavors described by Walusimbi extends to the perceived historical relationship between Ganda clans and the kingdom's well-being. Just as a kiggwa brings together a series of shrines to promote a clan's collective health, Baganda recall the historical contributions of their respective clans in promoting the kingdom's collective health. George William Kalule, a healer and head of a lineage in the Colobus Monkey clan, captured this connection in his description of the initial encounter between Kintu, the purported founder of Buganda, and Kasujja, the original ancestor of the Colobus Monkey clan. Kalule explained that Kasujja was already settled in Buganda when Kintu arrived in the area. Upon meeting Kintu, Kasujja gave him the skin of a leopard, which would protect the incoming ruler. This leopard skin was the territorial spirit (musambwa, pl. misambwa) Mayanja, who created the Mayanja River and appears in the form of a leopard. "Kasujja told Kintu that the leopard skin was now his musambwa," Kalule recounted, "and this is why it is Mayanja who protects Buganda . . . and all its people." He then reiterated that Mayanja was once Kasujja's musambwa and explained that the territorial spirit retains a connection to the Colobus Monkey clan, because its members are descendants of indigenous inhabitants of Buganda. Kasujja may have given the musambwa Mayanja to Kintu, Kalule concluded, but its power resides in the Colobus Monkey clan, which explains why "one of the misambwa that protects Buganda is the same as that which protects our clan."[3]

These two conversations highlight a central concern of this book: the shifting relationship between clanship, collective well-being, and political complexity in Buganda, a kingdom located on the northwestern shores of

Lake Victoria in present-day Uganda (see map 1). These conversations also point to the rationale for yet another study of Buganda, a kingdom that has one of the richest historiographies in East Africa and that in recent years has been the object of renewed interest.[4] Like other Great Lakes kingdoms, Buganda first appeared in historical texts in the latter nineteenth and early twentieth centuries, and the manner in which it appeared has had a profound effect on the drama that historians have projected onto the past.[5] As in other parts of Africa, the imposition of colonial rule in the Great Lakes region accorded to a specific category of African actors the authority to control the production of official knowledge about the past. Indirect rule required colonizers to know how power and authority worked, and for guidance and assistance with regard to the Great Lakes kingdoms colonial administrators turned to an obvious and familiar source of control, the royal courts. Lakes royal officials, however, often proved just as skilled in the art of indirect rule as their European counterparts, and the imposition of colonial rule therefore presented a particular set of Lakes historical actors with the opportunity to fortify their shaky foundations of power.[6] Just as colonial officials sought to legitimate their authority by appealing to existing notions of leadership and authority, the royal officials they consulted sought to present these notions in ways that would legitimate their positions in the emerging colonial order.

The works of Apolo Kaggwa,[7] the most influential Ganda intellectual in the first two decades of the twentieth century, tellingly illustrate how Lakes royal officials exploited the circumstances of colonial rule to present a particular vision of the precolonial past. Kaggwa, who served as prime minister (*katikkiro*) of Buganda from 1899 to 1926, produced the first written account of the kingdom's history, *Bakabaka b'e Buganda* (*The Kings of Buganda*), in 1901. In this work Kaggwa sought to present Buganda's past in a way that would both reinforce his position in the volatile Ganda political order and satisfy Western tastes and sensibilities regarding proper historical writing. As a result, he offered a royalist perspective of Buganda's past in which powerful kings and their representatives serve as the principal historical actors. Royal officials in other Great Lakes kingdoms followed Kaggwa's lead, in some cases responding directly to the Ganda prime minister's publications. Like their counterpart in Buganda, they produced dynastic histories of their respective kingdoms that sought to instill precolonial patriarchy and central authority in the colonial order.[8] These histories, which cut out actors at the margins of centralized power, have left a lasting legacy on subsequent scholarship.

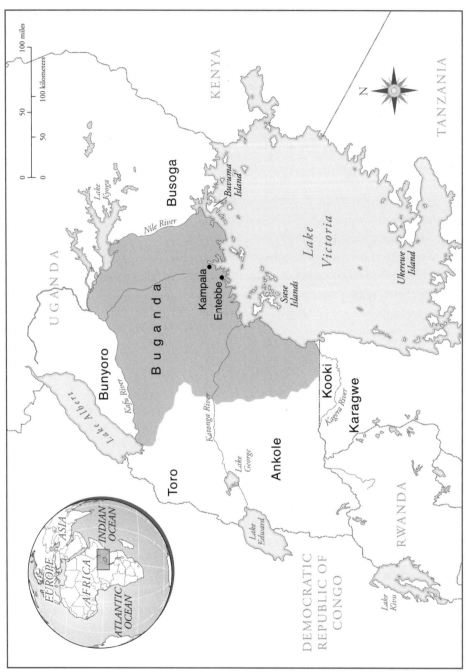

MAP 1. Buganda in the northern Great Lakes region

Writing during the early days of postindependence nationalism, the first generation of professionally trained historians to examine Buganda's past built upon the works produced by their intellectual predecessors. Their pioneering studies sought to differentiate the historical from the mythical in dynastic narratives and to trace Buganda's "territorial growth and expansion, the evolution of its organs of government and the triumph and decline of . . . political institutions."[9] In their focus on the political role of kings, chiefs, and other royal representatives, however, these studies reproduced the royalist perspective found in the dynastic narratives published in the early twentieth century.[10] More recent scholarship has reformulated the triumphant narrative of centralization and modernization that dominated this earlier generation of scholarship on Buganda. By emphasizing both the decentralized nature of the nineteenth-century Ganda economy and the instability resulting from Buganda's often violent territorial expansion in the eighteenth and early nineteenth centuries, this scholarship has transformed long-held perceptions of Buganda.[11] The once prevalent image of a highly centralized kingdom has begun to give way to a vision of a polity with multiple nodes of authority and power, paving the way for new and instructive avenues of inquiry into the deep past of one of the most well studied kingdoms in East Africa.

This book shifts the analytical perspective from which we view kingdoms by asking what Buganda looked like to people who were not of the center but nevertheless became central to the functioning of kingship. Specifically, the book examines the histories of Ganda clans and the clan concept in Buganda by recognizing the importance of historical visions that lie outside official, courtly histories. While there may not be a rigid division between clan and dynastic histories, which intersect in meaningful and instructive ways, viewing Buganda's history through the lens of clanship offers an alternative perspective onto the Ganda past. Ganda clan histories open up a new territory for discourses that lie outside of dynastic narratives because they lie partially outside the world of royal politics. This territory includes discourses about spirit mediums, public healers, and other wielders of authority on the local level. The entrance of these overlooked historical actors onto the Ganda historical stage does not simply fill an obvious gap in historical knowledge; it alters entirely the story of the Ganda state.

An examination of Ganda clan histories and the history of clanship shifts attention to the centuries preceding the better-studied period of state formation. Although Ganda clans and the clan concept continued to develop and change over the course of Buganda's territorial expansion in the eighteenth and early nineteenth centuries, the earliest processes of clan formation preceded this period by at least two centuries. A variety of types of evidence, ranging from informal conversations to historical linguistics to detailed clan histories, suggest that these processes might best be examined from the perspective of public healing. This evidence points to how shifting notions of collective well-being informed the character of political developments in the period preceding the emergence of an instrumentally powerful kingship in Buganda. It illustrates how in the distant past historical actors living along the northwestern shores of Lake Victoria drew upon the clan concept to mobilize dispersed bodies of knowledge in the service of cultivating the conditions in which communities could thrive. The clan concept, in other words, served as a vehicle for increasingly larger groups of people to conceive of their relationships to one another in unprecedented ways. In this manner, the language and practices of clanship provided the discursive and ritual cement with which communities sought to establish and then maintain the shifting connection between collective health and the composition of knowledge.

The early history of clanship in the area that would become Buganda reveals that the domains of public healing and politics were intimately entwined in practical ways. This observation furnishes new insights into the practice of politics in the distant Ganda past and also generates questions about the nature of the interactions between the new techniques of community building that began to emerge in the eighteenth century and these older, and previously overlooked, sources and forms of authority. In the periods preceding the emergence of an instrumentally powerful kingship, political leaders acted as public healers, seeking to ensure the well-being of increasingly complex and dispersed communities. The convergence of public healing and political authority in the distant Ganda past compels us to historicize the frequently observed divide between the authority of healers and the power of royals and their representatives. The gradual institutionalization of this divide occurred later as part of Buganda's violent and extractive formation. Throughout these momentous developments, however, efforts to ensure collective prosperity and perpetuity—usually expressed in the idiom of health and healing—continued to influence community-building processes. This book unearths these efforts by exploring how the shifting contours of clanship informed the historical formation of publics within which individuals strove to create healthy, knowledgeable, and vigorous communities. Changes in the range and scope of public healing practices, and the understanding of health to which they were directed, coincided with changes in the shape and character of the publics involved in these practices. Ganda clan histories and the history of clanship in Buganda illuminate these transformations and reveal the dynamic relationship between efforts to reconfigure the boundaries of public healing, the development of political complexity, and the expansion of political scale in the areas surrounding the northwestern shores of Lake Victoria.

CLANS, CLANSHIP, AND AFRICAN HISTORY

Recent scholarship in archaeology, history, and anthropology has begun to critique the deeply embedded link between the emergence of complex societies and evolutionary models of development. Rather than accepting centralization as an inevitable outcome of complexity, these works question the pervasive notion of complexity as "differentiation by political hierarchization"[12] and focus instead on the various strategies African communities have employed in constructing arenas of collective action. These critiques of social evolutionist scholarship point to the importance of examining multiple, interacting sources of power in order to understand the development of political complexity. The narrow, linear lines of organic growth that once dominated the literature on state development and complexity are rapidly disappearing, and scholars are now grappling with the task of proposing alternative explanations. This growing body of literature points to the importance of diffuse, heterarchic, and segmentary forms of power and to the significance of ritual, technological, and other types of knowledge in achieving complexity.[13] These works emphasize the need to consider different sources of power and to look for voices that chiefs cannot express. In so doing, they acknowledge the "creativity of power" by highlighting how efforts to establish control over material resources—an essential component of crafting polities—always relied on less visible resources, such as the capacity to manage the ideas underlying human actions intended to affect the relationship between the natural, social, and supernatural realms.[14]

Perhaps not surprisingly, this critique of social evolutionist scholarship has been accompanied by a thorough critique of lineage theory. In a critical retrospect published more than twenty-five years ago, Adam Kuper reflected upon what he considered the "long-evident bankruptcy" of the lineage model, which he declared of "no value for anthropological analysis."[15] For Kuper, the model's bankruptcy resulted from its lack of correspondence with either how actors viewed their societies or the actual organization of political and economic activities. Wyatt MacGaffey has recently elaborated upon and refined Kuper's critique of lineage theory as part of an examination of what he describes as the "historiographic burdens imposed by question-able anthropological models of kinship." According to MacGaffey, the pri-macy accorded to lineality and corporate kin groups in discussions of African history stems more from late nineteenth- and early twentieth-century anthro-pologists' preoccupations with explaining social evolution and the mainte-nance of order in so-called primitive societies than from the fact that lineage ideology and its accompanying institutions served as the foundation for social life in African communities. Despite this critique of lineage theory, however, MacGaffey declares that Kuper was "almost certainly wrong" in pointing to the lack of correspondence between actors' views of their social world and the lineage model. Rather than casting doubt on the existence or importance of descent groups, MacGaffey questions the primacy accorded to these groups in prevailing understandings of African social organization, declaring that "there is not and never was any such thing in Africa as a matrilineal society."[16] Like races and tribes, matrilineal or patrilineal socie-ties serve for MacGaffey as "imagined objects that made good myths for a while" but ultimately should be abandoned.[17]

Jane Guyer and Samuel Belinga have offered a different yet related expla-nation for the primacy of kinship in the study of precolonial Africa. In their examination of community-building processes in Equatorial Africa, Guyer and Belinga note how the commonly encountered assumption that kinship served as the guiding principle of African social life may in large measure reflect the effects of conquest and the implementation of colonial rule. They point out how the disorder and demographic collapse that accompanied the establishment of colonial rule in many parts of Africa rendered inoperable previous processes of social mobilization based on the complementarity of different bodies of knowledge. Kinship, on the other hand, survived this period of despair and loss and therefore rose to the forefront of ethno-graphic endeavors in the early colonial period. Rather than representing the fundamental building blocks of African social life, then, kinship constituted " 'what [was] left' in the organizational repertoire" when ethnographers crafted the earliest descriptions of African communities. When subsequent scholars turned their attention to examining the precolonial period, the models of community formation they developed preserved kinship's pri-macy. Whether based on the lineage mode of production prevalent in the

1960s or on the concept of wealth in people launched in the 1970s, these models focused on kinship as a means of managing processes of control and accumulation, a theoretical insistence that preserved problematic assumptions from evolutionary theory.[18]

Critiques of both social evolutionist scholarship and lineage theory correctly call into question the models scholars have most frequently employed to describe social organization and modes of order in Africa. In so doing, these critiques compel us to reevaluate the various components that have constituted the building blocks for these models. Many of these components —such as the ubiquitous references to the existence of "clans" in almost every region of the continent—have long occupied center stage both in the lives of Africans and in discussions about political complexity and the expansion of scale in early African history. In this regard, we might take care to distinguish between the models we have employed and their constituent parts. For while matrilineal or patrilineal societies may represent "imagined objects," matriclans and patriclans are certainly not a figment of professional historians' and ethnographers' imaginations; in the words of Vansina, they are "out there."[19] This raises the question of how we should make sense of these phenomena in the absence of the models that once gave them meaning.

The "clan" has long served as an important building block in reconstructing early periods in Africa's pasts. As Justin Willis has noted, the pioneering works of the 1960s on East Africa, most of which ostensibly were concerned with the histories of "tribes," actually drew upon the clan as a unit of enquiry and were written in terms of the origins and activities of clans.[20] For the Great Lakes region, scholars working in the 1970s at times turned to clan traditions as part of their efforts to compose historical narratives that traversed the boundaries of the region's well-known kingdoms.[21] The extensive references to clans in the historical literature on East Africa and the Great Lakes region in particular—and indeed on the continent more broadly—suggest the possibility of speaking generally about clans in Africa. As Willis has observed, however, the use of the English term clan as a translation for numerous different terms in African languages "covertly imposes an externally defined idea of hierarchy and order" onto a variety of diverse phenomena throughout the continent. According to this frequently encountered conception, clans are "composed of various sub-clans, which are composed of lineages, which are in turn made up of families."[22]

The widespread depiction of clans as the almost natural extension of kin groups poses a number of analytical problems.[23] As David Newbury commented in his examination of clanship in Rwanda, the "normative ideal" invoked in the descent model of clans often differs from the "behavioral norm," and "it is the incompatibility of empirical 'realities' within the conceptual framework used in most analyses which gives rise to the problem of clan analysis."[24] Considerable differences in the "empirical realities" of clanship also highlight how the use of the term *clan* serves to mask differences in the wide range of phenomena tagged as such in studies about Africa. The difficulties involved in treating "clanship" as a singular and overarching phenomenon become apparent even if we limit ourselves to a discussion of the Great Lakes, where geographically dispersed communities commonly referred to as "clans" appear throughout the region. The variety of terms designating these groupings in related Great Lakes Bantu languages—*umuryango* in Kirundi, *ubwooko* in Kinyarwanda, *ishanja* in Kihavu, *rugàndá* in Runyoro and Luhaya, and *kika* in Luganda and Lusoga—hints at differences in the types of collectivities grouped under the label "clan" in the region.

In searching for commonalities that would warrant the classification of these collectivities as "clans," we might follow Jean-Pierre Chrétien in pointing to how these groupings combine the language of kinship, reference to a collective name, and in most cases a totemic avoidance to indicate membership in some sort of social group.[25] While useful in some respects, such an attempt to pinpoint the defining features of "clans" in the region sheds little light on the various meanings these categories assume in different settings (not to mention how these meanings change over time) or the variety of forms, sizes, and shapes encountered even in a relatively circumscribed area such as the Great Lakes. For example, Bunyoro, Burundi, and Buha contain an extensive number of clans, with the number in Burundi alone totaling more than two hundred. By contrast, clans in Rwanda and Nkore are much larger but less numerous, with approximately twenty in the former and four in the latter. To further complicate matters, this variation in size and number does not take into account differences in the constituent components of clans, whose internal organization and structure vary throughout the region.[26]

Buganda's approximately forty clans comprise groups of people who perceive themselves as related by agnatic descent from a common male ancestor.[27] Each clan further comprises a descending series of subdivisions: *masiga* (hearthstones), *mituba* (fig trees), *nyiriri* (lines), *lugya* (courtyards), and *nnyumba* (houses). In anthropological parlance, the first three of these subdivisions correspond to maximal lineages, minor lineages, and minimal lineages. Baganda conceive of these subdivisions as descending from the clan's founder, and Ganda clan histories usually narrate their formation accordingly: the sons of the original founder become the *masiga* heads, his grandsons become *mituba* heads, and his great grandsons become the leaders of *nyiriri*. The estates associated with these subdivisions for any given clan in most cases lie scattered across Buganda in discontiguous distribution, a pattern usually explained by the movements of a clan's earliest ancestors as narrated in clan histories.

In addition to sharing a common male founding ancestor, Baganda clanmates also share a common totemic avoidance that defines the limits of exogamy and also provides the clan's name. This strict correspondence between totem and clan is unique to Buganda. Elsewhere in the region a clan might recognize more than one avoidance, or several clans might share a single totem. In the Soga states, to the east of Buganda, for instance, the name of a clan's eponymous ancestor, rather than a common totem, determines the limits of exogamy and distinguishes one clan from another. Thus, for example, while the abaiseKidoido clan—"those of the father of Kidoido" —recognizes the frog as its totem, its members may marry individuals from the several other distinct Soga clans that also claim the frog as their avoidance.[28] In Buganda, by contrast, each clan recognizes a unique avoidance (*muziro*), which also provides the clan's name, as well as an equally unique secondary totem (*kabbiro*).[29] We therefore find in Buganda the Sheep clan, which recognizes the lion as its secondary totem, and the Hippopotamus clan, which observes the elephant as its secondary totem. This convergence of clan and totem means that when inquiring about the clan to which a Muganda belongs, one simply asks "What do you avoid?" to which he or she responds, for example, "I avoid the mushroom."

Seeking to explore Ganda clan histories as an alternative avenue into Buganda's past, I engaged in an extended period of fieldwork in Uganda, from June 2001 to December 2002. During the first two months, I devoted the majority of my time and energies to intensive study of Luganda, the language spoken in Buganda. This language training, combined with a few private lessons from a Luganda speaker in Chicago, eventually allowed me to engage in casual conversations and to follow more in-depth discussions about Buganda's past. My Luganda skills, however, did not reach the point where I felt comfortable conducting interviews alone, and I therefore worked with research assistants throughout my period of fieldwork in Uganda.[30]

The process of identifying people to engage in discussions about the histories of their respective clans began with a series of visits to Bulange. Located on Mengo Hill, one of the seven hills that constitute the core of Kampala, Bulange serves as Buganda's administrative headquarters and houses the kingdom's parliament, the Lukiiko. Bulange also serves as a gathering place for Buganda's clan heads or their representatives, who began to convene regular meetings there following the restoration of the kingdom in 1993, after more than two decades of political instability in Uganda.[31] These gatherings presented opportune occasions to introduce myself to Buganda's clan leaders, many of whom invited me to attend one of the monthly clan meetings that usually occur in the vicinity of Kampala and today constitute a regular feature of clan activities. I attended many of these meetings, during which members discussed a variety of affairs ranging from fund-raising to inheritance disputes to the organization of Buganda's annual clan soccer tournament. Clans generally welcomed my presence, and on most occasions either the clan head or the presiding official invited me to make a presentation toward the end of the meeting. Speaking in a combination of English and halting Luganda, and with the help of a research assistant, I explained to those present that I was interested in learning more about the history of their clan and would like to arrange meetings with those who were knowledgeable in these matters. The recent restoration of the kingship in Buganda has been accompanied by a renewed interest in clanship and the publication of clan histories, and most clans were therefore more than willing to assist me.

As a result of presenting my research interests at clan gatherings, I was able to arrange meetings with the many individuals who volunteered to discuss the histories of their clans. These individuals included both people who occupied prominent positions within their clans and people who held no post. Since many of the people I met at clan gatherings did not reside in Kampala or its vicinity, I conducted interviews throughout mainland Buganda as well as on the Ssese Islands and Buvuma Island. These meetings, which ranged in length from thirty minutes to several hours, usually began with the person introducing him- or herself, an activity known as kulanya, in which Baganda name three or four generations of their genealogy, followed by the various branches of the clan to which they belong. I then asked the person I was interviewing to relate the history of his or her clan or of his or her branch within the clan. These histories, which often mirrored published versions of clan and royal traditions, included the well-known royal narratives about Kintu, the purported founder of Buganda, and Kimera, the third king in the Ganda royal genealogy, as well as the various clan narratives situated at the core of the following chapters. After these somewhat formal presentations of clan and dynastic traditions, I asked a series of questions prompted by the details offered in the particular history presented. By allowing me to explore the overlaps and discrepancies between the oral presentations of these traditions and accounts published by Ganda intellectuals during the first half of the twentieth century, this technique both provided insight into the transmission and circulation of historical knowledge in early twentieth-first-century Buganda and, as illustrated in the following chapters, opened up novel perspectives into the Ganda past.

My initial inquiries into the histories of particular clans most often resulted in descriptions of the internal architecture of Ganda clans. I listened patiently on countless occasions as people explained the various subdivisions that together constitute a Ganda clan in a manner similar to that described above. Many people sketched a pyramid-shaped structure depicting the organization of Ganda clans from the household level to that of the clan head, situated at the peak of the pyramid. These depictions were often followed by an explanation of where the person providing the description fit into this structure. The frequency with which I encountered such responses may have stemmed from the fact that most of the people with whom I was speaking presumed a complete lack of knowledge about these matters on my part. This type of explanation, however, might also have been the easiest way to respond to what I subsequently realized were exceedingly difficult questions about the meaning of clanship in Buganda.

While descriptions and depictions of the internal architecture of Ganda clans provided insight into the specifically Ganda manifestation of a familial model of clanship frequently employed by scholars, this model often obscured other, perhaps more revealing formulations. One particularly compelling aspect of the less formal conversations that followed the presentation of clan traditions was the recurring reference to the significance of biggwa, the sacred sites located on clan estates (butaka). Intrigued by these references, I made arrangements to visit numerous primary and secondary butaka, which lie scattered over sometimes large areas throughout Buganda. On most of my visits to butaka the caretaker or another knowledgeable individual guided me and those accompanying me through the various sites on the estate. These sites include prominent trees, hills, rocks, and other features of the natural environment that serve as storehouses of historical memory and house the area's most venerated spirits, as well as the burial grounds, which constitute an important feature of all *butaka*. Tours of *butaka* usually culminated with a visit to the *kiggwa* (sacred site), some of which included a shrine at which people engaged the area's spirits. In most cases I was granted permission to enter the shrine, where I engaged in conversations with priests, mediums, and other officials, and on several occasions my hosts insisted that we enter a shrine so that they could better explain both the activities undertaken in it and the narratives about its historical significance for Buganda and the clan.

During my tours of *butaka* I engaged in many conversations about the meaning of clanship. While these conversations usually did not result in the collection of oral traditions that were new to me, they did point to a novel way of approaching both the clan concept and the interpretation of more formal, structured clan histories. By bringing into focus the discursive, ritual, and political connections between shrines located on discontiguous clan estates, these visits to clan estates and discussions about clanship suggested a connection between clanship and public healing. In these conversations, I learned that sacred sites embedded in features of the natural landscape served as repositories for narratives about significant moments in a clan's history. As mentioned earlier, many people described how clanmates gathered at these sacred sites—and in particular at the shrines constructed on these sites—to talk about the past and engage in ceremonies designed to ensure their collective health. These conversations made it clear that I needed to examine transformations in public healing in order to understand shifts in the scope of political activities in the distant Ganda past. Thus, what initially began as an effort to employ clan histories as an alternative avenue into Buganda's past gradually evolved into an examination of the intersection between clanship, public healing, and political complexity in the areas surrounding the northwestern shores of Lake Victoria.

PUBLIC HEALING AND POLITICAL COMPLEXITY

Over the past two decades, a growing number of scholars have demonstrated the potential that a critical examination of health and healing holds for understanding a wide range of historical processes in Africa. These scholars have worked from a simple yet illuminating premise: because healing practices are rooted in the social, cultural, and material world, changes in these practices as well as the concepts supporting them can only be understood in the context of broader changes in areas such as farming, kinship, trade, and politics.[32] Rather than a separate domain of analysis, then, the history of healing, whether in the form of spirit mediumship, cults of affliction, divination, biomedical practices, or herbal therapies, necessarily becomes the history of social organization, agricultural production, intellectual innovation, and political activity. Far more than an epiphenomenon of these larger patterns of change, however, transformations in healing practices have influenced the nature of these broader developments in creative and crucial ways.

The most illuminating contributions to this burgeoning literature focus on the often dramatic transformations in conceptions of health, personhood, and the body that occurred in many African communities over the course of the twentieth century.[33] Many of these works examine how the implementation of colonial rule generated new sorts of tensions that ultimately led Africans to extract themselves from the mesh of relationships—social, spiritual, and political—that previously had constituted the domain of public health. These developments often resulted in the breakdown of long-standing systems of public health and the loss of efficacy, and therefore prestige, of practitioners of public healing. The nature of the sources available for examining early periods in African history, however, necessarily requires that historians of pre-twentieth-century Africa focus on the public aspects of healing rather than the experiences of individuals that characterize and make so compelling many of the most valuable studies of the twentieth century.[34]

The notion of social health, or what I here call (following Steven Feierman) public healing, revolves around the idea that communities can suffer the "collective analogues of illness" and that groups of individuals perceive the pursuit of well-being as a collective endeavor.[35] Prior to the imposition of colonial rule in the first half of the twentieth century, many Great Lakes communities—as well as communities elsewhere on the continent—drew upon intricate systems of public health as part of their efforts to manage social welfare. As Julie Livingston has noted in her illuminating study of debility in twentieth-century Botswana, the activities involved in promoting this understanding of collective well-being differed from those associated with the modern Western discipline of public health. Whereas the modern discipline "organizes knowledge and action around statistical and scientific understandings," systems of public health in many parts of precolonial Africa often focused on establishing productive relationships with a variety of spiritual entities and anchored the social health of communities in overlapping political, ecological, and cosmological domains.[36]

The study of public healing offers an opportunity to revisit some deeply entrenched ideas about enlargement of scale and the development of political complexity. Practitioners of public healing played a vital role in shaping public consciousness by stressing the connection between a community's moral economy and its continued well-being. These practitioners ranged from spirit mediums, diviners, and rainmakers to chiefs, military leaders, and ritualists at royal courts. The public-health practices coordinated by these actors exhibited a similarly broad range and encompassed activities designed to ensure the continued welfare of families, extended kin groups, healing associations, and even entire kingdoms. In other words, the practices of public healing and the manner in which communities conceived well-being varied depending on the publics involved. From a historical perspective, then, changes in the nature and shape of the publics involved in public healing necessarily coincided with shifting understandings of health and its necessary components as well as transformations in the scope of public healing. Any effort to treat public healing as a dynamic process therefore requires that we examine the history of public healing in dialogue with political complexity.

The practitioners of public healing discussed in this study—the mediums and the variety of spirits they embody—lie at the intersection of what David Schoenbrun, in his examination of ancient Great Lakes social history, describes as "creative" and "instrumental" power. For Schoenbrun, the notions of creative and instrumental power "represent different aspects of what Great Lakes Bantu speaking people thought power was and what it should do." Whereas creative power "operates in the words, pauses, and gestures that healers and political orators use to make people well and to sway opinion," instrumental power "operates in the exchange of gifts to build patron-client relationships or in the power of military threat to cause social change." The distinction between creative and instrumental power proves useful in that it highlights the "mercurial nature of power" and allows us to examine the various combinations of power, as well as potential challenges to power, at work in a particular historical moment.[37]

We must be careful, however, to avoid the overly simple association between instrumental power and the material world, on the one hand, and creative power and the metaphysical or spiritual realm, on the other hand. As Schoenbrun insinuates in his use of the term, creative power included the capacity to shape new realities in the earthly realm, a type of power that Kairn Klieman, in her study of the relationship between Bantu and Batwa communities in West Central Africa, describes as "transformative."[38] When mediums called upon their spiritual patrons, for example, they sought to provide for the material well-being of their community of followers. Similarly, the priests who served as translators for mediums combined their authority as guardians of the land or family heads—and the connections to territorial spirits that accompanied their positions—with the creative capacities of mediums in an effort to "create" new realities in the material world. The patron-client relationships these figures established with their followers were based on the notion that material prosperity required engagement with the appropriate spiritual entities. These engagements, which I here refer to as practices of public healing, were designed to ensure the continued fertility of banana trees, establish productive trade networks, and draw together the skills and knowledge of dispersed communities. The authorities who presided over these activities, in other words, sought to "heal" and provide for the well-being of the shifting publics over which they presided. They served as the dominant political figures in the period preceding the emergence of a state bureaucracy, and the ideas that motivated their political practices both withstood the challenges presented by the increasing power of royal authorities and influenced the development of the Ganda state in the eighteenth century.

The sorts of public-healing practices discussed here often surface in scholarly analyses under the rubric "religion." In many respects, however, scholars' use of the concept of religion in this context stems from the manner in which African elites and Europeans recorded their observations about African societies in the late nineteenth and early twentieth centuries. European missionaries were the first outsiders to record detailed descriptions of Ganda healing practices. While at times disparaging and undoubtedly misguided, missionary attitudes toward these practices were not entirely hostile. Missionaries most often did not approach these practices from the perspective of healing but instead regarded them as uncritical and irrational forms of religion designed "to fill the heart of the simple-minded native with awe and wonder and to captivate him with its charms."[39] As a form of worship, spirit possession and the propitiation of ancestors, although misdirected, gave missionaries hope that their proselytizing endeavors would succeed. At least initially, the acts of faith Baganda displayed in these practices proved encouraging to missionaries, who viewed their challenge as consisting in the channeling of these internal convictions toward an appropriate end. Baganda might have engaged in acts of spirit possession and made offerings at various shrines, but "that [they] prayed to the spirit, or probably to the Creator, [was] a fact."[40] For some missionaries, certain features of these practices even hinted at a possible ancient Christian presence in Buganda and, along with the inroads that Islam had already made in Buganda, signaled that Baganda had a spiritual thirst that only required proper quenching.[41]

Encouraged by the conviction Baganda displayed in their nonetheless misguided practices, European missionaries embarked on the formidable task of finding effective words with which to promote their message. They drew analogies between Christian and Ganda practices and searched for linguistic markers that could serve as useful conveyors for Christian teachings. These acts of massive cultural as well as literal translation, which often relied as much upon the efforts of Baganda converts as upon those of their missionary teachers, sought to classify Ganda practices into a coherent (if irrational, from the missionary perspective) system of beliefs from which useful elements could be extracted. Missionaries and Baganda converts compiled lists of Ganda spirits, their genealogies and effective capacities, the locations of their principal shrines, and the pedigrees of their mediums and priests. In this manner, early Baganda converts and European missionaries together searched for similarities between this refashioned Ganda system of thought and the Christian concepts missionaries sought to introduce.

The considerable documentary record that emerged in the rapidly shifting world of late nineteenth- and early twentieth-century Buganda has provided scholars with a relatively rich and easily navigated set of sources. For scholars interested in Ganda healing practices, the early ethnographies of the Baganda offer convenient chapters, such as "Historical Religion among the Baganda," "Religion and Magic," and "The Old Religion and Morals."[42] Both the missionary-ethnographer John Roscoe and the Ganda prime minister Apolo Kaggwa, the two figures who stood at the forefront of the ethnographic endeavor in Buganda and upon whom much subsequent scholarship would come to rely, included in their works a detailed taxonomy of the various Ganda spirits and the relevant practices involving each. Roscoe fitted a chapter entitled "Religion" between two entitled "Government" and "Warfare," while Kaggwa, whose conception of what an ethnographic report might look like undoubtedly drew upon Roscoe's, incorporated a section titled "National Gods and Diviners" ("Balubale na Balaguzi") between his descriptions of Ganda burial practices and court proceedings.[43] These chapter headings guide the researcher through the accounts produced by early travelers, missionaries, and ethnographers.

The relative ease with which historians can draw upon these early written sources, however, raises concerns regarding the relationship between the organization of source material and the types of narratives historians produce. In many respects, much of the scholarship that draws upon these early written sources has followed the analytical path forged in the specific circumstances of late nineteenth- and early twentieth-century Buganda. The publication of Ganda healing practices as "religion" extracted a complex cluster of activities deeply enmeshed in Ganda social life and sought to rearrange them into a distinct realm of experience. These acts of appropriation, propagated by Europeans and Baganda alike, have affected the way subsequent scholars have approached the study of Ganda healing practices. Historians of Buganda, for instance, have for the most part continued to treat these practices as forms of religious expression.[44] This metaphor, however, cannot capture the significance of public healing in the distant Ganda past.

The use of the concept of religion to describe Ganda public-healing practices poses particular problems for understanding their historical significance. Paul Landau has observed that the term *religion* represents as much an act of interpretation as one of translation.[45] As Anthony Appiah has commented, because of the differences between the Western concept of religion and African practices usually conceived as religious, "to report [these practices] in Western categories is as much to invite misunderstanding as to offer insight."[46] The problem with the term lies in its inability to capture the extent to which the various activities and philosophies grouped under this analytical umbrella once animated practices that most historians would not necessarily regard as religious in nature.[47] Abstracted from their social and historical contexts, the practices usually catalogued as "religious" serve as expressions of "faith" and "belief." As Feierman noted in his discussion of Nyabingi mediumship in southwestern Uganda and northern Rwanda, however, the religion metaphor proves inadequate because "[Nyabingi] mediumship was a form of practical reason, and only rarely do historians speak of religion in these terms. . . . Mediums and their followers were concerned not with expressing belief but rather with reorienting their situation in the world for practical ends—to cure the sick and to bring an end to famine and epidemic diseases."[48]

Ideas about health and prosperity were related in a similar fashion in the distant Ganda past. The semantic histories of words for medicines, different sorts of spirits, and healing techniques in the Great Lakes region reveal that Lakes historical actors thought about health and prosperity together. These histories suggest that efforts to promote conditions in which individuals and communities could thrive fell within the territory of healing.[49] Healers shaped and maintained the social order, and the discourse and practices of public healing therefore stood at the heart of political activities. The domains of public healing and politics were intimately entwined in practical ways; thus, treating Ganda healing practices as forms of religious expression often results in misguided and misleading interpretations. In order to recognize public healing as a critical element in the development of complex political, social, and moral communities, then, we must recognize the changing ways in which public healers acted as political leaders who sought to both fashion and preserve the conditions in which communities could prosper. Public-healing practices both steered transformations in material conditions and posited interpretations of changing realities. Their study therefore provides an entrée into the shifting worlds in which historical actors sought to establish the conditions in which both communities and individuals could thrive and prosper.

SOURCES, METHODS, AND THE PRODUCTION
OF HISTORICAL KNOWLEDGE

Researching and writing precolonial East African history presents a methodological challenge. The first written sources for most places in the interior did not appear until the second half of the nineteenth century. In the case of Buganda, the earliest documented description of the kingdom appeared in the British explorer John Hanning Speke's *Journal of the Discovery of the Source of the Nile* in 1863. Scholars of precolonial East Africa confront this challenge by employing a multilayered methodology that draws upon a variety of sources and disciplines. Historians compose narratives for the distant East African past based on evidence gleaned from oral traditions, historical linguistics, archaeology, and comparative ethnography. They place these different forms of evidence side by side in the hopes of perceiving various correlations, convergences, and divergences.

A critical approach to such interdisciplinary scholarship requires that scholars recognize and respect both the benefits and the limitations of disciplinary concerns.[50] Archaeological evidence, for instance, provides information about such things as technological change and material culture, but we can seldom comment on the cultural meanings associated with excavated materials without careful recourse to the ethnographic record. Similarly, oral traditions provide a finer resolution and a more textured description of processes deduced from archaeological and linguistic evidence, but they rarely provide any sort of reliable chronological anchor. For this we must turn to archaeological and historical linguistic evidence. The time frames and chronologies informing narratives supported by these types of evidence, however, must necessarily differ from those based on documentary sources. Studies of precolonial East Africa cover what for non-Africanists or historians of twentieth-century Africa may seem to be unusually expansive and sometimes vaguely defined periods. Moreover, these narratives often do not include individual historical actors, relying instead on units of agency such as "Ganda speakers" and "clans" or on composite images of persons or groups. Moreover, when we can speak of individual historical actors, these discussions often focus on the activities of spirits, a narrative genre and form of analysis that, while unfamiliar to some historians, perhaps best reflects both the nature of the available sources and the reality of the distant African past. The content and composition of precolonial East African historical narratives therefore differs in significant ways from those focused on places and periods for which we have a richer documentary source base.

Because of the interdisciplinary nature of researching and writing histories for places and periods for which there are few documentary sources, historians of precolonial East Africa necessarily rely upon the work of other scholars. While this study builds upon the considerable efforts of several scholars, I am particularly indebted to the work of four historians. First, David Schoenbrun's rich examination of ancient Great Lakes history, which draws in large part upon his exhaustive historical linguistic analysis of the region's Bantu languages, furnished the deeper and broader context for this exploration of Buganda's early history. Second, Renee Tantala's magnificent analysis of what she termed the "Kitara epic," the oral traditions relating the origins of the well-known kingdoms of western Uganda, provided much inspiration for my reexamination of the earliest sections of Ganda dynastic narratives. Third, Holly Hanson's consideration of the relationships of obligation at the center of the emerging Ganda polity and the subsequent unraveling of these relationships during the period of territorial expansion opened the door for many of the avenues of inquiry pursued in this study.

Finally, this study owes a considerable intellectual debt to Steven Feierman, whose thoughtful scholarship on the history of health and healing in Africa has shaped my ideas on the subject in profound ways.[51]

In many respects, however, the analysis of the distant Ganda past presented in this book is a testament to the continued value of conducting fieldwork for scholars of early African history. The possibility of collecting wholly new oral material relating to the precolonial past has diminished considerably in places such as Buganda, where published accounts of oral traditions produced in Luganda by literate Ganda intellectuals have circulated for more than a hundred years. Nonetheless, the process of engaging practicing intellectuals continues, at least in the case of Buganda, to prove an invaluable component in the production of knowledge about the distant past. For no matter how detailed and thorough the versions of oral traditions published in the early colonial period are, they necessarily reflect the particular circumstances of their production.

The impact of colonial policies aimed at eradicating what colonial officials in Uganda and elsewhere viewed as irrational practices was that particular locales, such as healers' shrines, suffered significant setbacks as sites of recollection during the colonial period, while others, such as missionary schools, emerged. The result of this process in Buganda was the relative absence, though not complete invisibility, of the roles played by spirit mediums, public healers, and other wielders of authority on the local level in determining the trajectory of Ganda history. Recognizing these colonial and postcolonial realities allows us to see why particular interpretations, and the sites of recollection in which they circulated, became dominant on the public level, while others became less visible (or audible) yet did not wholly disappear. The challenge for historians lies in excavating these often overlooked historical figures and the particular perspectives on the past they embody. I believe that we are now in a position to confront this methodological challenge, particularly the use of oral traditions to unearth developments in the distant past, in novel and creative ways.

Recent interpretations of oral histories in Africa have been based increasingly on the premise that each teller creates a unique oral text. Oral sources, according to this new formulation, should not be "flattened by transcription," with individual voices operating interchangeably.[52] Rather, these sources should be heard with all of the personal, subjective, ambiguous, and contradictory inflections with which they circulate in practice.[53] This emphasis on multiplicity, variability, and subjectivity represents a nota-

ble departure from earlier approaches to oral history that privileged "tradition" as a distinctive cultural form and, following a meticulous methodology
pioneered by Jan Vansina, sought to sift stable and verifiable elements from
the flux of performances.[54] Perspective and performance, once considered
antithetical to the pursuits of professional historians working with oral
sources, now occupy a privileged position in the analytical framework.

The growing body of literature that has accompanied this theoretical shift
urges historians to recognize the institutional structures in which Africans
crafted their histories and to adopt often unfamiliar epistemologies.[55] The
potential of such an approach to enable one to understand the past lies in the
perhaps not so surprising discovery that the truth regimes that operate in
these institutional structures often do not have an equivalent in Western
epistemologies about what constitutes "history." Or to rephrase the matter slightly, these truth regimes, like their Western counterparts, are consistently under construction. But rather than their serving as an obstacle
to historical analysis, recognizing how regimes of truth shape the meanings listeners or readers attach to texts unveils previously hidden aspects of
the past.

This reconfiguration of the premises undergirding the interpretation of
oral sources has opened up a host of new possibilities for "find[ing] ac-
curacy in unexpected places."[56] Vampire stories, paintings, and life histories,
as much as formalized poetic traditions and rehearsed oral epics, are now
the focus of investigations into African pasts.[57] The scholarship that has
resulted from this shift in focus has provided critical theoretical and methodological insights. We have learned, among other things, the value of arguing with informants, the significance of non-narrative modes of organizing
memories, and the importance of setting and audience in the meaning-
making process. Perhaps most importantly, this body of work has implored
us, in the words of Johannes Fabian, to "confront other searches for truth
and reality" and to "experience all these *representations* of reality as *realities*."[58]
Our understanding of Africa's multivocal pasts has been greatly enriched by
the works of those who have taken Fabian's call seriously.

Despite yielding remarkably rich theoretical and substantive insights,
however, the sustained challenge over the past fifteen years to previous approaches to oral history has in many respects resulted in a methodological
impasse. Perhaps not surprisingly, the recent focus in oral historical research on subjectivities, personal recollections, rumor, and interpretive
practices has coincided with a focus on Africa's most recent pasts.[59] Because

historians who employed African oral "traditions" in writing African history focused on the precolonial period, the move away from the study of oral "traditions" and its accompanying method appears to have coincided with a move away from using oral sources to write early African history.

In many regards, these simultaneous moves represent the result of shifting theoretical orientations and topics of scholarly interest as much as they do the outcome of methodological disagreements. Lost in much of the debate between the advocates of recent approaches to oral history and scholars who study oral "traditions" are the differences in the types of materials employed in their respective works and the potential of these materials as historical sources. For instance, Luise White describes her concern with rumors about blood-sucking vampires in colonial East Africa as resulting from her interest "not in what happened in Uganda or Kenya but in something that never happened."[60] But can we extend the same luxury to Vansina, for example, in his efforts to write the eighteenth-century history of the Kuba kingdom in central Africa?[61] White can adopt this analytical stance because she has many other sources with which to create the historical canvas that allows her to make sense of the fantastic stories that constitute the focus of her research. For Vansina, however, oral narratives such as those informing his history of the Kuba kingdom serve as much as a means for creating the historical canvas itself as they do as a source for uncovering new perspectives onto the past. White's pronouncement that "oral history and personal narrative may require as much methodological interrogation as oral traditions do" serves as an important corrective to the once prevalent notion that life histories and personal recollections allow subalterns to "speak for themselves."[62] But the sorts of methodological interrogations called for in the fascinating work on rumor, gossip, and personal narratives produced over the past fifteen years do not fully account for the differing challenges, both methodological and theoretical, involved in writing histories of Africa in the eighteenth century as opposed to in the twentieth. The revealing worlds opened up by the "undefining" of oral tradition, in other words, seem to have a limited time depth.[63]

Yet need this be the case? Has the theoretical shift in the interpretation of oral sources rendered their use impossible for writing early African history? Can the valuable insights derived from this new body of literature on oral-history practices be applied to oral narratives that in their early twentieth-century publications or current circulation are ostensibly neither personal recollections nor reflections on relatively recent happenings? This book offers a way of bridging recent approaches to oral history in Africa to an earlier set of concerns about oral "traditions" and the use of oral sources for writing histories of considerably earlier periods. The insights yielded by innovative approaches to the study of oral sources over the past fifteen years need not apply only to twentieth-century topics of analysis. The sensitivity toward genre, the focus on how different regimes of truth shape the content of stories, and the attention to the significance of sites of recollection displayed in recent work can also enhance the analysis of oral sources that claim to describe developments in the distant past. An interest in early African history, in other words, need not necessarily entail readopting the notion of fixed, stable, and bound "traditions."

Part of the recent critique of earlier oral historical practices in Africa revolves around the notion that what oral narratives purport to describe—the past actions and events that for scholars of oral "tradition" represented the substance of history—constitutes only part of their communicative force. Similar renditions of the same narrative can be read or heard on different levels, and there are different dominant interpretations depending on setting and audience. The most widespread interpretation at any given moment, or the interpretation propagated by those in dominant positions of semantic creativity, represents the outcome of considerable struggle. Unearthing these historical contests and the layers of meaning they engender for the more distant past is no simple matter, particularly when (as in Buganda) the locally constituted sites of production and reception in which they were actualized no longer function as they did in the past. Yet the benefits of embarking on such endeavors are substantial in that they open the door for new interpretations that provide novel insights into the histories of regions for periods not easily accessible by conventional methodologies.

In many respects, the fieldwork I conducted in Buganda did not result in the unearthing of a new archive. Many, though by no means all, of the oral traditions I listened to had been recorded by early missionaries, intellectually inclined colonial officials, and the first generation of literate Ganda elites. However, by listening to these stories in different settings, such as in healers' shrines or as people walked me through their clan estates, I learned new ways of interpreting and analyzing old stories. In addition, more informal conversations pointed to different ways of thinking about a seemingly well understood phenomenon—clanship—and forced me to consider the history of the clan concept itself rather than simply using clan histories as an alternative avenue into the Ganda past. The many lessons I received from my

Baganda teachers, in other words, brought into focus previously overlooked historical perspectives and presented a new set of levers for grasping historical transformations in Buganda. Applying these lessons to an examination of the distant Ganda past, and specifically to an interpretation of well-known oral traditions, often requires exercising our historical imagination. But as illustrated in the following chapters, it is an imagination bound by evidence drawn from historical linguistics and comparative ethnography and inspired by the words and activities of practicing intellectuals in contemporary Buganda. By historicizing and contextualizing our historical imagination, in other words, we can infer possible ranges of understanding from a limited set of conceptual tools that can be reconstructed to the time and place in which people listened to oral traditions such as those discussed in this book.

Perhaps, then, we have reached an appropriate moment for revisiting some of the well-known oral traditions that so intrigued historians of Africa in the 1960s and 1970s. Armed with the methodological techniques and analytical insights derived from the more recent work on oral histories, historians of Africa are now in a position to reexamine these traditions with an eye to their circulation in previously overlooked sites of production and reception. If oral narratives circulated in a variety of different manners and had a multiplicity of meanings and lives in the colonial and postcolonial periods, they also did so in the more distant past. Moreover, because of the multiple sites at which these narratives had life, "traditions" were diffuse and scattered rather than singular and concentrated. Oral traditions such as those describing Buganda's distant past provide illuminating insights into early periods in African history. But they can only do so if we exercise our historical imagination in an effort to understand the generic framework and the criteria of plausibility according to which various sorts of audiences might have understood them.

2 Genre, Historical Imagination, and Early Ganda History

Dynastic accounts of Buganda's origins revolve around the exploits of Kintu, the purported founder of the kingdom and quintessential Ganda hero. Perhaps the best known of these foundational narratives, "Kintu and Bemba the Snake," describes Kintu's arrival in Buganda and his eventual defeat of the tyrannical ruler Bemba at Buddo Hill, in southern Busiro. According to most accounts of this narrative, upon overcoming Bemba, Kintu embarked on a journey through a series of places before eventually reaching Magonga, in Busujju, where he settled and established his capital. After residing at Magonga for many years, Kintu disappeared following an altercation with Kisolo, of the Otter clan. But his spirit and the memory of his accomplishments endured through acts of commemoration performed at his royal tomb at Nnono, Magonga, which was tended by the priest Mwanje of the Leopard clan (see map 2).

This image of Kintu as a wandering conqueror-king dominates the master narrative running through most written versions of Ganda history. A careful probing of recollections about Kintu that weave in and out of this dominant trajectory, however, suggests that Kintu may not always have been regarded in this manner and that when he was, such a view was not the only one circulating with force. As George William Kalule, a prominent healer in the Colobus Monkey clan, explained, there were "two different Kintus: one who vanished and one who produced Cwa Nabakka, who succeeded his father Kintu as king."[1] Kalule sought to direct attention to two distinct yet layered aspects of Kintu's persona. Recollections of Kintu's having disappeared hint at an alternative conception of the most prominent figure in Ganda history, a conception not of the "first *kabaka* [king] to rule people," as one local historian explained, but of a powerful spiritual force.[2]

Descriptions of Kintu as a spiritual entity surfaced numerous times over the course of my conversations in Buganda, most often in shrine settings

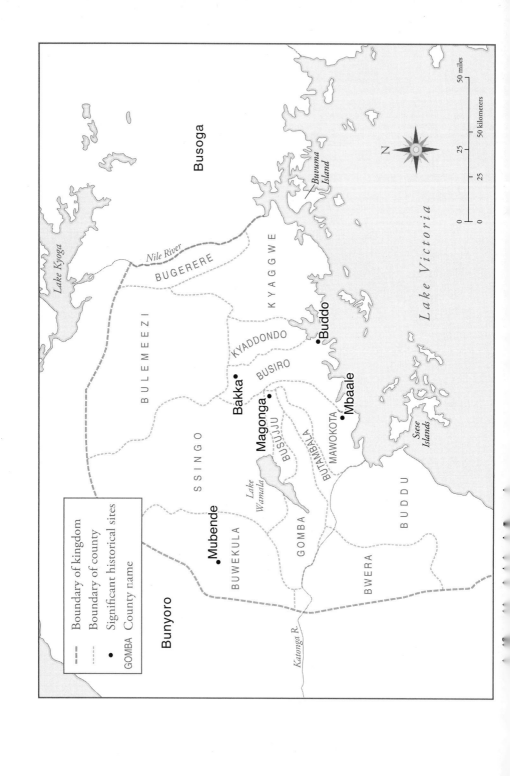

during discussions with healers who practice their profession through spirit possession. In pointing to these alternative conceptions I do not mean to raise questions concerning authenticity and veracity. Rather, I want to suggest that these variants provide insightful clues about an alternative arena in which stories about Kintu, as well as other prominent figures in Ganda historical discourse, once lived and circulated on a considerably larger scale than they do today. By exploring the relationship between *where* listeners engage with a story and *what* they hear, I show that the healer's shrine served as a prominent, perhaps even the oldest locale for generating the content and meaning of stories about Kintu and several other prominent Ganda historical personalities.

If Ganda healers suggest that there were two sorts of Kintus, then understanding the significance of each requires us to imagine how audiences at different locations might have understood the narratives about the Kintu persona. Such an exercise in historical imagination necessarily entails recognizing how historical actors exercised claims to truth quite different from those made by professional guilded historians. The first Kintu, the one who founded a royal dynasty and produced a successor to his throne, circulates within a familiar generic framework and has therefore figured prominently in Ganda historiography. The second Kintu occupies less familiar, less visible terrain and has barely made an appearance. In this chapter I seek to redress this imbalance by pursuing two related strands of argument. The first strand explores the intellectual history of colonial Buganda and the manner in which Ganda narratives about the past, and specifically about Kintu, were incorporated into the historical arena as written texts. As the first generation of literate Baganda intellectuals struggled to come to terms with a rapidly shifting world, they produced written accounts of Buganda's past that sought acceptance in an emerging discursive universe shared by elite Baganda, colonial officials, and European missionaries. These accounts suppressed particular understandings of narratives such as those about Kintu, and an examination of the intellectual politics surrounding their production paves the way for a rereading of these well-known foundational stories.

This historiographic excavation leads directly to the second strand of argument pursued in this chapter. Through a consideration of the three main narratives about Kintu, I examine how conceptual innovations in the institution of spirit mediumship and the expansion of territorial cults contributed to critical political developments in the distant Ganda past. By dislodging spiritual entities from their territorial bases, ambitious leaders inaugurated a series of intellectual and social transformations that would have widespread ramifications for the development of complex political communities. The concept of spiritual portability allowed initiated mediums to transport their spiritual patrons from one place to another and extended the territory for which a particular spirit and its earthly representatives might ensure collective health and prosperity. These developments led to a period of increased competition as well as alliance between rival healing complexes. During this period, healers' shrines emerged as sites of creative ambition where aspiring leaders fused ritual and political power and created stories to explain the nature of their authority.

KINTU AND BEMBA THE SNAKE

There are three main narratives in which Kintu serves as one of the primary characters: "Kintu and Bemba the Snake," "Kintu and Nambi," and "Kintu and Kisolo." Though not necessarily treated by either Baganda or outside scholars as individual elements of a single set of ideas, these three narratives constitute what I call the "Kintu Episode" in Ganda traditions. For the moment I will focus on the first of these narratives, "Kintu and Bemba the Snake":[3]

Bemba Omusota (Bemba the Snake)[4] ruled Buganda prior to Kintu's arrival in the country. He resided at Buddo Hill, which was then called Naggalabi Hill, from where he plundered his own subjects and caused the deaths of many people. Bemba's tyrannical nature even led him to kill a son of his prime minister, Mukiibi,[5] the head of the Pangolin clan, forcing him to flee the country along with his other sons. While in exile, Mukiibi met Kintu at Mangira, in Kyaggwe, where he offered to assist him in overthrowing Bemba and volunteered the services of two of his men, Nfudu (Tortoise) and Kigave (Pangolin).[6] Upon completing their meeting, Kintu, Mukiibi, Kigave, and Nfudu traveled together with the people of Mangira to Bukesa, where Kigave and his assistant Nfudu set up a base from which to attack Bemba.

One day Nfudu and Kigave visited Bemba's palace disguised as visitors. After spending a few days there, they told Bemba that people of high respect did not sleep with their heads intact and that he should take off his head at night as they did at their homes. Kigave demonstrated what they meant by pointing to his friend Nfudu, whose head had disappeared into his shell.[7] The following evening Bemba asked his guests to cut off his head so that he could sleep with a lot of respect just like them.[8] Nfudu and Kigave then chopped off Bemba's head and carried it to Kintu, who became the *kabaka* of Buganda and established his capital at Magonga, in Busujju.

KINTU, COLONIALISM, AND HISTORICAL ANALYSIS

That a "tradition" becomes a text that then circulates as "history" should not be taken for granted by historians investigating early periods of Africa's pasts in places where the culture of literacy emerged relatively recently.[9] In Buganda this process occurred in a volatile environment fraught with political and discursive restraints, both local and international. As Baganda intellectuals struggled to present their past in a manner that was palatable to those in power in order to win legitimacy in the colonial world, they sought to domesticate a European vision of what constituted proper subjects for historical inquiry and analysis. For our purposes, the significance of this process lies not so much in the nature of the competing political interests at play as in the effect these undertakings have had on historians' understanding of Ganda narratives about the past, particularly "Kintu and Bemba the Snake."

The first generation of literate Baganda intellectuals often included "Kintu and Bemba the Snake" and similar types of narratives in their presentations of the Ganda past. Over the course of colonial debates concerning the bounds of historical analysis, however, these stories were either relegated to the category of fable (*olugero*) or transformed into narratives that meshed with recently introduced European discursive constructs. The manner in which these narratives entered the historical arena as written texts has had a profound impact on subsequent analyses of the Ganda past, and any examination of these early glimpses into Ganda history must therefore necessarily begin with the kingdom's more recent experiences during the colonial period. Rather than serving as a means of transcending the colonial experience in order to reveal an "authentic," usable set of "traditions," however, this clearing of the "colonial clutter" recognizes how particular understandings of the Kintu narratives and the cultural domains in which they circulated became hidden during the colonial period.[10] Such recognition enables a rereading of the Kintu Episode in Ganda history and lays the foundation for an examination of earlier attempts at suppression, or at least reformulation, which predated the imposition of colonial rule by almost two hundred years.

The first published version of "Kintu and Bemba the Snake" appeared in

1901 in Apolo Kaggwa's *Bakabaka b'e Buganda* (*The Kings of Buganda*), followed a few years later by the colonial administrator J. F. Cunningham's account.[11] Over the next few decades several versions of the narrative appeared in the Luganda-language Catholic missionary newspaper *Munno*,[12] various clan histories,[13] and historical treatises written by Baganda intellectuals.[14] These renditions and their accompanying commentaries generated considerable debate among literate Baganda concerning proper historical practices. In this respect, the narrative served as one of the principal markers around which prominent Baganda sought in the colonial period to distinguish between "history" and other types of discourse. In a much broader sense, then, the incorporation of "Kintu and Bemba the Snake" into an emerging discursive universe shared by literate Baganda intellectuals, colonial officials, and European missionaries encapsulated the challenges elite Baganda faced in coming to terms with a rapidly changing world.

European missionaries were not the first outsiders to introduce reading and writing into Buganda. This distinction belonged to Arab and Swahili traders, who reached the court of Kabaka Muteesa in the mid-nineteenth century and taught a small number of Baganda how to read and write in Arabic. Literacy remained largely confined to speakers of Arabic, however, and not until after the entry of British colonial officials at about the turn of the century did Baganda begin to write histories and other types of treatises in Luganda. These developments closely followed the rise to power of a cohort of Protestant chiefs led by Apolo Kaggwa, whose intellectual outlook —like that of his contemporaries and future Baganda writers—owed less to a transition from an oral to a written culture than to their interactions with European missionaries and colonial officials.[15] In the midst of this shifting political and intellectual ground, Kaggwa and others, keenly aware of European notions of proper historical discourse, sought to secure Buganda's future by creating a space for the kingdom's past in the emerging colonialist historical vision. Such a task would no doubt have been all the easier if silly narratives such as that about a snake, a tortoise, and an anteater had lain beyond the bounds of "history."

Kaggwa did include "Kintu and Bemba the Snake" in the opening pages of his monumental history of the Ganda dynasty. But the story did not make sense to Kaggwa, who asked, "How could a mere snake have been the ruler of a country?"[16] Perhaps, Kaggwa conceded, Bemba and the other characters in the story were real human beings. As to the historical and human characteristics of Kintu, however, Kaggwa had no doubts. He preceded the story of

Kintu's defeat of Bemba and his conquest of Buddo (Naggalabi) Hill with a narrative about Kintu's early exploits during his journey to Buganda. This narrative traced Kintu's travels from a port called Podi, in Bunyoro,[17] to his eventual destination of Bukesa, in Butambula County, from where he set off to defeat Bemba. Along the way Kintu produced three children, to whom he distributed the countries of Buluuli, Bukedi, and Kibulala. Upon conquering Buddo Hill, Kintu left Bukesa, went to Nnono Hill, and settled at Magonga, where he established his capital.[18] No longer simply the protagonist in what European observers might have considered a children's tale, Kintu appeared in Kaggwa's history as a conquering hero who had successfully founded a kingdom in the distant past. By presenting Kintu's journey into Buganda in such explicit detail, Kaggwa depicted the founding king as a fully human historical figure who, quite sensibly, did not occupy the same discursive territories as cruel snake-rulers and crafty anteaters, headless or otherwise. His efforts reflected the manner in which the first generation of literate Baganda avoided discussing (or writing about) "Kintu and Bemba the Snake" as anything other than a mere fable or a story about a real, human conqueror-hero disguised in fablelike characteristics.

The missionary-ethnographer John Roscoe, with whom Kaggwa worked closely, echoed Kaggwa's depiction of Kintu as a conquering hero. While Roscoe acknowledged that some Ganda legends described Kintu as the first man to appear on earth, he pointed out that these "national" traditions required modification in light of the traditions about Kintu relayed by individual clans. From clan traditions, Roscoe wrote, "we may gather that Kintu was a powerful ruler, who invaded and conquered the land, and who by his superior skill incorporated the clans into one nation under his own government."[19] Statements such as these produced the framework within which several subsequent scholars situated their historical analyses of Kintu. Roscoe and Kaggwa, however, were not the first to propose the idea of Kintu as a conquering hero. In their efforts to consolidate the historical interpretation of Kintu, Roscoe and Kaggwa drew on earlier efforts to locate Kintu within Koranic and biblical histories and, as I discuss in chapter 5, perhaps even earlier ones to install him as the founder of the Ganda kingdom.

Upon their arrival in Buganda, Christian missionaries and colonial officials marveled at the sense of orderliness they found in the kingdom and immediately set about proposing explanations for this unexpected surprise. In 1878 Colonel C. E. Gordon wrote to his friend the Reverend H. Wright, "My belief is that Mtesa [Muteesa, the kabaka of Buganda] has the germs of

Christianity . . . from his Abyssinian ancestors, but he is not so situated as to feel his need, at any rate at the present."[20] If Buganda displayed the residue of a distant Christian past, then Kintu was the most logical candidate for explaining this remarkable phenomenon. A popular notion that circulated in missionary circles at the time was that Kintu had been a long-lost Christian priest who belonged to an ancient order of missionaries. Henry Morton Stanley was the first to postulate this conjecture, writing that Kintu's humane characteristics suggested that he had probably been "a priest of some old and long forgotten order."[21] As Henri Médard has noted, this theory resonated particularly well with the Catholic White Fathers missionaries, for whom a Kintu-as-priest figure served as a brilliant justification for their efforts to convert Baganda: while Baganda had a Christian background, their isolation from Rome, combined with natural human predilections, had resulted in the decaying of their Christian roots. According to this scenario, the European missionaries simply needed to demonstrate that Kintu had been a Christian and that his descendants—the Baganda—should return to their forefather's legacy. As in other aspects of the conversion process, early Baganda converts played a crucial role in the attempts to legitimate this notion. In 1894 a group of converts organized an archaeological expedition in search of proof of Kintu's origins. And Father Denoit reported in 1887 that some Christian chiefs had arranged an excursion to Kintu's shrine at Magonga, where it was thought that an old book wrapped in bark cloth, possibly a Bible, survived.[22] What they found, however, was a jawbone, and the task of converting Kintu into an adventurous early missionary proved more difficult than expected.

Another theory to which both missionaries and colonial officials turned to explain Buganda's complex administrative structure was the now infamous Hamitic hypothesis. Drawing on the revised version of this theory, in which Noah's son Ham was transformed from the progenitor of all black Africans to a movement of light-skinned peoples who had brought "civilization" to African societies, colonial officials began to look for early residue of a Hamitic presence in Buganda. Kintu played a crucial role in this search for historical traces of outside influence, as Baganda administrators, European missionaries, and colonial officials together worked to transform Kintu into an immigrant state-builder.[23] Under these circumstances, elite Baganda embarked on an effort to trace Kintu's journey from Abyssinia, a search for which the ethnographic observations of Baganda officials sent to administer other parts of the protectorate provided crucial clues. The existence of Kintu shrines throughout Busoga, the similarity of Luganda to the languages spoken in eastern Uganda, and traces of Ganda cultural practices found in the customs of the people who lived in this area all indicated to these Baganda clerks and administrators that Kintu must have passed through the Masaba area around Mount Elgon before reaching Buganda.[24] "Kintu and Bemba the Snake" did appear in the articles written by these administrators and published in vernacular missionary newspapers, but only either in muted form, in which Bemba appears as a chieflike ruler whom Kintu defeated in battle, or as an example of the tales once told by people of old.

As Michael Twaddle has noted, J. T. K. Gomotoka, the head of the Princes clan in Buganda, played a crucial role in establishing Kintu as a fully human historical character. In a series of articles published in *Munno*, Gomotoka denied the existence of Bemba, much as Kaggwa had, and upheld Kaggwa's version of the Kintu story.[25] Adopting the views of Tobi Kizito Wampamba, a frequent contributor to *Munno*, Gomotoka flatly rejected the assertions of other contributing writers that Bemba the snake had been the last in a line of pre-Kintu kings, writing that such a thing "cannot be accepted and has never been heard of in Buganda."[26] Instead, he argued that Bemba had been merely a snake, one of a series of characters in a type of story told in days gone by. "Although those who spoke in riddles in the old times said that the snake Bemba was the kabaka of Buganda," he wrote, "we very well know that these were jokes and fables. How could a snake rule people? It is possible that the reference was to the devil who had become notorious all over the world."[27] Guided by his Christian upbringing, his familiarity with European historical models,[28] and his position in the volatile Ganda political world, Gomotoka provided royal endorsement for the idea of Kintu as a foreigner and dismissed "Kintu and Bemba the Snake" as not worthy of proper historical analysis.

Professional historians working during the late colonial and postindependence periods have to a certain extent followed the various analytical paths established by Kaggwa, Roscoe, Gomotoka, and others during the first few decades of the twentieth century. In their efforts to navigate the divide between myth and history, scholars have proposed a host of interpretations of "Kintu and Bemba the Snake."[29] Those inclined to treat the narrative in a historical manner have built upon the work of their intellectual predecessors in the colonial period and have portrayed Kintu as an immigrant conqueror (or, in some cases, as a "condensed personification" of a series of immigrant conquerors) from either the east or the west who defeated a number of petty kings on his way to establishing Buganda as a kingdom.[30] Others have dismissed the migration theme in favor of less historically situated analyses, the most elaborate of which has been forwarded by Christopher Wrigley.[31] In his efforts to provide an explanation for why the "majesty of Ganda kingship [would] have been enhanced by the telling of a silly story about a tortoise and a snake," Wrigley remarked how the story, which for him signified the universal lessons related to puberty initiation, lent a dignity to the Ganda monarchy by associating it with an "emotional charge generated by the profoundest of human experiences." Wrigley embarked on the correct path in asking why Baganda should narrate the story of their kingdom's founding in the manner they did, but the symbolic universe into which the narrative's signifiers point reflects regional practices and epistemologies more than those associated with the Genesis tale of Adam and Eve or the Mesopotamian story of Gilgamesh. In this respect, three aspects of the Kintu conquest story deserve particular attention: Kintu's appearance in the broader regional setting; Bemba's portrayal as a snake, often as a python; and the role of the Mukiibi, Kigave, and Nfudu characters.

KINTU: THE REGIONAL SETTING

While the image of Kintu the conqueror-king dominates historians' accounts of Buganda's origins, the Kintu figure circulates in a broader regional context that extends beyond the borders of Buganda. The derivation of the name Kintu, in fact, suggests a far more humble and familiar origin for Buganda's founding hero than that found in Ganda dynastic narratives. Consisting of the prefix ki and the root -ntu (person), Kintu designates the "Big Person," an honorific title that may once have served as a generic designation for every prominent founder of a clan, lineage, or other sort of social collectivity. In this regard, there were many different Kintus, or "Big People," in the region prior to the collapsing of these personages into the Kintu-as-dynastic-founder figure in Buganda. The transition from Kintu the "Big Person" to Kintu the dynastic founder, however, did not occur throughout the region. A brief examination of the Kintu character in the histories of the Soga states, to the east of Buganda, illuminates regional transformations in the character's significance and function.[32]

As part of the process of clan formation in Busoga, a specific category of spirits was created there designed to perpetuate the memories of the eponymous founders of Busoga's numerous clans. Known as nkuni, these spirits resided in areas where a particular clan first settled or arrived in Busoga and presided over the community's continued well-being. Clan members consulted nkuni and made offerings at the nkuni shrines located on these original settlements. These activities granted firstcomer status and the entitlements that accompanied such a distinction to participating clan members. However, while nkuni sites anchored a clan's discursive and ritual acts in a primary geographical location, clan members could carry their nkuni with them as they moved into new areas and established new settlements.[33]

In Busoga, some nkuni spirits became more prominent than others and "were often associated with such important forces as fertility and death, and such important events as birth and marriage." Basoga referred to these spirits as misambwa, and Kintu proved the most revered in southern Busoga. In most parts of the Great Lakes region, misambwa referred to a category of territorial spirits that manifested themselves as wild animals—usually leopards, snakes, and crocodiles—and resided in features of the natural environment such as trees, rivers, hills, and stones. In his examination of early Soga history, David Cohen noted that in addition to misambwa such as Kintu, there were also in Busoga "older misambwa" that resembled those described above. Shrines at which people made offerings and sought assistance by consulting the musambwa Kintu through the services of a medium appeared throughout Busoga, where people also planted a tree in honor of the spirit before erecting a new house.[34] In southern Busoga, then, Kintu appears to have undergone a transformation from a nkuni, a spirit designed to perpetuate the memory of a clan's founding "Big Person," to a musambwa, a more wide-ranging spiritual entity associated with a category of experience (e.g., fertility or death) or a particular territory.[35]

The meanings attached to the Kintu figure in southern Busoga shed light on Kintu's significance in Buganda prior to his transformation into dynastic founder. Baganda legitimate and perpetuate the memories of notable historical figures and spirits by anchoring them in specific sites of reminiscence embedded in the landscape. Such a place exists for Kintu at Magonga, an area just west of the Mayanja River in Busujju. Situated on the eighteenth-century border with the kingdom of Bunyoro, Magonga lies quite a distance from the fertile lakeshore where Kintu defeated the tyrannical Bemba at Buddo (Naggalabi) Hill. As a ritual site dedicated to the musambwa Kintu, Magonga brought together a complex configuration of communities comprising ritual specialists, herders, cultivators, and healers.

Perhaps the most striking feature of the activities undertaken at Magonga, or more specifically the plot called Nnono at Magonga, was the number and diversity of participating clans.[36] At least a dozen clans contributed to the ritual center's functioning, some of which later emerged as among the most prominent in the kingdom.[37] These clans established a variety of ritual and discursive connections with Kintu at Magonga. The Frog clan, for example, maintained its principal estate several miles northeast of Magonga, at Bukerekere (Land of the Frogs), in Busiro, home of its leader, Nankere. However, at each new moon the clan's leader and his followers journeyed from Bukerekere to Magonga, where they performed a series of rituals at Kintu's shrine. All of Nankere's "children," along with their *misambwa* spirits of Bukerekere and those housed at another Frog clan estate near Magonga, attended these rituals, after which they returned to their home in Bukerekere. The clan also maintained additional connections to Magonga. The clan's main drum, for instance, was presented to the head of clan after a series of activities beginning at Magonga and ending at Bukerekere. In addition, Kintu's estate at Magonga housed the Frog clan's horned charm (*jjembe*) Nawanga, whose caretaker carried it to the Kikasa celebrations performed at the clan's main shrine in honor of Mukasa, the powerful spirit associated with Lake Victoria.[38]

The Frog clan's connections to Kintu at Magonga illustrate not only the ritual center's integrative capacity but also its links to wider ritual networks. The clan's spiritual home remained at Bukerekere, where clan members gathered at the estate's shrine to honor the *misambwa* spirits that inhabited the area. Yet the clan's ritual tentacles stretched south to Magonga, where Frog clan members participated in ceremonies at Kintu's estate. These ceremonies served as occasions when Frog clan members interacted with people belonging to a number of different clans, which themselves formed part of social, ritual, and discursive networks reaching in a variety of directions. In this regard, Kintu the *musambwa* spirit did not "belong" to any particular clan. Mwanje, of the Leopard clan, who served as the shrine's main priest, held the most exalted position in the ritual complex at Magonga.[39] His association with the leopard, which circulates widely in the region as a symbol of royalty, suggests the emergence of an early "kingdom" at Nnono centered around the *musambwa* Kintu.[40] But Kintu's life-sustaining capacities resulted from the participation of a number of different groups of people, and Mwanje played but one role, albeit a critical one, in activating Kintu's powers.

In the mid-eighteenth century, leaders of the Leopard clan played a crucial role in the discursive and ritual transformation of Kintu into Buganda's dynastic founder. Their efforts resulted in the establishment of a new royal installation rite at Buddo Hill and prompted the incorporation of "Kintu and Bemba the Snake" into the emerging Ganda dynastic narrative (see chapter 5). Prior to attaining the status of Buganda's first king, however, Kintu the *musambwa* serviced Magonga as a spiritual entity toward which communities directed practices designed to ensure continued prosperity and abundance. These communities sought to maintain their well-being by consolidating their intellectual energies and productive capacities around their spiritual patron. They participated in collective ritual practices, such as those that occurred at each new moon, at the *musambwa* Kintu's "home" at Magonga. But each also formed part of a wider network of alliances that stretched beyond Magonga. This understanding of the Kintu figure opens the door for an alternative reading of "Kintu and Bemba the Snake," and a similar analysis of the Bemba character lends further insight into the shifting political and intellectual environment in which Baganda crafted what would eventually become their kingdom's founding narrative.

BEMBA: PYTHONS, PROSPERITY, AND LAKE VICTORIA

As a counterpart to the benevolent protector Kintu, Bemba appears as a tyrannical ruler who plunders his subjects and brings harm to surrounding communities. While this depiction of Bemba dominates all accounts of the Kintu and Bemba narrative, ethnographic evidence from Buganda as well as other areas in the Great Lakes region suggests that Bemba—or the form of authority that he personifies—probably did not always appear in this manner to Baganda historical actors. This evidence hints at how Bemba's despotic characteristics represent the outcome of a struggle that resulted in the reorientation of the healing capacities of particular ritual centers and the spirits associated with them. Before considering this transformation itself, however, we must first examine the nature of the authority that Bemba represents. Two particular features of the Bemba character stand out and warrant further attention: Bemba's appearance as a snake, often a python; and the location of Bemba's "capital" at Buddo Hill, close to the shores of Lake Victoria (see map 2). Taken together, these two features furnish insight into both the type of authority Bemba held over his subjects and the nature of the social and intellectual transformations that his defeat entailed.

In their efforts to promote and maintain social health and continued prosperity, the communities living along the western shores of Lake Victoria from the fourteenth to the sixteenth century drew upon an ancient intellectual tradition inherited from their distant ancestors. For Ganda communities, these collective endeavors included the practice of directing acts of sacrifice and dedication to territorially based spirits known as *misambwa*. These spirits resided in features of the natural environment and presided over the success of fishing, hunting, and farming endeavors. *Misambwa* spirits oversaw these activities in localities occupied by several lineages. However, particular lineages or families, those designated as having been the first to arrive in the area, maintained authority over these local spirits. These lineages displayed their status as firstcomers in ritual settings by providing the priests or mediums at important *misambwa* shrines and by coordinating acts of sacrifice and dedication to *misambwa* on behalf of all members of the community.[41]

Ethnographers working in the Great Lakes region in the late nineteenth and early twentieth centuries noted that *misambwa* spirits frequently manifested themselves as snakes, most often as pythons. These early ethnographers also observed that the lineages or families who directed acts of sacrifice and dedication toward *misambwa* spirits often performed these rites at locations where powerful pythons dwelt. John Roscoe provided perhaps the best account of these practices in his early twentieth-century observations of the activities undertaken at Bulonge, a locality near the shores of Lake Victoria in Buddu. Roscoe described a series of activities centered around a shrine located in a forest on the shores of Lake Victoria near the banks of the Mujuzi River. Members of the Heart clan cultivated the areas surrounding the shrine and provided its priest, a hereditary office within the clan occupied by the estate's principal caretaker. In addition to his role in the area's ritual activities, the estate's caretaker was also responsible for maintaining the shrine. On one side of the shrine's interior were the resting places of the python Sserwanga and his guardian, while the other side included a sleeping area for the medium and his assistant, both of whom lived at the shrine.

Ritual practices directed toward Sserwanga sought to ensure the well-being and prosperity of the entire community as well as of its individual members. Fishermen requested success in their expeditions from the shrine's medium, who sought to meet these requests by tying fowls on the riverbank for the python to devour. Successful expeditions were followed by a feast, for which the medium prepared the fish and the estate's residents provided cooked vegetables and beer. In addition to fishermen, newly married men desiring children or those whose wives had not yet produced any also sought the python's blessing. Sserwanga's ability to secure abundance for its devotees, however, relied on rituals carried out on behalf of the community by the shrine's medium and priest. These rituals occurred at the appearance of a new moon, and Roscoe's account deserves a rather lengthy quotation:

> For several days before the moon became visible the people made prepa-
> rations because there was no work allowed to be done on the estate for
> seven days. Directly after the new moon appeared the drums were beaten
> and the people gathered for the worship; those who had requests to make
> brought offerings for the god; they were chiefly beer, cowrie shells, and a
> few goats and fowls. The priest always came with a large following of
> smaller chiefs. The priesthood was hereditary, and the holder of it was
> always the chief of the estate. When the priest had received the offerings
> from the people and told the python what had been brought and the
> number of requests, he dressed the Medium in the sacred dress ready for
> the python to take possession of him. . . . When the priest had thus
> dressed the Medium, he gave him a small gourd full of beer to drink, and
> afterwards some of the milk mixed with the white clay from the python's
> bowl; the spirit of the python then came upon the man, and he went down
> on his face and wriggled about upon his stomach like a snake, uttering
> peculiar noises, and speaking in a tongue which required an interpreter
> to explain to the people. The people stood around and looked on whilst
> the drums were beaten and the python gave its oracle. The interpreter,
> named Lukumirizi, stood by listening until the Medium had ended his
> speech; when he finished his talk he fell down like a person in a sound
> sleep for a long time utterly overcome with his exertions. Lukumirizi the
> interpreter then explained what had been foretold, and told the fortunate
> persons whose requests had been granted what they were to do in order
> to obtain their desire, and what was the medical treatment which the wife
> was to undergo, &c. This ceremony was repeated each day during the
> seven days feasting.[42]

Roscoe's description of the activities related to Sserwanga at Bulonge reveals several crucial features of misambwa practices in general and those involving pythons more specifically. The conflation of the offices of priest-interpreter and family head of the estate's principal lineage illustrates the fusion of ritual and political authority that occurred at places of creative power, such as Sserwanga's shrine.[43] Sserwanga's priestly interpreter held the title Lukumirizi, an honorific designation derived from okukumiriza, the causative form of the verb okukuma, "to heap up, pile together, concentrate."[44] The title Lukumirizi also, however, plays on the verb okukuumiriza, the causative form of okukuuma, "to guard, protect, watch over." As the person endowed with the capacity to gather together people as well as offerings, and as guardian of Sserwanga's shrine and the community's interests, Lukumirizi, in his role as intermediary between Sserwanga's medium and devotees, was in an advantageous position from which to steer the moral content of residents' behaviors.[45] Lukumirizi's role as priest-interpreter also explains the effective significance of firstcomer status. Like the priests at almost all misambwa shrines in Buganda, the priest at Sserwanga's shrine came from a family claiming a long-term relationship with the spirit. This creative combination of ritual, political, and material power meant that any challenge to existing authority would necessarily have to overcome the compelling connection between positions of leadership and the ability to direct a community's collective well-being. Attempts to supplant a priestly lineage's claim to this status would inevitably run the risk of offending the local musambwa and would require that skilled priests or mediums persuade local residents of the superior efficacy of an alternative spirit.[46]

The practices centered around Sserwanga also illustrate the limitations inherent in the musambwa concept. As spiritual entities resident in the land and associated with particular features in the natural environment, misambwa necessarily remained attached to specific localities. In addition, because misambwa manifested themselves as animals, a particular musambwa's authoritative reach extended, in a sense, only as far as the territory covered by its animal host. The territorial limitations placed on misambwa also applied to their priests and guardians, whose responsibilities for maintaining a community's well-being, like those of the spirits they served, covered a specific territory and its residents. As the priestly representative of the musambwa Sserwanga and a prominent member of the Heart clan, Lukumirizi exercised authority over residents living at Bulonge, an area over which his clan claimed firstcomer status. But the fusion of political and ritual authority personified in his role as priest at a specific sacred site would make it difficult to extend the range of his influence to surrounding communities. These conceptual limitations, combined with the redistributive obligations enacted at feasts such as those undertaken at new-moon ceremonies, placed significant constraints on the ambitions of prominent priests and the misambwa spirits they represented.

When presenting their requests to a *musambwa*, local residents offered gifts and made sacrifices at sacred sites in hopes of engaging the territorial spirit and its earthly representatives in a mutually beneficial relationship based on notions of reciprocity and redistribution.[47] As Roscoe's account illustrates, however, ritual practices involving *misambwa* that manifested themselves as pythons also included the ancient practice of spirit possession known throughout the Great Lakes region as *kubándwa*. The widespread analogy in the Great Lakes region between the manner in which a spirit possesses a person and that in which a python seizes its prey hints at the historical depth of this connection. Baganda living along the shores of Lake Victoria, for example, drew upon this analogy in naming the sea serpent associated with the lake's principal spirit, Mukasa. Baganda refer to the act by which a spirit possesses a person as "seizing" the victim's head, *kukwata ku mutwe*, a phrase from which they derived the lake monster's name, Lukwâta.[48] The complex conceptual overlap between *misambwa*, their animal hosts, and spirit possession found throughout the region, along with the equally widespread analogy between the acts of marrying and initiation as a *musambwa*'s medium, further suggests that the connection between pythons and spirit possession constituted part of an ancient intellectual tradition.[49] As indicated in the likely derivation of the term *musambwa* from the verb *okusamba*, "to judge," the significance of the connection between spirit possession and *misambwa* for the early history of Buganda as well as other parts of the Great Lakes region may have rested in the ability of mediums and priests to influence political and intellectual developments through the rendering of justice.[50]

In attributing to Sserwanga the capacity to ensure successful fishing expeditions, residents of Bulonge demonstrated the common association between pythons and bodies of water, in this case the Mujuzi River and, by extension, Lake Victoria. Similar associations appeared throughout the Great Lakes region: the Kafu and Muzizi rivers reportedly housed powerful pythons responsible for maintaining high water levels; a spirit that manifested itself as a python controlled Kisengwe, an ancient node of ritual authority on the upper reaches of the Nguse River; the islands of Lake Victoria were thought to transform themselves into giant pythons; and a forceful python provided abundance and prosperity to the people living on the northeastern shores of Lake Victoria, in Kavirondo.[51] Great Lakes historical actors also broadened this ancient connection between pythons, abundance, and natural bodies of water to include wells and pools of water found in caves.[52] Thus the python spirit Magobwe resided near a well situated on top of Kagaba Hill, and the *musambwa* Nakamwana, which prevented the principal well from drying up at the Dog clan estate of Kiggwa, in Busujju, appeared in the form of a python.[53] The association of pythons and bodies of water drew upon the ancient conceptual connection between ancestral ghosts (*mizimu*) and snakes in general. When a living body died, its life force (*mwoyo*) continued to operate by bestowing the gift of life upon the disembodied spirit, the *muzimu*.[54] As the disembodied life force, a *muzimu* entered the underworld, which served as its permanent abode, according to conceptions developed in western Uganda, or a mere stopping point on the journey to its burial ground, according to Ganda formulations.[55] And since some *mizimu* could manifest themselves as snakes, most often as pythons, the bodies of water around which they usually dwelt—lakes, rivers, wells, pools—appeared as conduits to the underworld.[56]

Python centers similar to the one described by Roscoe dotted the shores of Lake Victoria in the distant past. These centers formed part of an intellectual network that elaborated upon the connections between pythons, the life-sustaining qualities of water, and the capacity of water to function as a mediatory substance and a vehicle for ontological transformation.[57] An example drawn from the history of the Genet Cat clan, in Buganda, demonstrates how canoes transported, both in a literal and a metaphorical sense, this complex association of ideas from the Ssese Islands, in Lake Victoria, to estates on the mainland. According to Genet Cat clan histories, the clan played a crucial role in Kabaka Nakibinge's well-known campaign against the Banyoro, Buganda's western neighbors. As Nakibinge prepared for his journey to the Ssese Islands to seek assistance in his campaign, a diviner told the king that when he reached Bussi Island he would hear someone chopping trees in the forest. The diviner told the king that this person would ferry him in a canoe to Bukesa Island, where the spirit Wannema would provide him with a brave young man to assist him in his battle against the Banyoro. Upon reaching Bussi Island, Nakibinge heard a man named Nakiiso, of the Genet Cat clan, chopping wood in the forest, just as the diviner had foretold. The king approached Nakiiso, who as it turned out was constructing a canoe to return to his home on Zzinga Island. Nakiiso ferried Nakibinge to Bukesa Island and then back to the mainland in a canoe called *Nakawungu* (from *okuwunguka*, "to cross over a body of water, be ferried, transport across a body of water"). As a sign of gratitude for the service he had provided, the king bestowed upon Nakiiso the name Kabazzi, an honorific title derived from the verb *okubajja*, "to chop into shape, engage in carpentry work," which came to designate the head of the Genet Cat clan.[58]

Nakiiso's canoe, *Nakawungu*, eventually achieved prominence as part of the royal naval fleet.[59] The name Nakawungu, however, circulates in a different fashion at the Genet Cat clan's principal estate, on the mainland at Kyango, in Mawokota. A giant incense tree (*Canarium schweinfurthii*) called Nakawungu stands at the center of the estate and functions as a sacred site where individuals seek assistance from the area's spiritual forces and residents gather to "beat drums and call the spirits." The tree acquired the name Nakawungu on account of its growing on top of the grave of a prominent woman named Nakawungu, whose ancestral ghost became a territorial spirit that continues to inhabit the tree and grant the gift of childbirth. One of the tree's several visible roots resembles Nakawungu's outspread legs, and there women who have not yet conceived place offerings and make their requests. Some of the other roots resemble snakes, and in the shrine situated close to the tree the *musambwa* Nakawungu manifests herself in the form of a python.[60] Nakawungu's spirit also appears at the estate of the Kasendwa subbranch of the Genet Cat clan, where it resides in a well thought to contain healing substances and serves as the vehicle through which members of patrilineages (*masiga*) "link up to the clan's spirits."[61] Finally, the Genet Cat clan presides over an estate named Nakawungu in coastal Kyaggwe, from where in the past its residents crossed the lake to "fetch" the spirit Mukasa.[62]

Nakawungu's enduring presence as a spiritual entity in the Genet Cat clan provides a telling example of how lacustrine historical actors transported a complex set of ideas relating fertility, abundance, pythons, and the powers of Lake Victoria from the Ssese Islands to settlements on the mainland. In his examination of the powers associated with Lake Victoria, Michael Kenny noted that the people living along the eastern lakeshores believed their canoes to be inhabited by spirits. These canoe spirits originated in the trees used to construct the canoe's keel, where the spirits resided, and manifested themselves as pythons to receive offerings as directed by the people whom they possessed. Residents also attached to their canoes "hair" made from the cloth streamers of old canoes in order to create a resemblance to the lake's giant sea serpents.[63] Building upon this image and the example from the Genet Cat clan, we can easily imagine a scenario in which residents of lakeside communities, traveling in serpentlike canoes between the Ssese Islands and various points along the lakeshores, carried with them critical ideas and practices associating notions of abundance and fertility with spirit possession, pythons, and the powers emanating from the bodies of water in which pythons often dwelt. Members of the communities to which they journeyed would have then drawn upon existing conceptual categories—the ancient notion of ancestral ghosts, the well-established idea of consecrating a person to a spirit, and the connection between these two concepts and a community's well-being—to translate and extend these ideas and practices further inland.

In their broadest sense, then, the python centers that dotted the shores of Lake Victoria formed part of an ancient intellectual complex combining the connection between ancestral ghosts, territorial misambwa spirits, and pythons with spirit possession, fertility, and the mediatory nature of water. Situated in close proximity to Lake Victoria on the Busiro shoreline, Buddo Hill—home of the python named Bemba—was just such a center.[64] Because of the clanless nature of the kingship in Buganda, most dynastic accounts of the Kintu and Bemba narrative depict Bemba as having no clan, so as to avoid associating the kingship with a specific indigenous clan. However, a combination of evidence drawn from clan histories and descriptions of the royal-accession rites at Buddo Hill in the mid-eighteenth century suggests that the Lungfish clan may have presided over a python center there in the distant past.

Among all Ganda clans only the Lungfish clan claims Bemba as one of their ancestors, a claim that resonates with the clan's contributions to the lacustrine cultural complex along the northwestern shores of Lake Victoria.[65] The Ssese archipelago formed part of a network of economic relations that included people living on the lakeshores to the west, north, and possibly as far east as Ukerewe.[66] The Lungfish clan played a prominent role in canoe-borne economic activities between the Ssese Islands and coastal Busiro, and clan members presided over a diffuse network of estates along the lakeshore as well as on Lake Victoria's major islands.[67] Some of these estates functioned as centers of canoe construction, where skilled professionals engaged in the complex craft.[68] These early canoe builders and oarsmen appear as the ancestral figures in Lungfish clan histories in Buganda, where Lungfish clan members later provided the main canoe men for the royal fleet, which was headed by the clan's leader, Gabunga.[69]

In addition to playing a major role in lacustrine canoe-building and trading activities, the Lungfish clan stood at the heart of the region's intellectual and ritual complex. The clan contributed to the administration of the principal shrine dedicated to Mukasa, the lake's primary spirit. Mukasa's mother, Nambubi Namatimba, reportedly belonged to the Lungfish clan, as did his medium as well as several other prominent individuals with connections to Ssese. In addition, the clan's leader, Gabunga, served as an intermediary between the *kabaka* and Mukasa's earthly representatives. When Mukasa's principal shrine required repair or rebuilding, for example, Gabunga ferried a royal attendant to Bubembe Island and presented him to the spirit, whose priest accepted the *kabaka*'s offerings before summoning the island's residents to begin the restoration.[70] Gabunga's intermediary role was reinforced by the clan's lungfish totem, whose anomalous characteristics seem to have inspired metaphorical associations with the spiritual realm. An air-breathing creature that inhabits the mudflats along the lake and resembles a snake, the lungfish provided oarsmen traveling between ritual centers on the Ssese Islands and lakeshore settlements with a totemic symbol capable of capturing the metaphysical capacities of their intermediary role.[71]

The royal-accession rites instituted at Buddo Hill in the mid-eighteenth century ultimately transformed the sacred site from a python center into a venue for the *kabaka*'s inauguration (see chapter 5).[72] Some of the details of these rites, however, contain the residue of Buddo Hill's previous existence and further suggest an association with the Lungfish clan. When the *kabaka*-elect and his entourage arrived at Buddo Hill, they were met by the hill's guardian, a Lungfish clan member who served as the hill's priest, along with a clanmate. The guardian-priests blocked the king-elect from entering the compound, and after engaging the *kabaka*'s men in a mock battle, they permitted the royal entourage to enter the site. The two guardians then led the king-elect to a house called Buganda, which was regarded as the former dwelling of Bemba and his predecessors. There the king-elect participated in a series of ceremonies, including one in which he sharpened a brass spear on the living body of a python. He then spent the night in the house before undergoing the remaining ritual activities the following day.

The most venerated drum in the Ganda royal battery also reveals a connection between the Lungfish clan and python centers such as Buddo Hill. Known as Ttimba, the Luganda word for "python," this drum acquired its name from the relief of a serpent carved on its body. A member of the Lungfish clan who lived on Bugala Island, in the Ssese archipelago, served as the drum's guardian and later became a member of the royal navy. The drum's name and its association with the Lungfish clan and the Ssese Islands suggests that prior to becoming part of the royal battery of drums known collectively as Mujaguzo, Ttimba was employed by mediums and priests at the possession rituals that occurred at python centers.[73]

The numerous linkages between the Lungfish clan, Buddo Hill, and the lacustrine cultural complex suggest the following scenario: Ssemanobe, the Lungfish guardian-priest at Buddo Hill, managed a drum similar to Ttimba as part of his priestly duties. At public ceremonies akin to the one Roscoe described at Bulonge, residents of Buddo Hill assembled to perform a series of rituals designed to ensure the community's continued prosperity. The hill's Lungfish clan guardians directed the community's offerings and ritual efforts toward a spiritual entity named Bemba, which manifested itself as a python and drew on a complex set of ideas connecting fertility, the mediating powers of Lake Victoria, and the spirit Mukasa. Bemba's demotion in Ganda dynastic and clan histories to the role of tyrannical ruler, then, represented the outcome of profound changes linking Kintu's "home" at Magonga and the lacustrine cultural complex on Lake Victoria's northwestern shoreline. As suggested in "Kintu and Bemba the Snake," the capacity to connect these two nodes of authority rested with the Pangolin clan leader, Mukiibi, whose role in the narrative requires further explication.

MUKIIBI: MEDIUMSHIP AND SPIRITUAL PORTABILITY

One of the striking features of "Kintu and Bemba the Snake" is the geographical distance separating Kintu's inland "home" at Magonga and Bemba's lakeside dwelling at Buddo Hill (see map 2). Building on the argument presented above that the Kintu and Bemba characters represent territorial misambwa spirits at their respective abodes, we can imagine Kintu's defeat of Bemba as the enlargement of the territory of healing over which Kintu and his representatives exercised authority. As other scholars have noted, the key to understanding how territorial spirits could have become portable rests in the connection between mediums (mmándwa) and the institution of spirit possession (kubándwa), through which community members could communicate with territorial spirits at public gatherings such as those described by Roscoe at Bulonge.

Historical linguistic evidence suggests that in the thirteenth to sixteenth centuries the ancestors of the Baganda and neighboring communities instituted an intellectual innovation that enabled the portability of territorial misambwa spirits.[74] By joining spirits to their mediums rather than to a specific territory, these historical actors severed the limiting conceptual connection between spiritual and territorial authority. The concept of spiritual portability allowed initiated spirit mediums to transport spirits from one place to another, a process that extended the territorial range over which a particular spirit and its earthly representatives might ensure collective prosperity. If listened to carefully—imagining how listeners might have understood it in a shrine setting—"Kintu and Bemba the Snake" appears to be describing just such a process: the enlargement of territories of healing and the concomitant suppression of local spirits. As mentioned above, itinerant mediums were the key figures in this transformation, a development captured in the activities of the intermediary character Mukiibi.

Significantly, in the story of Kintu and Bemba the conqueror-king Kintu did not personally defeat the tyrannical Bemba. Instead, he enlisted the assistance of the Pangolin clan leader, Mukiibi, and his representatives Nfudu and Kigave, who intervened on Kintu's behalf in order to protect the people from Bemba's misdeeds and restore order to the community. That the person or creature who mediated between Kintu and Bemba belonged to the Pangolin clan provides a compelling hint regarding the setting in which "Kintu and Bemba the Snake" emerged. In explaining the significance of the totems associated with Ganda clans, Baganda healers describe a world in which all nonhuman forms of life fall into five categories (endyo): animals (ensolo); creatures that fly (ebibuuka), including birds; insects (biwuka); creatures of the lake, including fish (byenyanja); and plants (kimera).[75] Often perceived as a cross between a mammal and a reptile, the pangolin, a type of white, scaly anteater, has many features of aquatic creatures yet lives exclusively on land. As such, it does not fit any of the prescribed categories according to which Baganda healers and others classify nonhuman forms of life, a characteristic that lent the pangolin to particular metaphorical associations. As an anomalous creature that eluded categorization according to the Ganda taxonomy of nonhuman beings, the pangolin possessed the necessary metaphysical associations required of a mediatory figure.[76] The same quality—the ability to serve in a mediating capacity—presumably was imparted to the leaders of those who adopted the pangolin as their totem.[77]

Viewed in the context of Great Lakes healing practices, the role of the Mukiibi and Kigave characters resembled that played by mediums throughout the region, with the additional flourish that these characters could transport their mediating skills, along with the spirits they represented, to new areas. According to "Kintu and Bemba the Snake," the Pangolin clan leader Mukiibi first "met" Kintu at the Leopard clan estate of Mangira, in Kyaggwe, where he introduced Kintu to his two representatives Kigave and Nfudu. From Mangira, they journeyed together to another Leopard clan holding at Bukesa, in Busujju, which served as the base from which Kigave and Nfudu formulated their plan to defeat Bemba. Viewed from the perspective of transformations in regional healing practices, these meetings might be regarded as representing the induction of a group of mediums headed by the Pangolin clan leader Mukiibi into a regional healing complex centered on the spirit Kintu and connected to groups of people who recognized the leopard as their totem. Armed with newly acquired mediating skills and the backing of their spiritual benefactor, Kintu, Kigave and Nfudu set out for Buddo Hill, where they encountered the followers of the *musambwa* Bemba. Kigave and Nfudu managed to convince the area's inhabitants of Kintu's superior healing capacities, a process that may have hinged on the greater access to wider productive, trade, and therapeutic networks offered by portable spirits and their representatives.[78] The success of Kigave and Nfudu resulted in Bemba's depiction as a tyrannical, malevolent ruler and his defeat at the hands of Mukiibi's representatives. Bemba's decapitation served as a narrative device symbolizing the suppression of Bemba's medium, who could no longer be "seized by the head" and direct the community's activities on Bemba's behalf.[79] In presenting Bemba's head to Kintu, Kigave and Nfudu transferred Bemba's responsibilities to Kintu, the mediums through whom he spoke, and the priests who presided over his shrines.

KINTU AND NAMBI

The second main narrative involving Kintu describes the circumstances of his marriage to his wife, Nambi:[80]

Kintu arrived in Buganda with nothing other than his one cow. As there was no food in the country, he lived off of only what his cow provided. After some time, Nambi and her brothers came down from the sky and eventually stumbled across Kintu. Nambi was captivated by the stranger of unknown origins and informed Kintu that she wished to marry him. Upon hearing of his daughter's intentions, Nambi's father, Ggulu—the ruler of the sky country—ordered his sons to steal Kintu's cow and bring the animal to the sky. Fearing that Kintu would die of hunger and thirst, Nambi returned to Kintu and informed him of what had happened. She then invited him to the sky to retrieve his cow and to take her away. When Kintu arrived in the sky, Ggulu subjected him to a series of impossible tasks: consuming enormous amounts of food, cutting firewood from solid rock, filling a pot with dew, and picking out his cow from Ggulu's considerable herd. Kintu succeeded in each of these tasks, after which Ggulu presented him with his daughter Nambi and provided the couple with cows, goats, fowl, and plantains. Ggulu, however, warned Kintu and Nambi that they should depart quickly before Nambi's brother Walumbe (Death) found out about their marriage. He also ordered the couple never to return so that they could avoid Walumbe.

Kintu and Nambi immediately embarked upon their journey. Along the way, however, they realized that they had forgotten the grain for the fowl. Nambi insisted on returning for it, and despite Kintu's protestations, she journeyed back to the sky against Ggulu's order.[81] When Nambi arrived at her father's place, her bother Walumbe spotted her and insisted on accompanying her back to earth. Nambi and Walumbe returned to earth, where Nambi planted her garden and where she and Kintu produced a number of children. The couple lived happily until Walumbe asked Kintu to let one of his children serve as a cook for Walumbe. Kintu refused Walumbe, who then threatened to kill Kintu's children. Kintu did not understand what Walumbe meant and ignored his threat. But when his children began to fall ill and die, he returned to the sky and appealed to Ggulu for help.

Upon hearing Kintu's plea, Ggulu sent Nambi's other brother, Kayiikuzi (The Digger), to fetch Walumbe. Walumbe, however, refused to return to his father's abode, and despite Kayiikuzi's efforts, he managed to escape his brother's grasp and flee into the underworld at a place called Ttanda. Twice Kayiikuzi managed to drag Walumbe out, but each time he escaped. Kayiikuzi then devised a plan: he directed Kintu to order everyone to stay indoors for two days and to remain quiet even if they caught a glimpse of Walumbe. Perplexed by the quiet, Walumbe emerged from the underworld to investigate. Just as Kayiikuzi was about to capture Walumbe, however, two of Kintu's children took their goats to pasture. These two children cried out in fear when they saw Walumbe, who immediately returned to the underworld at Ttanda, where he was beyond Kayiikuzi's reach. Kayiikuzi became angry with the children, declared himself too tired to continue chasing his brother, and returned to the sky. Kintu accepted his fate and declared: "Let Walumbe continue killing my children if he must. I will never cease begetting children, so Walumbe will never be able to make an end of my people."

KINTU AND NAMBI: THE BIBLICAL INTERPRETATION

Like "Kintu and Bemba the Snake," "Kintu and Nambi" has much to tell us about early Ganda history. But as with "Kintu and Bemba the Snake," we must first briefly examine the narrative's role in shaping early interactions between European missionaries, colonial officials, and Baganda converts, whose initial recordings and commentaries have had a marked impact on subsequent analyses. "Kintu and Nambi" first appeared in written form in both Luganda and English in 1882. The Catholic White Father Le Veux published the Luganda version as part of his *Manuel de langue luganda*, while a shorter English version appeared in the travel accounts of the Anglican missionaries Charles Thomas Wilson and Robert William Felkin.[82] The narrative next emerged in print almost twenty years later, in the works of John Roscoe, whose first of three separate accounts published in the early twentieth century appeared in 1901.[83] His fellow researcher Apolo Kaggwa included the story in his collection of Ganda folktales published a year later, as did the colonial official Harry Johnston in his pseudo-ethnographic writings about his experiences in Uganda published in the same year.[84] One of Kaggwa's adversaries, the historian-politician James Miti, and the Protestant clergyman Bartolomayo Zimbe—who together provided perhaps the best sources on Ganda history in the latter part of the nineteenth century—included revealing interpretations of the narrative in their respective works.[85] Finally, contributors to the Catholic newspaper *Munno* and its Protestant counterpart *Ebifa* contemplated the narrative's meaning in their musings about the ancient roots of Christianity in Buganda.

While both Baganda and European intellectuals argued that "Kintu and Bemba the Snake" could, if stripped of certain elements, serve as a historical account of past events, no such claims circulated with regard to the "Kintu and Nambi" narrative, which all literate Baganda intellectuals regarded as either myth or fable. Despite its relegation to mythical status, however, the story of Kintu and Nambi did provide Baganda Christian converts with a recognizable drama that they could employ to cement their relationships with their European counterparts. In their efforts to establish common ground between themselves and European missionaries, these intellectuals focused a Christian lens on "Kintu and Nambi." In so doing, they inaugurated a particular understanding of the narrative that would dominate subsequent analyses.

In the commentaries that accompanied their accounts of Kintu and Nambi's activities, Baganda intellectuals writing during the early twentieth century drew parallels with the biblical account of Adam and Eve, which, like the Ganda narrative, blamed a woman's disobedience of a sky-dwelling god for bringing death into the world. Kaggwa noted that the narrative closely resembled "the works of the Holy Bible of God where we read about Adam and Eve. We see how Eve, the wife of Adam, brought death in the same way that Nambi, the wife of Kintu, brought death."[86] James Miti, a rival of Kaggwa's and one of the most prominent Ganda politicians and intellectuals during the early colonial period, reached a similar conclusion. After relating his version of the narrative in the first chapter of his comprehensive history of Buganda, Miti commented: "It is through the disobedience of Muntu Beene (Kintu) and Namuntu Bandi (Nambi) to the voice of the Lord God that we are subjected to death. They brought Walumbe along with them to the earth because of Nambi's returning to heaven to get the corn of her chickens. She did not bring death to men only, but also to every creature that did not know death before." Like Kaggwa, Miti concluded his presentation of "Kintu and Nambi" by drawing a parallel to the biblical story of Adam and Eve. "After we have learnt about Christianity," he wrote, "we are amazed to see that there is some similarity between this story and that we read in the Bible. The two stories are based on this point that both Nambi Nantuttululu and Eve yielded to temptation through the question of food and it was that that caused death to come into the world."[87]

In arriving at their respective conclusions, Kaggwa and Miti perhaps drew on the teachings of their missionary educators who indulged in similar comparisons. Le Veux, who as mentioned earlier published the first Luganda version of the narrative in 1882, commented in a footnote that Ggulu resembled the biblical Creator-God; Kintu, the first man; Nambi, his female companion, provided by God; and Kayiikuzi, the "Son of the Sky dedicated to abolishing death on earth."[88] Comparisons such as these clearly indicate early missionary receptiveness to historical speculations about Buganda's possible connection to a Christian past, a theme that would come to characterize the works of several prominent Baganda Christian converts, including the contributors to *Munno* and *Ebifa*.[89]

Of course the parallel with the story of Adam and Eve proposed by several Baganda writers necessitated that the blame for bringing death into the world fall upon Nambi, as illustrated in the writings of Kaggwa and Miti described above. In a later work, Kaggwa invoked Nambi's act of disobedience to explain, among other things, "the suffering of women" in Buganda, and his research partner Roscoe extended this line of reasoning further by describing Nambi as "the cause of all evil, sickness, and death."[90] In a similar vein, the missionary C. W. Hattersley followed his presentation of the narrative by commenting on the "very remarkable similarity between [the Kintu and Nambi] story and our own account of the Creation. Death is represented as coming into the world through the disobedience of the woman."[91] Buganda's Eve did not always occupy this ignominious position, however. In both Le Veux's and Johnston's versions of the narrative, it was Kintu who returned to the sky to fetch the chicken feed despite Nambi's ardent protestations, thus inviting Death (Walumbe) into the world. That early Baganda Christian writers ultimately blamed Nambi for this misdeed reveals their complicity in translating a religiously inspired patriarchy into a Ganda idiom.

Efforts to domesticate biblical teachings constituted a critical part of the process according to which the first generation of Christian Ganda intellectuals struggled to reconcile their recently acquired role as leaders both of Buganda's flourishing Christian communities and of a kingdom with considerably deeper historical roots. The conflation of these leadership positions inspired speculation that Buganda's position at the forefront of both Christianity and civilized life in Uganda was the inevitable result of the kingdom's exposure to Christian teachings in the distant past. Thus a contributor to *Munno* wrote in 1916 that "our religion [Christianity] did not teach us something new [about God] but reminded us of something we already knew."[92] For their part, European missionaries offered few objections to the Christianization of "Kintu and Nambi," as the process of adapting the story to the Genesis account transformed the Ganda narrative into an effective tool for conveying the Christian teachings that they sought to instill in their Baganda students.

Christian interpretations of "Kintu and Nambi" continue to circulate in Buganda and have had a significant effect on scholarly analyses. While academically trained scholars have not always adopted the Christian framework employed by Baganda intellectuals and European missionaries in the late nineteenth and early twentieth centuries, they have inherited from their predecessors the inclination to treat the story as a fable expressing some basic sociological and ontological truths but devoid of any historical meaning.[93] An alternative interpretation of Kintu and Nambi's exploits becomes possible, however, if we focus a different sort of analytical lens on accounts of the couple's activities. When Kintu and Nambi first made their way into print in the latter part of the nineteenth century, the account of their accomplishments certainly appears to have belonged to a national, though not necessarily royal, tradition widely known throughout the kingdom. Like most such traditions, however, the story of Buganda's primordial couple seems to have emerged from more modest beginnings. In Buganda, perspective and performance relied largely on the language and lens of clanship, which if focused properly can yield alternative understandings of Kintu and Nambi's significance in early Ganda history. The route back to the beginning of "The Beginning," then, follows the path of Ganda clanship, and perhaps no path is more revealing than that marked by the Colobus Monkey clan.

KINTU AND NAMBI: THE CLAN PERSPECTIVE

The plot of "Kintu and Nambi" revolves around the division of space into three realms: heaven/sky (Ggulu), the domain of the father god Ggulu; earth (Nsi), the domain of Kintu and his living descendants; and the underworld (Magombe), the domain of Walumbe and all ancestral ghosts. These three realms form the basis of Ganda cosmology and, as discussed earlier, figure in the most crucial feature of Ganda metaphysical thought. When people die on earth, their disembodied spirits enter the underworld and present themselves to Walumbe (Death) before returning to earth as ancestral ghosts. This ontological transformation allows ancestral ghosts to continue to exert their influence on earth, where they linger about the shrines built near their respective burial sites and receive offerings from living descendants.[94]

As part of this general conception of the ontological transformation that occurs upon a person's death on earth, Walumbe's abode necessarily possesses the abstract qualities that characterize all cosmogonic dimensions. In the story of Kintu and Nambi, however, the entrance to the underworld receives a specific geographical location, at Ttanda Hill in Ssingo, where a series of more than fifty pit shafts dominate the surrounding landscape. During the colonial period these shafts, which range from ten to thirty feet deep, attracted the attention of several observers, who concluded that they probably served as sites for excavating kaolin, a fine white clay that was rubbed on a person's body to induce possession.[95]

The place name Ttanda, a reflex of the archaic Luganda word lutanda, meaning "crack" or "rent," draws upon the common regional conception of cracks in the earth as passageways to the underworld.[96] At Ttanda, on a ridge overlooking these shafts, stands Walumbe's principal shrine, whose priest,

Nakabaale, belongs to a section of the Colobus Monkey clan. This hereditary position, which figures as a source of pride for Colobus Monkey clan members and features prominently in the clan's history, hints at the nature of the authority that the leaders of those who eventually adopted the colobus monkey as their totem once held.[97] Colobus Monkey clan histories suggest that as the guardian of Walumbe's shrine at Ttanda, Nakabaale served in the distant past as one of a line of priests whose authority rested on their ability to communicate with the ancestral ghosts that resided in the underworld. This understanding of Nakabaale's authority accords with widespread symbolic associations attached to the colobus monkey, whose black and white fur was a mark of prestige, protection, and mortality throughout the region.[98] These associations drew on the symbolic distinction between whiteness and blackness embedded in regional ritual practices. Great Lakes historical actors associated whiteness with notions of purity, order, indigenousness, and prosperity.[99] In contrast, blackness evoked images of impurity, disorder, foreignness, and misfortune.[100] Thus Mukasa, the "white" spirit of life and abundance who received offerings of a white he-goat and a white cock, stood in contrast to Walumbe, the "black" spirit of death.[101] As an emblem that combined both of these qualities, the colobus monkey's black and white fur served as an apt symbol for the delicate and contingent nature of human life, and ritual leaders endowed with the authority to adorn themselves with this skin enjoyed the ability to navigate between Life's domain on earth and Death's underworld abode. This ability granted significant healing capacities, as journeys to the land of ancestral ghosts enabled these ritual experts to identify sources of misfortune and illness and to provide their patients with appropriate remedies.

The narratives about the Tembuzi leader Isaza, who according to the Cwezi traditions of western Uganda operated in the Kisengwe area, to the west of Buganda, prior to the arrival of the Cwezi, further elaborate upon the connection between colobus monkey fur and guardians of portals to the underworld.[102] Cwezi traditions bestowed upon Isaza the praise name Muhundwangeye (One Adorned with the Colobus Monkey), a reference to the colobus fur chinstrap supporting the headgear worn by priests in western Uganda whose duties included communicating with ancestral ghosts residing in the underworld.[103] Renee Tantala has suggested that this category of ritual experts might have evolved in the distant past from the authority of elders who, close to becoming ancestors themselves, assumed responsibility for communicating with the ancestors on behalf of their families. The priest's colobus fur chinstrap, which flowed like a white beard, quite possibly alluded to the ability elders once had to communicate with and propitiate ancestral ghosts. As part of the broader cultural process according to which ritual specialists assumed the responsibilities once held by elders, the Tembuzi leader Isaza represented a line of priests in the Kisengwe area whose authority derived from their connection to the underworld. According to Tantala, Isaza's eventual demise, which was depicted in oral traditions by his descent into the land of ancestral ghosts and his ultimate inability to escape, signaled the waning of the influence held by this category of priests.[104]

The symbolic and ritual overlaps between the Isaza figure and the priest Nakabaale suggests that "Kintu and Nambi" emerged in the context of a regional decline in the status of ritual leaders whose ability to communicate with ancestral ghosts was the basis for their positions of authority. The nature of this decline in Buganda, which included acts of alliance as much as suppression, emerges in another critical connection between "Kintu and Nambi" and the Colobus Monkey clan. According to Colobus Monkey clan histories, the clan's founder fathered Nambi and eventually offered her in marriage to Kintu.[105] Unable to make sense of this well-known detail in Colobus Monkey clan versions of the narrative, most scholars have either ignored it altogether or dismissed it as a "curious anomaly" that does not accord with the generalized social circumstances within which they argue the narrative should be analyzed.[106] Those who have taken this feature seriously have done so in a somewhat literal fashion, positing a possible marriage alliance between Kintu's followers and Nambi's extended kin.[107] In claiming Nambi as one of the clan's daughters, however, Colobus Monkey clan histories provide a critical clue about how audiences at a site of healing may have understood the nature of the developments depicted in "Kintu and Nambi," the first hint of which appears in the name of Nambi's father, Kawooya Ssemandwa.

The name Kawooya derives from the verb kuwooya, which carries two meanings: "to speak softly to, to lower one's voice" and "to calm, appease."[108] Significantly, both of these meanings characterize the activities of spirit mediums, who speak in a deep, low voice while in a state of possession and whose pronouncements include instructions on how to placate neglected ancestral ghosts.[109] Nambi's father's second name, Ssemandwa, further suggests a connection to mediumship. The name Ssemandwa derives from the noun mmandwa, an ancient word found throughout the Great Lakes region that means "a person possessed by a spirit."[110] In Luganda the noun prefixes *sse-* and *ssa-* serve as honorific prefixes meaning "head," "chief of," or "father of," thus yielding the meaning "head of the spirit mediums" for the name Ssemandwa. If, as his name suggests, Kawooya Ssemandwa once served as the head of the spirit mediums, we must now turn to the question of the significance of his daughter Nambi's marriage to Kintu.

The key to understanding Kawooya Ssemandwa and Nambi's relationship to Kintu hinges on our understanding of the verb *marry*. Upon initial consideration, Kawooya Ssemandwa's offering his daughter Nambi in marriage to Kintu seems to record a relatively straightforward development: that members of the Colobus Monkey clan formed an alliance with Kintu and his followers, a relationship cemented, in a practice common throughout the region, through the bond of marriage. While not wholly incorrect, this conclusion, which other scholars have quite sensibly reached, fails to capture the nature of the alliance represented by Kintu and Nambi's union.[111] Political alliances cemented by the language and practices of marriage did at one time establish a broad set of relationships between large groups of people. Yet the type of relationship signaled by the marriage metaphor varied according to the circumstance in which it operated. Given Nambi's father's position as the leader of a group of spirit mediums, the meaning of marriage within Great Lakes healing complexes deserves further attention.

Throughout the Great Lakes region, marriage served as a common metaphor referring to both initiation as a spirit medium and a medium's relationship to the spirit that possessed him or her. Iris Berger has suggested that the use of this metaphor in the organization of the region's territorial cults may have emerged from the widespread, apparently archaic practice of dedicating girls and women to spirits as "spirit wives." The power associated with spirit wives related to the general connection between women, fertility, and the continuity of life. Women dedicated to a spirit were supposed to remain chaste for the remainder of their lives, the idea being that a spirit wife's fecundity could be redirected for the benefit of a particular individual or community.[112] Extensions of this principle appear consistently in ethnographic descriptions of regional possession practices. These descriptions relate that both male and female novices were referred to as "brides" while undergoing a series of initiations rituals that mimicked marriage practices.[113] Upon the completion of these rites, mediums were treated as "wives" of their disembodied husbands, thus rendering the initiation as a form of "marriage."[114]

Early ethnographers working in Buganda recorded a metaphorical relationship between marriage and mediumship similar to that found elsewhere in the region. Baganda referred to a person's first possession experience as "being married to a spirit," a metaphor that continues to operate today.[115] A practicing medium explained to me that upon a *kabaka*'s death and the removal of his jawbone, his ancestral ghost immediately sought out a person whom the king wished "to marry." The selected person then appeared before the other royal mediums while possessed by the *kabaka*'s ancestral ghost and answered a series of questions in a manner that imitated the tone, gestures, and expressions of the late king. If the initiate's answers and behaviors drew approval from the gathered crowd, the royal mediums prepared a meal befitting a newlywed and "married" the initiate to the deceased *kabaka*.[116] The principal medium at Kabaka Ssuuna's royal jawbone shrine, an elderly woman who at the time of our conversation had served in this capacity for thirty-two years, described such a process. She recounted that the former king's ancestral ghost "came and touched [her] heart" and carried her to his royal jawbone shrine, where Kabaka Ssuuna has served as her "husband" ever since.[117]

Viewed within the metaphor of marriage as the union between a medium and a spirit, Nambi's marriage to Kintu takes on a rather different meaning from that proposed by other scholars. The "marriage" of Nambi, "daughter" of Ssemandwa, "Head of the Mediums," might best be regarded as recalling her initiation as a medium of the *musambwa* spirit Kintu. The connection between Nambi, the Colobus Monkey clan, and regional practices of spirit possession suggests the following scenario: Nambi's union with Kintu—a narrative description of a process that most likely unfolded over an extended period of time—resulted from the inability of ritual specialists who guarded the portals to the underworld to continue to provide for a community's collective well-being. These failures led to the emergence of alternate sources of assistance and the concomitant demotion in status of healers whose authority resided in their connections to the land of ancestral ghosts. Faced with such a situation, the network of mediums encapsulated in the figure of Kawooya Ssemandwa sought an alliance with Kintu, a union that in this situation involved harnessing their mediating skills to a more effective spiritual entity. This reconfiguration brought considerable rewards, as even Walumbe, the personification of Death, could not prevent the continued perpetuity of this prominent network of healers—Kintu and Nambi's "children."

The third main narrative involving Kintu tells of his altercation with Kisolo, the founder of the Otter clan:[118]

Kintu left Bukesa and settled at Nnono Hill following the defeat of Bemba. Several years later he shifted his residence to Magonga and then decided to embark on a journey of inspection in his territories, leaving his deputy Kisolo in charge of his household.[119] Upon returning to Magonga, Kintu found his wife, Nambi, pregnant and immediately questioned her as to who was responsible for her condition. Nambi referred Kintu to his deputy Kisolo, who informed his master that he had not told him about Nambi's pregnancy because he had not wished to bother him after such a tiring journey. Incensed by his deputy's words, Kintu picked up a spear and stabbed Kisolo in the foot. The wounded Kisolo fled to the home of his son Ssenkungu, who had earlier left his father's home at Bweza, in Busujju, and settled at Lumuli, in Mawokota. Ssenkungu took his father to his son Ddamulira's place at Ffunvu, in Mawokota. Ddamulira healed his grand-father's wound, and as a result of this act Kisolo bestowed upon him the name Muganga (Healer). After a short while, Kisolo journeyed to his grandson Katwere's place at Buzungu.

Meanwhile, Kintu's men chastised him for injuring Kisolo and forcing him to flee, whereupon Kintu sent some messengers to look for his deputy. The messengers journeyed to Buzungu, where Kisolo told them to inform Kintu that he would return after a short while. When after several days Kisolo had not returned, Kintu sent out a different group of messengers. Kisolo met these messengers on the road, and they went to the home of his grandson Muganga, the son of Ssenkungu. Kisolo agreed to return with the messengers but then noticed a cloud of smoke in the direction from which the messengers had come. Taking this as a sign that Kintu still wished to kill him, Kisolo slipped away from the messengers and disappeared into the bush, never to be seen again. A conscience-stricken Kintu disappeared shortly thereafter.

KINTU AND KISOLO:
MUWANGA, MEDIUMSHIP, AND MARRIAGE

Perhaps because they could find neither a biblical counterpart to nor a politically useful historical interpretation of "Kintu and Kisolo," Baganda intellectuals working in the colonial period directed considerably less attention to this narrative than they did to either "Kintu and Bemba the Snake" or "Kintu and Nambi." In his dynastic history, Kaggwa presented the narrative as part of Kintu's continuing exploits after defeating Bemba, a shameful episode in Buganda's early royal history. He elaborated upon this theme in his later work on Ganda clan histories, and his political interpretation, which, if anything, reinforced the notion of Kintu as a fully historical conquering king, generated little debate in the intertwined Ganda, missionary, and academic circles during the first half of the twentieth century. The narrative provided continuity to the early period of official Ganda dynastic history and explained Kintu's disappearance, but its inability to support either chiefly or missionary claims rendered it a less effective vehicle for engaging in the coincident debates about Buganda's history and its position in the emerging colonial political order.

Like their intellectual predecessors in the colonial period, recent scholars have focused less attention on Kintu's encounter with Kisolo than on his more widely known adventures with Bemba and Nambi. Those who have examined the narrative have presented widely varying interpretations. Despite their differences, however, these analyses share a common point of agreement. Implicit in all of them lies the notion that while "Kintu and Kisolo" illuminates some general features about Ganda kingship and human nature, it does not shed light on any specific historical developments in early Ganda history.[120] Like the first two Kintu stories, however, "Kintu and Kisolo" can illuminate previously overlooked aspects of Buganda's past if it is read with sensitivity to regional clan histories and idioms. Much like his experiences with Bemba and Nambi, Kintu's encounter with Kisolo reveals a world in which competition between territorial healing complexes and their leaders characterized an increasingly contentious political environment.

While the founders of the Pangolin clan play the leading role in Kintu's defeat of Bemba and those of the Colobus Monkey clan feature in his exploits with Nambi, the early leaders of the Otter clan occupy center stage in Kintu's altercation with the Otter clan founder, Kisolo. As with the pangolin and the colobus monkey, the otter's symbolic significance in the Great Lakes region situates it within the realm of healing practices involving acts of spirit possession. A mammal that spends a considerable amount of time in water, the otter lends itself to particular metaphorical associations. Throughout the region, Great Lakes historical actors viewed the otter as possessing metaphysical capacities, and groups who acknowledged the otter as their totem played a prominent role in the early histories of several kingships in the area surrounding Lake Victoria and beyond.[121]

The history of the Ganda Otter clan further attests to the connection between the otter as a totemic symbol and healing practices, specifically those involving spirit mediumship. The full name of the clan's founder—Kisolo Muwanga Ssebyoto—points to the clan's origins as a *musambwa*-type territorial cult aligned with a node of ritual authority in Mawokota. The name Kisolo derives from the Luganda word *nsolo*, "animal," a reference to the common occurrence throughout the region of *misambwa* spirits manifesting themselves in animal form. The name Muwanga, however, provides perhaps a more telling clue about the type of authority that the Otter clan's early leaders exercised in Mawokota and westward into Busujju. While today Baganda regard Muwanga as a *lubaale*, one of the kingdom's national spirits, the Otter clan holds a particularly close affiliation with this highly revered spirit. According to Otter clan histories, Kintu was initially attracted to Kisolo because he possessed the spirit Muwanga, who settled problems and brought peace to the land. Eager to court Kisolo's patronage, Kintu offered him a plot of land at Bweza, in Busujju, opposite his abode at Magonga. In return, Kisolo offered his son Lutaya to perform the ritual weaving of the roof for Kintu's house, suggesting an alliance between the territorial cult associated with Kintu and that aligned with Kisolo and the *musambwa* Muwanga.[122]

One of the Otter clan's most important sites lies at Nseke, in Mawokota, where Ssemwanga, the head of a prominent lineage (*mutuba*), maintains a shrine dedicated to Muwanga. According to the lineage's history, the shrine served as Kisolo's principal home before he settled near Kintu at Bweza, in Busujju. After quarreling with Kintu, Kisolo returned to his original home at Nseke, where he "disappeared and became a *musambwa* just as Kintu became a *musambwa* when he disappeared at Magonga."[123] Despite his disappearance, Kisolo Muwanga continued to exert his influence on the community at Nseke. His departed spirit spoke through mediums operating at the shrine, to which the area's residents brought offerings intended to ensure the multiplication of their herds and the fertility of their women.[124]

The earliest parts of Otter clan histories in Buganda suggest that the clan played a prominent role in the area's healing complexes in the distant past. These histories indicate that the Otter clan may have presided over an early node of ritual and political authority connecting the Ssese Islands, where the clan claims indigenous status, and mainland Mawokota. The link joining the Otter clan's influence on the islands with its influence on the mainland is the spirit Muwanga. This revered spirit occupies a prominent place in the Ssese pantheon, and as mentioned above, his main shrine operates on the mainland at Nseke, Mawokota, under the direction of a priestly guardian from the Otter clan. When considered with sensitivity to the nature and language of the region's early political history, Otter clan histories in Buganda furnish the following insight: in the distant past, the Otter clan in Buganda functioned as a prominent network of healers whose practices included the use of spirit possession, whose authority at some point became merged with their control of the spirit Muwanga, and whose healing networks extended into Mawokota and possibly into Busujju.

This interpretation of early Otter clan histories in Buganda makes possible a different reading of the confrontation between the clan founder, Kisolo, and Kintu. As with "Kintu and Nambi," the key to understanding the significance of "Kintu and Kisolo" rests on an awareness of the language of initiation as a spirit medium in one of the region's many healing complexes. According to the narrative, the violent altercation between Kintu and Kisolo occurred as a result of Kintu's accusing Kisolo of having impregnated his wife, Nambi. As discussed earlier, in the context of regional healing practices the term *wife* referred to both initiation as a spirit medium and a medium's relationship to the spirit that possessed him or her. Nambi's "marriage" to Kintu and her status as his "wife" therefore indicated her position as a medium of the territorial spirit Kintu. Viewed from this perspective, and listened to with sensitivity to the language and practices of spirit possession, the gravity of Kisolo's indiscretion in "Kintu and Kisolo" acquires an alternate meaning. If aspiring mediums were born into the profession through the "marriage" of an initiated medium and her spiritual patron, then Kisolo's impregnating Nambi—a medium of the *musambwa* Kintu—constituted an affront to the authority of Kintu's representatives. Significantly, mediums who acted as "wives" might eventually acquire status as "mothers," a critical element in attracting the patronage of women who had experienced difficulties conceiving. And since any "children" born to Nambi would add to the number of representatives in her "husband"'s network, the identity of the "father" in this scenario becomes crucial in determining the reach of a particular healing network. The story of Kisolo's impregnating Nambi, then, may quite plausibly have been understood as the efforts of Kisolo Muwanga's followers to usurp the ritual and political authority of Kintu's supporters by "marrying" her into their organization and staking a claim to her "children." In response, Kintu speared Kisolo in the leg, forcing him (and his mediums) to flee the area and seek refuge in the homes of his "children" and "grandchildren" in Mawokota. The violent altercation might therefore be regarded as the severing of an alliance between the musambwa Kintu's followers and those of the Otter clan founder, Kisolo Muwanga Ssebyoto.

CONCLUSION

The literate Baganda who published and argued over the significance of the Kintu narratives in the early colonial period were recent converts to Christianity, government clerks, and active politicians. Similarly, those who narrated various stories about Kintu to me during my stay in Buganda included practicing Christians and devout Muslims who had made the pilgrimage to Mecca. Some of their narrations included the residue of unmistakably recent discursive developments, as well as feedback from Ganda histories published in Luganda. Much of what they narrated did not differ, at least in formal content, from the accounts recorded in the early and mid-twentieth century. Yet these narrators also served their communities as healers, and their references to Kintu and Kisolo as misambwa, their statements about there having been two Kintus—one who founded a royal dynasty and one who disappeared—and their descriptions of Kintu as the first kabaka "to rule people" (compared with his predecessors, who had controlled only misambwa) opened up new avenues of interpretation.

Listening to these narratives in healers' shrines provided insight into the overlapping contexts in which Ganda heard these traditions. This in turn opened up the possibility of imagining how they might have been understood in similar settings in the distant past. I could then draw upon evidence from historical linguistics, early ethnographic writings, my conversations with Ganda healers, and other scholarly works to present an interpretation of how an audience seated at a shrine might have understood these narratives in the distant past. Such an endeavor necessarily requires exercising our historical imagination. But it is an imagination that reflects regional sensitivities and whose contents and contours derive from evidence generated by historical linguistics and comparative ethnography.

When viewed with sensitivity to their circulation and meaning in shrine settings, the Kintu narratives capture a series of momentous developments in the realm of public healing in the distant Ganda past. By dislodging spiritual entities from their territorial bases, ambitious leaders extended the territory over which a particular spirit and its earthly representatives might ensure collective health and prosperity. While these converted *misambwa* spirits continued to operate at shrines located in specific territories and to bestow upon their representatives the authority derived from firstcomer status, their newly achieved mobility allowed for the extension of the powers of particular shrines over increasingly larger territories. These transformations reconfigured the boundaries of public healing in Buganda and undergirded the development of complex political communities along the northwestern shores of Lake Victoria. The Kintu narratives, which encapsulate the nature of these intellectual and political transformations, constituted part of these efforts. The telling and retelling of these and similar narratives at the various shrines dotting the Ganda landscape served as a fundamental means of enlarging the territorial range of a spirit's effectiveness and formed part of a broader campaign to recast the composition of local communities in the areas that would become the Ganda kingdom.

The Kintu figure and the narratives describing his exploits underwent several transformations and reinterpretations in the periods that followed the intellectual and political developments discussed in this chapter. In the mid-eighteenth century, royal chroniclers incorporated "Kintu and Bemba the Snake" into a dynastic narrative. In so doing, they bestowed an additional interpretation upon the narrative that transformed Kintu from *musambwa* spirit to dynastic founder. The Kintu figure also featured prominently in subsequent Ganda efforts to make sense of rapidly shifting realities.[125] John Yoder has argued that in the tumultuous period preceding the establishment of the Uganda Protectorate, Baganda leaders reshaped the stories of Kintu's actions in order to express concerns about the increasing incidence of state violence in the latter part of the nineteenth century.[126] Later, in the early twentieth century, the impassioned debates over whether Kintu was an indigenous Muganda clearly drew upon emerging tensions between Baganda chiefs who had benefited from the agreement they had signed with the British in 1900 and those leaders who had lost most in the settlement.[127] As discussed in this chapter, the Kintu figure also played a critical role during this period in the efforts of Baganda Christian writers to domesticate biblical teachings and consolidate their position at the apex of the reconstituted political order.

Rather than effacing prior interpretations, however, these adaptations added an additional layer of meaning to the Kintu narratives. In a sense, this process of reinterpretation preserved the narratives, which retained the "residua of previous presents"[128] and continued to circulate in nonroyal, non-Christian arenas where alternate epistemologies shaped the meaning listeners attributed to them. The silencing efforts of Christian missionaries, colonial officials, and elite Baganda converts marginalized the role of healers in shaping discursive contours. The narratives about Kintu that continue to circulate in healers' shrines, however, illustrate that they did not wholly succeed in their task. In this regard, the Kintu narratives serve as a palimpsest whose layered contents reflect the accumulated historical record of Kintu's transition in Buganda from one of several "Big People," to a *musambwa* spirit, to the founder and first king of Buganda.

In many respects, a sense of inevitability often pervades discussions of Kintu's exploits. Because Buganda eventually emerged as a centralized state, scholars have been tempted to view the narratives about its purported founder as necessarily describing the beginnings of this centralizing process. The analysis of the three main Kintu narratives offered in this chapter is an attempt to overcome this teleology by providing a sense of the multifarious nature of Kintu's existence. That Baganda remembered the period preceding Kintu's emergence as Buganda's founding monarch in narratives describing conceptual innovations in the institution of spirit mediumship points to the intellectual currents that undergirded, and perhaps even motivated, the enlargement of political communities. The timing of these developments, the shifting material conditions in which they occurred, and the relationship between healing practices and the historical formation of publics constitute the topic of discussion in the following chapter.

3

CLANSHIP
AND THE PURSUIT
OF COLLECTIVE
WELL-BEING

In the previous chapter I argued that when listened to as an audience seated at a healer's shrine might have done, the Kintu narratives can be understood as describing a series of changes in the practices of spirit mediumship and the expansion of territorial cults. As narrative accounts of the process according to which itinerant mediums sought out alliances by transforming territorial *misambwa* spirits into regional, portable spirits, these narratives highlight the confluence of public healing and politics in early Ganda history. Converted *misambwa* spirits continued to operate at shrines located in specific territories. Yet the authority they initially derived from their connections to the particular territories with which they were associated now extended beyond the locations of their principal shrines. This chapter builds upon the insights gleaned from the Kintu narratives by examining why their principal characters also figure as the founders of Ganda clans. Why, in other words, do our earliest glimpses into the distant Ganda past appear in the form of clan histories? And what do clans have to do with transformations in public healing practices?

The answers to these questions guide our efforts to set the Kintu narratives into historical motion and represent the opening phases in the long and winding history of clanship in Buganda. At the center of this story lies the relationship between clanship, transformations in public healing, and the development of a banana-based farming system in Buganda. The many conversations I engaged in about the meaning of clanship revealed a connection between clanship and Ganda notions of individual as well as collective well-being. These conversations both suggested that we might best examine the clan concept from the perspective of public healing and also pointed to a novel way of approaching the interpretation of more formal, structured clan histories.

David Schoenbrun's historical linguistic work on the history of spirit mediumship and banana cultivation in the Great Lakes region and Holly Hanson's examination of the transformations in productive, social, and spiritual relationships that accompanied the transition to land-intensive banana farming in Buganda offer a way to anchor the insights derived from Ganda clan histories and less formal conversations about clanship within a broader regional narrative. The combination of these various sources of evidence and scholarly insights suggests the following scenario: Beginning about the fifteenth or sixteenth century, Baganda expanded upon earlier knowledge of banana cultivation to develop a land-intensive banana-farming system. The opportunities for permanent settlement and the accumulation of wealth in the form of perennially fruiting banana trees rendered bananas a potentially lucrative long-term investment. The gradual transition to intensive banana farming, however, also generated social tensions related to property inheritance and succession that posed significant challenges to the communities living along the northwestern shores of Lake Victoria. In the face of these challenges, Baganda developed dispersed therapeutic networks that reconfigured the boundaries of public healing. They did so by transforming previously territorial spirits into portable spirits capable of ensuring the health of disconnected groups of people. This process drew upon the talents of itinerant mediums and lay at the core of clan formation. The webs of shrines situated on clan estates drew together communities whose leaders possessed a variety of skills, thus forging a powerful connection between clanship, collective health, and the composition of knowledge.

Treating clans as compositions of knowledge shifts attention away from the focus on kinship that dominates conventional explanations of clan formation. By discarding the commonly encountered notion of clans as gradually expanding kin groups, this chapter allows alternative historical explanations of clanship and clan formation in Buganda and elsewhere. For the people living along the northwestern shores of Lake Victoria about the sixteenth century, the clan concept facilitated the composition of knowledgeable communities through a reconfiguration of the boundaries of public healing. Mobile spirits ranged over sometimes vast geographical spaces, extending the reach of their effective capacities and drawing dispersed communities into a collective endeavor cemented by the language and practices of clanship. In a gradual process that coincided with significant changes in agricultural production, the disembodied life forces of deceased leaders were transformed from ancestral ghosts into territorial spirits and then into mobile spiritual entities before finally achieving status as the founders of clans. As the guarantors of peace and prosperity, the spirits of these clan founders sought to ensure continued prosperity by harnessing the knowledge and skills of their dispersed communities of "grandchildren."

"THE *KIGGWA* BRINGS TOGETHER THE OWNERS OF SHRINES": CLANSHIP AND THE FORMATION OF THERAPEUTIC NETWORKS

That the construction of clan histories depended upon the presence of clans perhaps seems obvious. Yet in simply scanning clan histories for clues about Buganda's past, most historians have failed to account for the fact that these histories exist in the first place. The question what holds clans conceptually together—what, essentially, enabled historical actors to compose clan histories—compels us to consider clans as something more than groups of people who share a common history. Treating clan histories as the outcome of historical processes, in other words, urges us to contemplate the circumstances that made possible the very construction of these histories. At the core of these historical processes lies the relationship between clanship and Ganda practices of public healing.

The convergence of clan name and totem, along with a distinctive series of subdivisions conceived through the idiom of kinship, distinguishes Ganda clans from seemingly similar phenomena found throughout the Great Lakes region. These two features also provide the conceptual framework for the narration of Ganda clan histories. The presentation of these histories, which describe the movements and activities of clan founders and their descendants, suggests an enticing mode of analysis by offering the possibility of tracing the gradual dispersal of Ganda clans from their central estates (*butaka bukulu*) to their numerous scattered and discontiguous settlements. This reasonable prospect presents itself wherever people employ the idiom of kinship as a means of narrating clan histories and has indeed seduced scholars working in Buganda and neighboring areas.[1] The problem with this approach lies in its failure to distinguish between the language of clanship and the types of relationships embedded in this language, a failure that results in the privileging of a model of clan formation based on notions of kinship and descent to the exclusion of other, perhaps more revealing formulations.[2]

Ganda discourse on clanship, as opposed to the narration of clan histories, suggests an alternate manner of conceiving the philosophical and historical underpinnings of clan formation. When Baganda speak about clanship, they offer a conceptual map that differs from more familiar familial models. Whereas Ganda clan histories invoke the image of a gradually expanding family tree sprouting from the clan's founder, more informal and less formulaic discussions of clanship describe a ritual web made up of dispersed yet connected therapeutic networks. In placing emphasis on the integrative capacity of the shrine centers located on scattered and discontiguous clan lands, Baganda squarely situate the concept of clanship within the realm of public healing. This discourse provides insights into the manner in which Baganda perceive clanship and allows for a novel approach to examining the clan concept.

Over the course of my stay in Buganda, I engaged in many discussions, both formal and informal, about the meaning of clanship. These discussions differed from those in which I encouraged people to narrate the histories of their clans or their particular branches. They were more personal, more about how people located themselves, in an existential sense, within the discursive and practical boundaries offered by the clan concept. Some of these conversations occurred in casual settings, almost accidentally or unintentionally at times, while others unfolded as people guided me through their clan estates. Many of the people I spoke with had had a Christian or Muslim upbringing, a factor that, along with a justifiable skepticism about both my interest in such matters and my ability to grasp their significance, initially hindered some aspects of these exchanges. Yet after much persistence and a few stumbling demonstrations that I did, in fact, have some knowledge about the rudiments of Ganda clanship, many of my hosts elaborated upon the importance of the shrines and other sacred spaces located on clan estates. The head of a lineage (mutuba) in the Colobus Monkey clan, for instance, related the following personal narrative:

> I was living a good life but had one problem—I did not have a child. I had wives and money but no children. My father was still living and I asked him why I had money and other things but could not have children. He took me to Bussi, where our clan's main shrine is located. The people at the shrine told me to construct a branch of the Bussi shrine at my house. They instructed me that after putting up the roof I should slaughter a cow, a goat, a sheep, and a chicken to distribute to people. I was told that I would not have children if I did not do these things. I want to assure you that I did not take any medicine, and now I have thirty children. I constructed a branch of the Bussi shrine here at my home in order to provide

an opportunity to those who cannot cross the lake to reach Bussi. I then became a medium without succeeding or inheriting the position.[3]

In an effort to explain to me the efficacy of ancestral ghosts (mizimu), the head of the patrilineage (ssiga) of Mbajja in the Lungfish clan offered a similarly personal story:

I grew up lonely and not knowing that my father loved me. But I later learned that he had placed trust in me. I was not aware that he had considered me in his will, since he passed away after I had already gone to Tanzania. Before I left, however, he told me that there was a territorial spirit in a rock at the place where I should construct the shrine for our patrilineage. Now, in his will he mentioned that upon his death the headquarters of Mbajja, the head of the patrilineage, should be constructed at Najja Mpwedde, the place where we are currently seated. This was an amazing request, since my father had never lived at this place. I was not aware of the contents of the will since I was already in Tanzania.

When Museveni's war began,[4] I joined the rebels in the bush. My father appeared to me three times while I was fighting in the bush. . . . On his third appearance he told me that the war had ended but that I had neglected my house, my headquarters. I did not know what he meant, since before entering the bush I had laid the foundation for my house and set six thousand bricks in place. My father said to me, "You have neglected Mbajja's headquarters; it is overgrown by bush." I told him, "No, father. I have finished laying the foundation and making the bricks." He said, "Is that the house of Mbajja? Is that Mbajja's place? Do not return to that place. From now on I want you to stay at Najja Mpwedde."

The place where we are currently sitting [Najja Mpwedde] was very inhospitable at the time. The people who had settled here in the past were not from the line of Mbajja and had suffered and died along with their children. But my father told me not to go back to the other place. His ancestral ghost told me. . . . So I settled here and then built this shrine. My father was captured by religion [Christianity] and it was up to me to rebuild the shrine. When I became the head of the patrilineage, people approached me and said, "Sir, we are dying"; "Sir, these things are being demanded"; etc. So I was forced to intervene in these matters. And I am assisted by those who are possessed by the spirits, such as the woman you spoke with inside the shrine.[5]

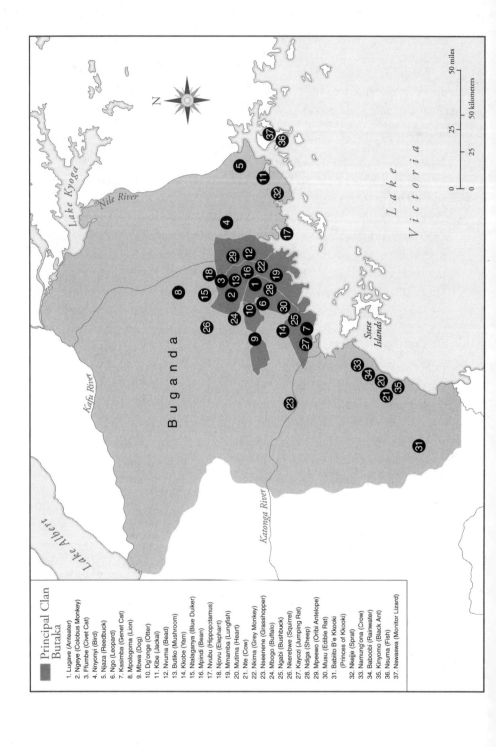

Principal Clan Butaka

1. Lugave (Anteater)
2. Ngeye (Colobus Monkey)
3. Ffumbe (Civet Cat)
4. Nnyonyi (Bird)
5. Njaza (Reedbuck)
6. Ngo (Leopard)
7. Kasimba (Genet Cat)
8. Mpologoma (Lion)
9. Mbwa (Dog)
10. Dg'onge (Otter)
11. Kibe (Jackal)
12. Nvuma (Bead)
13. Butiko (Mushroom)
14. Kkobe (Yam)
15. Ntalaganya (Blue Duiker)
16. Mpindi (Bean)
17. Nvubu (Hippopotamus)
18. Njovu (Elephant)
19. Mmamba (Lungfish)
20. Mutima (Heart)
21. Nte (Cow)
22. Nkima (Grey Monkey)
23. Nseenene (Grasshopper)
24. Mbogo (Buffalo)
25. Ngabi (Bushbuck)
26. Nkerebwe (Squirrel)
27. Kayozi (Jumping Rat)
28. Ndiga (Sheep)
29. Mpeewo (Oribi Antelope)
30. Musu (Edible Rat)
31. Babiito B'e Kkooki
    (Princes of Kkooki)
32. Nkeije (Sprat)
33. Namung'ona (Crow)
34. Baboobi (Rainwater)
35. Kinyomo (Black Ant)
36. Nsuma (Fish)
37. Nswaswa (Monitor Lizard)

While these sorts of narratives did not provide any specific details regarding the distant histories of a particular clan or segment of a clan, they did highlight the intriguing connection between the concept of clanship, the shrines located on clan estates, and Ganda notions of personal as well as collective well-being. Over the course of listening to several similarly autobiographical narratives, I gained glimpses into how people perceived and experienced clanship beyond the conventional and much-documented (though far from insignificant) discourse about succession and inheritance disputes in twentieth-century Buganda.

When the people I spoke with reflected more generally upon the manner in which clanship operated as a guiding principle in their lives, they frequently pointed to the significance of *biggwa* (s. *kiggwa*), the sacred sites located on clan estates (see map 3). Many people described *biggwa* as places where individuals sought diagnoses of personal problems such as illness, infertility, poverty, or faltering relationships. But they also described how clan members gathered at these sacred sites, more so in the past than today, to remember their ancestors at their place of origin.[6] Prior to the dramatic changes in public healing practices that accompanied the imposition of colonial rule and the spread of Christianity, most *biggwa* included a large conical shrine that housed a clan's most prominent spirits during these public clan gatherings. These spirits usually resided in nearby features of the natural environment and regularly manifested themselves in animal form. But they could also be called upon by trained mediums with the assistance of the priests who lived on clan estates and looked after *biggwa*. Baganda in fact drew upon the imagery of spirit possession in naming the locales at which these public meetings occurred. They derived the word *kiggwa* from the verb *okuggwa*, "to be exhausted or worn out," thus designating these sites of (re)collection as places where mediums, following a practice common throughout the region, fell to the ground in exhaustion after a possessing spirit exited their bodies.[7]

Clan members converged around *biggwa* to feast, drink, and recite historical narratives. Most importantly, however, they gathered to seek solutions to collective problems (*ebizibu ebwawamu*) such as famine, epidemics, and warfare.[8] These conditions required that clan members collaborate in a concerted effort to ensure their collective well-being. They pursued this objective by engaging the area's dominant spirits, which maintained a connection to the clan's founding ancestors whose graves were located at the nearby burial ground, the *kijja*. These two features—a sacred site and a burial ground—

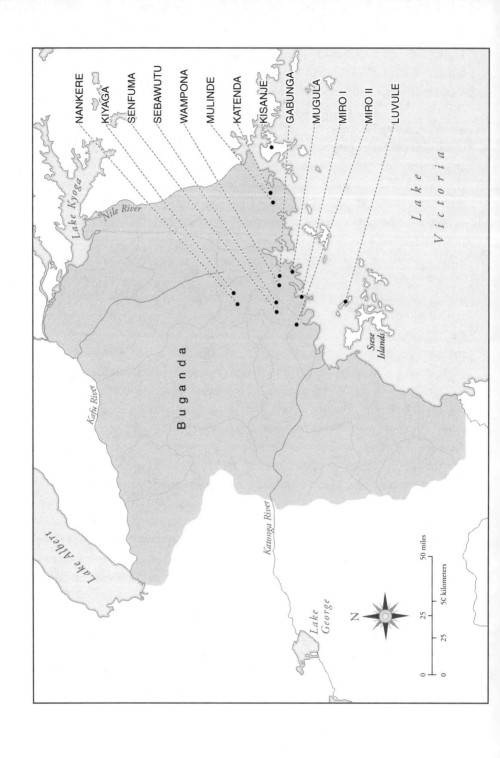

NANKERE
KIYAGA
SENFUMA
SEBAWUTU
WAMPONA
MULINDE
KATENDA
KISANJE
GABUNGA
MUGULA
MIRO I
MIRO II
LUVULE

Lake Victoria

Lake Kyoga

Nile River

Buganda

Kafu River

Ssese Islands

Lake Albert

Katonga River

Lake George

N

0   25   50 miles

0   25   50 kilometers

together constituted a clan's primary estate, which "belonged to the whole clan" and served as a meeting point for "those who believed in their totems" to "beat the drums and call the spirits which protected the lives of all descendants."[9] The activities undertaken at these gatherings, which included large-scale practices of spirit possession, drew upon the idea that the public recognition of common spirits generated the conditions for collective prosperity.

As the sites of these collective endeavors, *biggwa* functioned as ritual arenas where clan members assembled to seek life, peace, and collective good fortune.[10] The shrines located at *biggwa*, which were often situated on hilltops, dotted the areas along the northwestern shores of Lake Victoria and anchored people, in both a discursive and a visual sense, within dense healing networks. A series of dependent shrines (*masabo*), each connected to a branch of a particular clan at the level of the maximal lineage (*ssiga;* pl. *masiga*), the minor lineage (*mutuba;* pl. *mituba*), or the minimal lineage (*lunyiriri;* pl. *nnyiriri*), lay scattered on discontiguous secondary clan lands (see map 4). These dispersed shrines constituted ritual networks that shaped the framework within which communities sought their collective health. They formed the ritual rungs of therapeutic ladders that stretched across the Ganda curative landscape, with each upward movement representing both an act of ritual escalation—the shifting of ritual activities to ever more important shrines—and a metaphorical step toward the spiritual powers housed at the clan's original home. Statements such as "The *kiggwa* unites all [clan members] from different patrilineages [*masiga*]," "The *kiggwa* brings together the owners of shrines [*masabo*]," and "The *kiggwa* brings together people from different areas," which surfaced repeatedly during my conversations in Buganda, testified to this connection between clanship and public healing.

CLANSHIP, COLLECTIVE HEALTH, AND THE COMPOSITION OF KNOWLEDGE

The personal narratives and more general ruminations about clanship that I heard over the course of my stay in Buganda offer insight into why the principal characters in the Kintu narratives, which describe transformations in the realm of public healing, also figure as the founders of Ganda clans. In the period preceding the emergence of the Ganda state apparatus in the eighteenth century, Baganda employed the language and practices of clanship as a means of constructing healthy political and social bodies. As the discursive and ritual cement joining people living in discontiguous territories, the ideology of clanship guided the historical formation of publics over which spirits, as well as their earthly representatives, sought to extend their efficacy. In this manner clanship was critical in shaping the publics within which early Ganda communities sought to ensure their collective well-being, and the remembered founders of some of the earliest communities represent increasingly portable spirits (or their human vehicles) who joined people living in dispersed therapeutic networks.

A revealing illustration of this process appears in the history of the Otter clan. The Otter clan claims indigenous status in Buganda and, as described in the previous chapter, maintains an enduring connection to one of the main narratives about Kintu.[11] Clan members trace their ancestry to the clan's founder, Kisolo Muwanga Ssebyoto, bearer of the spirit Muwanga, father of the hearths (byoto), who domesticated wild bananas.[12] The clan's history begins with Kisolo's journey from his home at Nseke, in Mawokota, to Bweza, in Busujju, where he established a settlement close to Kintu's abode at Magonga. As discussed in the previous chapter, Kisolo's capacity to possess the renowned spirit Muwanga attracted the attention of Kintu, who had recently settled in the area. Eager to court Kisolo's patronage, Kintu granted him a plot of land at Bbongole, opposite his home at Magonga. In return, Kisolo offered Lutaya, the oldest of his three sons, to perform the ritual weaving of the roof for Kintu's house.[13] Lutaya's successors preserved this position within their patrilineage by performing subsequent weavings during the repair or rebuilding of Kintu's shrine, thus ensuring the clan's continued link to the ritual complex surrounding Kintu as well as their own control over the nearby estate at Bbongole.[14]

Following his violent confrontation with Kintu at Magonga (see chapter 2), Kisolo fled to the home of his second son, Ssenkungu, at Kyanja, in Mawokota. When Kisolo reached Kyanja, his son Ssenkungu, the inventor of the grooved mallet used for beating out bark cloth, directed his father to the home of his eldest son (Kisolo's grandson), Katwere Muganga, at Ffunvu, in Mawokota. A talented doctor, Katwere Muganga gathered some herbs and treated the leg wound inflicted upon his grandfather by Kintu.[15] After his wound healed, Kisolo returned to his original home at Nseke, in Mawokota, where he "disappeared and became a musambwa [territorial spirit]."[16]

Despite his disappearance, or perhaps precisely because of his disappearance and subsequent new standing as a spiritual entity, Kisolo continued to exert influence on his descendants. His departed spirit, known as

Muwanga, spoke through the medium operating at the shrine built for Kisolo at Nseke. Muwanga "looked after the well-being of the [Otter] clan, multiplied their cattle, and made their women fruitful," and the shrine at which Muwanga possessed the resident medium was a site to which mothers who had recently given birth brought offerings of beer, cattle, and firewood.[17] Ssemwanga, another son of Ssenkungu's and grandson of Kisolo's, served as priest and caretaker of this shrine, a position that has remained in his lineage ever since.[18]

Kisolo's third son, Kinkumu Kitumba, remained at Bweza, in Busujju, when his father fled to Mawokota following his confrontation with Kintu. Kinkumu Kitumba succeeded Kisolo after his disappearance at Nseke and retained control over the estate at Bweza, which became the clan's principal estate and the burial ground for subsequent heads of clan. Bweza's proximity to Kintu's shrine at Magonga further reinforced the clan's link to the ritual complex surrounding Kintu. The estate also served as the clan's principal gathering spot and contained the clan's main shrine, where clan members gathered to honor the spirit of their founder. In this respect, the shrine at Bweza provided a discursive and ritual connection to Kisolo's shrine located on his grandson's estate at Nseke as well as to those situated on the clan's other secondary estates.

The history of the Otter clan provides a valuable glimpse into the early dynamics of Ganda clanship. As discussed in the previous chapter, the otter's anomalous characteristics lent the animal to particular metaphorical associations. Throughout the Great Lakes region, historical actors viewed the otter as possessing metaphysical capacities. The animal frequently appeared in the regalia of spirit mediums and served as a potent symbol for people whose authority drew upon their skills in the craft of spirit mediumship. The name of the Ganda Otter clan's founder—Kisolo Muwanga Ssebyoto— further hinted at the clan's origins as part and parcel of the expansion of the spirit Muwanga's territory from the Ssese Islands to the mainland. Building on this suggestion, we might regard Kisolo Muwanga Ssebyoto as a disembodied spiritual entity rather than the embodied person who founded the Otter clan. Viewed from this perspective, Kisolo's journeys as recorded in Otter clan narratives appear as the gradual movement of the spirit Muwanga from his "home" in the Ssese Islands, where the Otter clan claims indigenous status, to the coastal province of Mawokota and then further inland into Busujju. Made possible through the work of itinerant mediums, the spirit's journey resulted in the emergence of dispersed therapeutic networks whose members turned to the powers of the spirit Muwanga for their well-being and drew upon the familiar idiom of kinship to describe their relationship to one another. In this regard, rather than preserving a record of the migration and segmentation of kin groups, the genealogy embedded in the Otter clan's history represents the outcome of historical alliances between dispersed communities cemented by the intimately connected practices of clanship, spirit possession, and public healing.

The spirit Muwanga's journey resulted, however, in more than simply the establishment of a series of dispersed shrines devoted to his continued perpetuity. The immediate descendants of Kisolo Muwanga Ssebyoto together constituted a network of knowledge that included a priest, a critical figure in the ritual complex surrounding Kintu at Magonga, a talented doctor, a craftsman who made mallets used in bark-cloth production, a well-known bark-cloth artisan, and a famous diviner.[19] The accounts of their individual talents and undertakings preserved in Otter clan narratives, along with the ritual activities undertaken at the shrines located on Otter clan estates, provide further insight into the intellectual principles informing the clan concept. These accounts suggest that the general notion of collective well-being situated at the core of clanship drew upon the connection between collective health and the effective composition of knowledge. In other words, the practices of public healing undergirding the clan concept served as a form of practical reason that linked a community's collective health to the ability of its leaders to bring together various sorts of knowledge and skills.

The history of the Pangolin clan, another of the principal clans associated with the Kintu narratives, further attests to the connection between clanship, the portability of spirits, and the composition of knowledge. As described in the previous chapter, the pangolin, like the otter, did not fit into the categories employed by Ganda healers to describe nonhuman beings and served as a symbol for the capacity to mediate between the human and spirit worlds. The earliest remembered leaders of the Pangolin clan, who played the critical mediating role in "Kintu and Bemba the Snake," enjoyed these same qualities. Like Kisolo, the founder of the Otter clan, then, Mukiibi Ndugwa, the founder of the Pangolin clan, might best be regarded as either a mobile spirit or a group of itinerant mediums whose efforts cemented a series of alliances between dispersed communities. Mukiibi Ndugwa's journeys as preserved in Pangolin clan histories covered a wide geographical expanse. According to these narratives, Mukiibi's adventures took him from his original home at Wassozi, in Busiro, to Malanga Island in Ssese, Mangira in Kyaggwe, Bukesa in Butambula, Kapeeka in Busiro, and a host of other locations. Some of Mukiibi's children and grandchildren settled at the sites visited by their wandering ancestor, while others fanned out even further and occupied a series of widely dispersed estates in Busiro, Kyaddondo, Kyaggwe, Ssingo, and Busujju.

In addition to describing the movements and activities of the clan's founder, Otter clan histories relate how Mukiibi's children and grandchildren became the heads of the clan's *masiga* and *mituba*. These descendants represent the earliest generations of Pangolin clan leaders, who formed a talented network of individuals wielding a variety of skills. They included the caretaker of the powerful *jjembe* Nantaba;[20] a renowned drummer;[21] the medium at the spirit Nagawonye's shrine in Bulemeezi, where devotees congregated in times of drought and famine; a ritual specialist who contributed to the upkeep of Kintu's shrine at Magonga; the first person to take care of the spirit Kitinda after it left Ddamba Island in Ssese; one of the people responsible for carrying the celebrated spirit Mukasa from Bubembe Island to the mainland; the priest who maintained the shrine dedicated to the spirit Wamala at Ssekiwunga Hill; and the guardian of Ssumba Hill, in Busiro, a prominent site in the royal installation ceremonies.[22] The composition of these individuals—or rather the nodes of authority they represented—into the Pangolin "clan" served as the signal achievement of the earliest historical actors who adopted the pangolin as their totem. Their efforts resulted in the fashioning of a knowledgeable community whose diverse talents strengthened the capacity of its constituent members to ensure both their collective health and their continued perpetuity in the human and spirit worlds.

The networks of knowledge embedded in Pangolin and Otter clan genealogies represent the outcome of considerable efforts to mobilize different bodies of knowledge into healthy communities that shared in a collective endeavor and, eventually, a common history. The therapeutic networks forged by the spirits Kisolo Muwanga Ssebyoto and Mukiibi Ndugwa or their earthly representatives formed the skeletons around which communities composed clan narratives, whose recitation ultimately constituted part of the process of clan formation. In this regard, the identification of Kisolo Muwanga Ssebyoto and Mukiibi Ndugwa as clan founders necessarily occurred long after the death of the historical actors whose ancestral ghosts were transformed into the territorial spirits that mediums ultimately transported from their "homes" to new areas. Moreover, clan narratives and their corresponding genealogies underwent periodic modification as people cultivated new skills or communities incorporated new forms of knowledge through the recruitment of new members. Though this process is difficult to detect for the earliest periods of clan formation in Buganda, two examples drawn from the histories of the Pangolin and Otter clans provide suggestive illustrations.

As part of a wave of territorial expansion in the late seventeenth century, Kabaka Mutebi incorporated the territory of Busujju into the growing Ganda kingdom. The king then replaced the area's existing chief with Kalali, a political ally and member of the Pangolin clan, and made him the Kasujju, chief of Busujju. Judging by clan as well as dynastic narratives, the Pangolin clan was well established by the time of Kalali's rise to prominence as chief of Busujju. In Pangolin clan narratives, however, Kalali Kasujju appears as the grandson of the clan's founder, Mukiibi Ndugwa. His place in the upper echelon of the clan's structure indicates the significance accorded to Kalali Kasujju's position as chief of Busujju and the manner in which his newfound status was incorporated into Pangolin clan networks and genealogies. Otter clan genealogies reveal a similar process of incorporation during the reign of Kabaka Jjunju, who in the late eighteenth century embarked on a campaign to conquer the territory of Buddu, to the south of Buganda's heartland. Jjunju received advice and military assistance from Kajabaga, a member of the Otter clan and leader of a pastoralist community near the banks of the Katonga River. Kajabaga later received the name Kiganda in recognition of his role in Jjunju's conquest of Buddu and his newfound status in the Ganda kingdom. He also achieved a prominent position in the genealogy of Otter clan leaders, where he appears as a grandson of Ssenkungu and a great-grandson of the Otter clan founder, Kisolo Muwanga Ssebyoto.[23]

The examples of Kalali Kasujju and Kajabaga Kiganda illustrate how the composition and recomposition of clan narratives constituted an essential element of community-building processes and strategies. The ideology of clanship offered both a language and a set of practices for incorporating and preserving new sorts of skills and statuses into social collectivities. As the histories of the Otter and Pangolin clans suggest, the concept of spiritual portability made possible the establishment of more expansive and diverse social networks. Each person or node of authority recruited into the therapeutic networks cemented by portable spirits and their earthly representatives brought a new element into an expanding body of knowledge. In this manner, healthy communities resulted from knowledgeable communities. The networks of knowledge achieved through this process of composing communities connected centers of production and exchange whose successful coordination drew upon the language and practices of clanship and contributed to a community's well-being.

LOCATING KINTU: THE PRACTICE OF SPIRIT POSSESSION IN THE GREAT LAKES REGION

Like the Kintu narratives, the histories of the principal clans associated with these narratives point to the considerable intellectual and social changes that accompanied a series of innovations in the practice of spirit mediumship. To better understand these historical developments in Ganda public healing, however, we must locate them within a broader historical framework. How, then, do we set about situating these narratives within the region's social and cultural history? From a reading of the narratives alone we cannot determine when the developments described in them occurred or when the stories were first crafted. We must therefore search other sources of evidence for a historical hook with which to secure these narratives to an identifiable temporal framework. Historical linguistics, which furnishes an independently derived body of knowledge, provides just such a hook.

If the Kintu narratives and the histories of the clans associated with them contain the historical residue from a period of innovations in the institution of spirit mediumship, then the linguistic evidence relating to the history of this practice provides an appropriate starting point for situating these narratives in a historical context and evaluating the transformations they describe. This evidence indicates that spirit possession served as one of the oldest techniques Great Lakes historical actors employed to meet a variety of intellectual and material needs.[24] As Schoenbrun demonstrates, the practice originated in the very distant past, as evidenced by the distribution of the root *-bándwa, "to be consecrated to a spirit," in Great Lakes Bantu languages. Forms of this root appear in all five branches of these languages with meanings related to spirit possession, suggesting that the experience of being possessed by a spirit probably constituted a part of the ancient Great Lakes Bantu cultural world.[25] Great Lakes historical actors derived the verb *ku-bándwa from its older transitive form *-bánda, which appears most widely in Bantu languages with the meaning "to begin" but also occurs in a narrower distribution (though still wider than the Great Lakes Bantu meanings relating to spirit possession for *-bándwa) with the meaning "to split." In its Great Lakes Bantu forms, *-bánda appears with the meaning "to press down or knock down," a semantic narrowing that hints at the connection with spirit

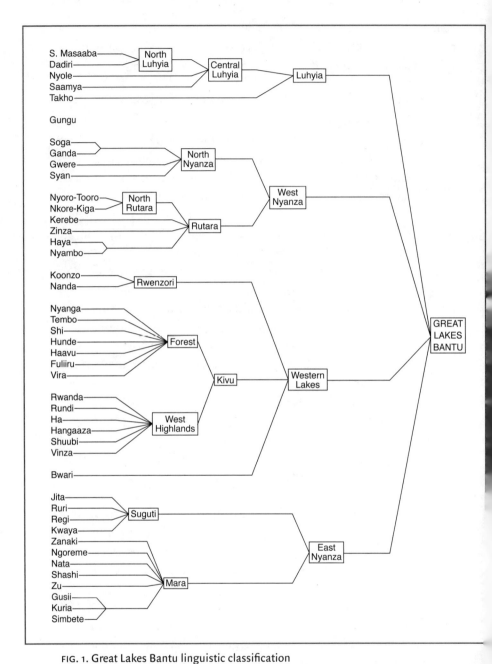

FIG. 1. Great Lakes Bantu linguistic classification
(After *A Green Place, A Good Place: Agrarian Change, Gender, and Social Identity in the Great Lakes Region to the 15th Century* by David Lee Schoenbrun, 89. Copyright © 1998 by David Lee Schoenbrun, published by Heinemann, Portsmouth, NH. All rights reserved)

possession. The rich ethnographic record in the Great Lakes region consistently describes the state of possession as being seized on the head by an overpowering force. As the passive form of the verb *kubánda, "to press down or knock down," *kubándwa described the experience of being knocked down by an overwhelming spiritual force that had mounted one's head.[26]

Despite displaying general similarities inherited from a period of common development in the era of Proto–Great Lakes Bantu, the kubándwa practices described in the ethnographic and oral historical records exhibit considerable differences both in their organization and in the types of spirits to which adherents directed their activities. These differences point to the radical adjustments this ancient practice has undergone as part of the regionally distinct reorganizations of social, political, and spiritual life in Great Lakes societies. As Schoenbrun points out, that these societies retained the term kubándwa with similar meanings related to spirit possession tells us only that they shared in common the notions of consecrating an individual to a spirit and possession by a spirit. Moving beyond this observation requires that we consider the linguistic evidence that marks the subsequent development of this ancient practice into its various institutional forms.

Two related and overlapping processes marked critical transformations in kubándwa early in the second millennium AD: the institutionalization of spirit possession practices and the transformation of territorial spirits into portable spirits. The ethnographic record for the Great Lakes region provides a bundle of linguistic markers related to institutional forms of spirit possession. These markers include terms for different types of mediums and other personnel, the material items they employed, and the ideas that undergirded their practices. Their distribution within Great Lakes Bantu languages reveals clusters of co-occurring regular correspondences only in KiHaya, Runyankore, and Runyoro, all of which fall within the Rutara subgroup of West Nyanza languages (see map 5 and fig. 1). Because these three languages form a block of contiguous languages, this clustering of terms within the Rutara subgroup suggests that the earliest possible period for the emergence of an institutional form of spirit possession coincided with the beginning of the dissolution of the Rutara dialect chain, early in the second millennium AD.[27] Some of these terms, however, overreach the Rutara subgroup and appear in languages belonging to such neighboring subgroups as Rwenzori, West Highlands, and North Nyanza. As Schoenbrun observes, their sporadic presence in these subgroups indicates that parts of the institution of spirit possession spread from societies that spoke languages de-

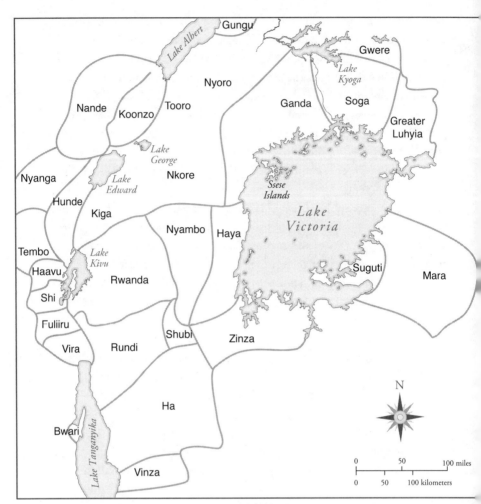

MAP 5. Linguistic geography of the Great Lakes region
(After *A Green Place, A Good Place: Agrarian Change, Gender, and Social Identity in the Great Lakes Region to the 15th Century* by David Lee Schoenbrun, 23. Copyright © 1998 by David Lee Schoenbrun, published by Heinemann, Portsmouth, NH. All rights reserved)

scended from Proto-Rutara into neighboring societies, such as those that spoke Luganda. Schoenbrun correctly asserts that these developments most certainly took place after the thirteenth century, when Rutara had begun to split into its northern and southern branches,[28] but they could have occurred as late as the sixteenth century, when Luganda, a member of the North Nyanza subgroup, emerged as a distinct language.

North Nyanza and Rutara communities employed the bundle of terms associated with the institution of spirit possession to mark the status of a specific type of medium, the mbándwa. The connection between the institutionalization of spirit possession and mbándwa mediums highlights another critical innovation in the ancient practice of kubándwa. In their capacity as public healers, spirit mediums performed crucial diagnostic services and relayed requests on behalf of the spiritual guardians of a particular social group (mizimu, or ancestral ghosts) or geographical location (misambwa, or territorial spirits). However, at some point following the dissolution of the Rutara and North Nyanza dialect chains between the fourteenth and sixteenth centuries, historical actors speaking North Nyanza and Rutara dialects instituted an intellectual innovation that enabled the portability of territorial misambwa spirits. By joining spirits to their mediums rather than to specific territories—as evidenced in the fact that the word mbándwa named both a medium and a spirit, while musambwa named a spirit and its territorial location but not its medium—these historical actors severed the limiting conceptual connection between spiritual and territorial authority. No longer tied to a particular locality, these transformed territorial spirits could extend the range of their healing capacities through the substantial efforts of professional itinerant mediums, who carried these portable spirits to new settlements and drew upon their expanded capacities to meet the needs of larger communities. Moreover, some of these portable spirits came to represent entire categories or fields of efficacy (fertility, war, hunting, fishing, etc.), an innovation that led to the emergence of shrines that served these needs in far-flung, discontiguous places.[29]

Mediums' endeavors to promote the efficacy of their spiritual benefactors undoubtedly involved the suppression or cooptation of local territorial spirits residing in the territories into which they traveled. Renee Tantala examined such a process in western Uganda, where itinerant mediums promoted the powers of a new category of spirits known as cwezi. The signal innovation differentiating cwezi kubándwa from possession practices involving other sorts of spirits hinged on the ability of cwezi to return from the underworld, where ancestral ghosts resided, even if they had no heirs to look after in the world of the living. Cwezi kubándwa thus provided hope for kinless, heirless, and childless people, who sought to overcome the social challenges accompanying their condition by becoming mediums for cwezi spirits.[30] The proliferation of cwezi kubándwa in the periods preceding the emergence of the well-known Great Lakes kingdoms signaled what Iris Berger has referred to as the democratization of *kubándwa*.[31] In contrast to the restrictive member-ship practices that characterized local territorial cults, *cwezi* cults offered membership to anyone willing to undergo the initiation rituals, which were performed by acknowledged experts. This democratization process resulted in the proliferation of *cwezi* adherents and the increasing political significance of prominent *cwezi* sites such as those at Masaka and Mubende hills.

In many respects, the broad outlines of the social and intellectual pro-cesses situated at the heart of the *cwezi kubándwa* revolution—the enlarge-ment of territories of healing and the concomitant suppression of local spirits—also characterize the historical developments embedded in the Kintu narratives. The concept of spiritual portability, a key component of both the Cwezi and the Kintu narratives, constituted part of a profound transforma-tion in public healing practices in both the central grasslands to the west of Buganda and the areas closer to the older settlements near Lake Victoria. These efforts to alter the boundaries of collective health, however, unfolded differently in different settings. In Buganda, for example, clanship played a far more significant role in these developments than it did elsewhere in the region. The histories of the Ganda clans associated with the Kintu narratives suggest that the process of clan formation constituted an essential part of this transformation in public healing. As aspiring political leaders converted territorial *misambwa* spirits into portable spirits, the effective range of these new spiritual entities extended over increasingly larger areas and led to the development of widespread therapeutic networks whose members came to consider themselves as belonging to various clans. This emphasis on clan networks resulted largely from the different sorts of pressures faced by those living in what would become Buganda's heartland compared with the occu-pants of the grasslands to the west. While the proliferation of *cwezi kubándwa* in the central grasslands was a means of coping with the tensions generated by the emergence of an increasingly aggressive pastoralism, the establish-ment of therapeutic networks in the areas along the northwestern shores of Lake Victoria accompanied a quite different shift in productive practices, the gradual development of land-intensive banana cultivation.[32]

THE DEVELOPMENT OF INTENSIVE BANANA CULTIVATION: A REGIONAL PERSPECTIVE

The innovations in spirit possession gleaned from the historical linguis-tic record and described in the Kintu narratives constituted part of a broader set of historical developments in the area surrounding the northwestern shores of Lake Victoria. Historical linguistic evidence suggests that these transformations in public healing occurred during a period in which Baganda were conducting critical experiments with intensive banana cultivation. Bananas (*Musa* spp.) came to Africa from Southeast Asia, where numerous wild species occur in an area stretching from Papua New Guinea to India. Two of the crop's three families—AAA "bananas" and AAB "plantains"—occur in Africa, and cultivars of each variety appear in the Great Lakes region.[33] In contrast to in western and central Africa, however, the banana variety predominates in the Great Lakes region despite having entered Lakes food systems later than plantains.[34]

Given the banana's origins outside the region, the terms for its various cultivars as well as those related to the cultivation process either were obtained from elsewhere as the crop and its cultivars spread to new areas or came into existence locally following plant mutations and the subsequent introduction of new names. The distribution of the terms surrounding banana cultivation in Great Lakes languages therefore provides an outline of the crop's spread in the region. The histories of these terms illustrate that the incorporation of the banana into the diverse and productive Great Lakes Bantu food systems occurred gradually and took on various regional inflections. As Schoenbrun has illustrated, three broad stages of development characterized this long and progressive process.[35]

A handful of widely distributed terms demonstrating familiarity with varieties of beer and cooking bananas (AAA), as well as the West Nyanza innovation of a new kind of billhook (*-pabíó) for pruning banana trees, trace the initial stage of experimentation and sporadic cultivation to the second half of the first millennium AD. A period of increased specialization, during which Rutara, West Highlands, and Forest communities elaborated upon their earlier knowledge about banana varietals, followed from 800 to 1300.[36] Finally, beginning in the thirteenth century a few societies speaking West Highlands, Rutara, and North Nyanza languages embarked upon the third stage in the development of banana farming. These communities formulated simultaneously the concepts of the banana plantation and generic names for bananas according to their uses, a pair of innovations that ushered in the intensive use of the banana in Rutaran and North Nyanzan societies in the fourteenth through the sixteenth century.

Linguistic evidence for the development of banana farming indicates, then, that while the sporadic cultivation of bananas had occurred in the Great Lakes region since at least the second half of the first millennium AD, the period of intensive development came considerably later.[37] The large number of unique terms for varietals in modern Great Lakes Bantu languages suggests that the land-intensive practices familiar today in Buganda, Buhaya, and parts of Kivu developed relatively recently, beginning after the breakup of West Highlands communities in the fifteenth century. The greatest number of these terms appears in Luganda, whose sixty unique terms for banana varieties suggest that cultivation may have been most intensive in the areas that would become Buganda. Since Luganda and its closest genetic neighbor, Lusoga, began to differentiate into distinct languages in the sixteenth century, Schoenbrun reasonably traces the development of Buganda's land-intensive banana farming system to around this period.[38]

The recent history of *Musa* in Africa requires that we temper historical claims based on the distribution of names for varieties. As Gerda Rossel has correctly pointed out, the widespread introduction of banana cultivars in East Africa during the colonial period blurred the picture of previous distribution patterns. Moreover, identical cultivars are sometimes known under a multitude of names, reflecting linguistic diversity rather than *Musa*'s diversity in a given area.[39] Scholars should therefore proceed cautiously when employing the terms for cultivars as historical evidence. The integrity of the narrative presented above, however, rests on the histories of terms related to the development of the concept of the banana plantation as much as on the histories of those designating cultivars. Perhaps the most telling linguistic evidence for the growth of intensive banana farming relates to the development during the North Nyanza–Rutara period of a set of terms denoting perennially cropped land. These terms suggest that the increasing emphasis on banana farming among certain groups of North Nyanzan and Rutaran farmers led to the creation of fields that were never fallowed. These fields were instead devoted to the planting of perennial crops such as bananas, an innovation that signaled intensive banana farming from the fourteenth to the sixteenth century. The greatest diversity in varietals, however, came after this period.[40]

LAND TENURE, PATRIARCHY, AND THE BANANA ECONOMY

Linguistic evidence related to both banana farming and spirit possession indicates that the gradual development of intensive banana farming in the area that would become Buganda coincided with the transformation of previously territorial spirits into mobile spirits capable of ensuring the collective health of larger, increasingly dispersed communities. Public healing practices, in other words, became de-territorialized as banana cultivation became highly territorialized. This paradoxical development requires closer analysis. Linguistic evidence merely suggests that these two processes coincided and does not indicate any sort of relationship. Holly Hanson's examination of the reorganization of social relations that accompanied the transition to land-intensive banana farming, however, offers some substantive historical premises for connecting these overlapping developments.

From the fourteenth to the sixteenth century the communities living along the western shores of Lake Victoria gradually incorporated a system of land-intensive banana cultivation into an already diverse farming base that included the cultivation of tubers, legumes, and cereals.[41] The fertile soils along the lakeshore were far more conducive to banana farming than the grasslands further west. As Hanson and others point out, however, certain regions were particularly well suited to this agricultural innovation, and the crescent-shaped stretch of land along the northwestern shores of the lake provided an exceptionally favorable setting. The upper and middle slopes of this area's many hills were covered with particularly productive soils capable of supporting heavy cultivation in moderate climates with adequate and evenly distributed rainfall. Temperatures varied little in this area, and while the total annual precipitation may have been as high or higher in other areas, the rainfall in the more narrowly equatorial region surrounding Lake Victoria was more evenly distributed throughout the year. A short dry season followed each of the region's two rainy seasons, but even these dry seasons were rarely without rain. This relatively evenly distributed rainfall made possible a kind of permanent cultivation that relied on a perennial crop.[42]

While the combination of rich soils, reliable rainfall, and a moderate climate created an exceptional environment for the cultivation of bananas in the area along the northwestern shores of Lake Victoria, the development of land-intensive banana farming in this fertile crescent occurred only gradually, passing through many modes of mixed farming.[43] According to Hanson, this process "would have involved a period of time in which members of a household allotted their time among many different kinds of work," including clearing fields, weeding, herding, harvesting, threshing grain, and preparing food. Banana farming, however, offered some distinct advantages over the cultivation of other crops: banana gardens involved considerably less labor than planting pulse and cereal crops; the perennially fruiting banana tree bore fruit year-round and continued to yield for several decades; and the fact that bananas were harvested year-round alleviated worries about storage and the risk of hunger faced by communities dependent on grains. As Hanson notes, these advantages eventually would have led mixed-farming communities to rely increasingly upon the banana as a staple food.[44]

The transition to land-intensive banana farming slowly transformed the rhythms and routines of agricultural production. Although we cannot comment definitively on the gendered division of labor in the distant past, we know from ethnographic observations that tending banana groves was women's work in Buganda in the late nineteenth and early twentieth centuries. While young men cleared the land of secondary thicket and set out banana rootstocks, they left the maintenance of groves almost entirely to women. Hanson suggests that during the opening phases of the gradual transition to land-intensive banana farming, "women may have paid attention to bananas during the slack times in the agricultural calendar when root and grain crops had been harvested and men concentrated on hunting." As communities slowly turned to bananas as a daily food, however, women would have devoted increasing attention to the maintenance of their groves. This shift in crop priorities, Hanson observes, may have prompted alterations in the gendered division of labor. As mentioned earlier, banana trees produced fruit year-round and continued to yield for a considerable period of time if properly mulched. Banana farming therefore involved a relatively light labor requirement compared with planting annual grain and pulse crops, and there was also less of a harvest bottleneck than in mixed-farming communities dependent on cereal agriculture. These alterations in labor patterns meant that as communities made bananas a central part of their food system, men would have been able to devote an increasing amount of time to activities beyond the agricultural domain.[45]

In addition to transforming productive rhythms, the gradual development of a banana-based economy in Buganda also contributed to momentous changes in settlement patterns. Hanson notes that whereas farmers who practiced banana cultivation prior to the transition to land-intensive banana cultivation "broke new fields every few years and moved their homes about every decade," those who came increasingly to rely on bananas as a staple food established new types of settlements. Although banana trees could be propagated relatively simply through cutting, banana suckers required one to three years to reach fruition.[46] This extended interval between the time of planting and the appearance of the first crop, combined with the fact that fully grown banana trees continued to produce fruit for many years, meant that people developed more permanent settlements as they came to rely on bananas for a larger portion of their food. Banana farming represented a good investment and fostered deeper attachments to productive land than did the cultivation of either grains or tubers. Unlike cropland that would be fallowed after three or four seasons, the land dedicated to the maintenance of banana groves remained under continuous cultivation for decades and even generations. As a result, Hanson suggests, "the period between moves might have grown longer" until eventually "Baganda stopped moving their homes."[47]

The development of more permanent communities resulted in the emergence of larger and more densely populated settlements. As communities came to depend increasingly on the banana as a staple food, the previously dispersed societies living along the northwestern shores of Lake Victoria began to concentrate themselves around the best banana lands. The growing importance of banana plantations made these lands attractive places for settlement and most likely resulted in increased population densities. While we cannot know how many people lived in the communities surrounding the best banana-bearing lands, Hanson's observations about the higher food yields resulting from land devoted to banana cultivation suggest that these communities were certainly more heavily populated and more densely settled than those located on lands unable to raise and sustain banana gardens. These higher food yields may also have resulted in an overall increase in population levels and the establishment of new settlements on previously unoccupied ridges.[48]

The stability of the settlements on the lands best suited to intensive banana cultivation meant that the stakes involved in securing continued access to these lands increased dramatically. Not all land in this region, however, was equally conducive for banana farming. Variations in soil quality and rainfall in the region that became Buganda determined the differing potential of land for banana cultivation, and the best plots often were not contiguous but were separated by swamps and stretches of rocky hilltops.[49] The establishment of permanent settlements around the best banana-bearing lands prompted competition for these resources and generated newfound concerns regarding the related matters of inheritance and succession. The increased economic and therefore political value of banana lands meant that these plots were guarded more closely than other areas. While community leaders used their control over productive banana lands to attract followers who sought access to them, they simultaneously developed ideologies and institutions designed to preserve these repositories of wealth within particular social groups. These efforts to secure and maintain access to banana groves resulted in an increased emphasis on lineality.[50] Banana gardens represented "invested labor and generations of surplus value stored in the form of perennially fruiting trees," and prominent farmers drew upon recently developed inheritance ideologies to transmit these valuable lands to designated heirs.[51] The new stress banana farmers placed on inheritance and lineality also led to an intensification of patriarchal forms of authority. As patrilineages sought to establish banana lands as lineage property, patrilocal women became dependent on male lineage members for access to banana groves. These developments would have been accompanied by an increasing emphasis on childbearing as well as male efforts to exert control over women as childbearers, a crucial component in the reproduction of lineage and property rights.

PUBLIC HEALING, CLAN FORMATION, AND LAND-INTENSIVE BANANA CULTIVATION

The earliest processes of clan formation in Buganda coincided with the reorganization of communities that accompanied new land tenure practices stemming from the shift to banana farming. Perhaps not surprisingly, the few scholars who have discussed the role of clans in early Ganda history have presented functionalist interpretations of clanship that revolve around competition for material property. The related matters of inheritance and succession have guided these discussions, which have focused on how clans and their constituent patrilineages served as the preeminent vehicles both for converting disconnected stretches of fertile land into banana gardens and for directing land-use rights. Scholars have for the most part conceived of clanship as a tool for managing social relationships and have treated clans as functional bodies that preserved sources of wealth and political standing for some people and limited the ambitions of others. They have examined how the concept of clanship, by providing a language and a set of practices for supervising access to the richest farmlands, enabled people to attend to the pressures that accompanied the changing material circumstances of intensive banana farming. According to this model, male leaders sought to employ their authoritative positions within patrilineages to control access to valuable clan lands and to distribute strategic resources, an enduring form of political power that would come to characterize the Ganda state.[52]

Discussions of Ganda clanship focusing on the simultaneous emergence of patriarchalism, lineality, and a land-intensive farming system have provided critical insights into the historical circumstances that led communities to develop social boundaries distinguishing insiders from outsiders, and they have shed light on some of the benefits that insiders could expect to receive. Yet the kinds of connections most often drawn between clanship, land-use rights, and inheritance would apply equally to lineages, clans, or any sort of social collectivity that drew upon notions of unilineal descent. As discussed earlier, however, Ganda clans were not simply lineages writ large. The ideology and practices of clanship in Buganda built upon transformations in public healing practices that posited a connection between health, wealth, and the effective composition of knowledge. Understanding the relationship between the process of clan formation and the transition to intensive banana cultivation therefore requires that we situate the discussion of banana farming in Buganda within the context of the shifting boundaries of public healing.

While banana gardens anchored the land-intensive farming system in the areas that would become Buganda, their significance stretched far beyond their serving as a source of food or beer. Hanson notes that "the settled, fixed quality of intensive banana cultivation" provided people with a new means—and a new vocabulary—for establishing relationships of obligation, both with the ancestors and between leaders and followers. Like their Great Lakes neighbors, Baganda had long recognized the importance of maintaining healthy relationships with their ancestors. But the development of more permanent communities both transformed the character of these relationships and increased their significance. As Hanson describes, "the presence of . . . graves in a place that people stayed for decades . . . added a dimension to the way [Baganda] remembered ancestors." In these circumstances, maintaining control over valuable plots came to revolve around the ability to establish widely recognized connections with ancestors, whose ghosts hovered around burial sites, ensured the land's continued fertility, and invited a host of prestational actions. People chose to live in close proximity to the graves of important ancestors in hopes of securing such linkages, and the continuous cultivation of the banana groves surrounding these graves "became in itself a way of remembering those ancestors."[53]

Hanson's work on the social and spiritual transformations that accompanied the development of land-intensive banana farming reveals that as communities stabilized around the best banana-bearing lands, "the power of the dead over land" provided the conceptual framework within which contests for the control of these fertile estates occurred.[54] Those who emerged victorious in these contests—the people who successfully managed to secure connections with the ancestors buried in a particular settlement—acquired the power to allocate land and to rule the people who cultivated the banana gardens on that land. They used their positions of authority to attract followers both by granting smallholdings and by acts of generosity made possible by the surplus products of banana trees. These social and political transformations characterized what Conrad Kottak described more than thirty years ago as the "shift from egalitarian to rank-organized society."[55]

By situating the struggles for the control and successful maintenance of fertile estates within the realm of public healing, we can better perceive the connection between the development of land-intensive banana farming, the process of clan formation, and innovations in the practice of spirit possession. The establishment of dispersed therapeutic networks that reconfigured the boundaries of public healing—the core of the earliest processes of clan formation in Buganda—served as a means of contending with the challenges and opportunities that accompanied the development of land-intensive banana farming. The opportunities for permanent settlement and the accumulation of wealth in the form of perennially fruiting banana trees rendered bananas a potentially lucrative long-term investment. The surpluses derived from banana cultivation may also have stimulated experiments and growth in practical knowledge of various arts, thus making a place attractive to newcomers and potential followers. As discussed above, however, the gradual transition to intensive banana farming also presented significant challenges to the communities living along the northwestern shores of Lake Victoria. The increased value of land generated contests concerning land-use rights and property inheritance. These contests unfolded within the realm of public healing and were mediated by the historical actors, whether spirits or their human embodiments, best situated to both shape and manage the shifting boundaries between the material and spiritual realms.

Kisolo Muwanga Ssebyoto and Mukiibi Ndugwa, the remembered founders of two of Buganda's earliest clans, represented just such figures. As either increasingly portable spirits or their human vehicles, these figures sought to manage the opportunities and challenges that accompanied land-intensive banana farming by securing a more widespread and increasingly diverse community of followers. The gradual transformation of spirits such as Kisolo Muwanga Ssebyoto and Mukiibi Ndugwa from ancestral ghosts into territorial spirits and the subsequent movement of these spirits from their "homes" to new areas resulted in the extension of the power associated with their principal shrines through the establishment of a series of connected ritual centers. This process drew upon the skills of itinerant mediums and was at the core of clan formation. The webs of shrines situated on clan lands drew together dispersed communities, whose leaders possessed a variety of skills. The proper management of these skills—the effective arrangement of various forms of knowledge distributed over wide geographical areas—resulted in the formation of more complex and efficacious social and productive networks. The individuals and communities recruited into these expanding networks of knowledge brought links to new territories, facilitated the establishment of trade networks, and provided access to new forms of agricultural production and healing practices. This gradual process resulted in the reconfiguration of the publics involved in public healing and offered a means of alleviating the pressures generated by the transition to banana cultivation. In this manner, the establishment of these shrine networks forged a powerful connection between clanship, collective well-being, and the composition of knowledge.

Rather than reproducing the instrumental character of existing arguments linking clanship to resource control in Buganda, this understanding of the connections between clan formation and the development of intensive banana farming points to how public healing served, in Steven Feierman's words, as a "form of practical reason" designed to "[reorient peoples'] situation in the world for practical ends."[56] The relationship between clan formation, transformations in public healing, and land-intensive banana farming suggests an understanding of public health in sixteenth-century Buganda as a condition characterized by the continued prosperity resulting from the forging of favorable relationships with the appropriate spiritual entities. The communities that emerged along the northwestern shores of Lake Victoria might have been born of their productive bases, but rich agricultural yields, and the opportunities for political advancement that these yields provided, were as much a sign of successful relationships with the appropriate spiritual entities as they were of effective farming practices. Agricultural abundance, in other words, was both a yield and a sign; it was something in and of itself and also indicated a condition of collective health. In this respect, the maintenance of collective health revolved around the successful arrangement of the skills required for a community's continued prosperity, and the composition of networks of knowledge from skilled individuals and their followers served as a marker of effective political leadership. At the heart of these endeavors stood the ideology and practices of clanship, which shaped the historical formation of publics within which Baganda pursued collective well-being. The social organization of knowledge, the spatial organization of clans, and material prosperity were intimately entwined in sixteenth-century Buganda.

CONCLUSION

In this chapter I have explored the connection between clanship, collective health, and the effective composition of knowledge in sixteenth-century Buganda. Faced with the social tensions generated by the increased value of land that accompanied the development of land-intensive banana farming, Baganda built upon recent innovations in the realm of spirit mediumship to develop dispersed therapeutic networks that reconfigured the boundaries of public healing and informed the earliest processes of clan formation. This understanding of clanship compels us to rethink the problem of scale identified in the case of Buganda by Christopher Wrigley. According to Wrigley, the reliance on ritual forms of authority necessarily limited the size and reach of the communities that preceded the development of states. For Wrigley, these communities, which included the many small kinglets in the Great Lakes region, "could not work unless most of the people were present at the rituals that were the reason for [their] existence."[57] The dispersed clan networks described in chapters 1 and 2, however, illustrate the capacity of ritual practices to forge relationships among communities whose members did not necessarily share face-to-face interactions. By extending the territorial scale over which a particular spirit might ensure collective health, itinerant mediums managed the composition of communities comprising people living in discontiguous territories. The discourse and practices of clanship thus furnished a critical vehicle for the development of larger, more mobile, and increasingly complex communities along the northwestern shores of Lake Victoria.

The focus in this chapter on the relationship between the process of clan formation, public healing, and the development of land-intensive banana farming in sixteenth-century Buganda also limits the tyranny of state formation in the history of banana cultivation. Discussions regarding the role of the banana in Buganda's history appear in just about every examination of the kingdom's past. These discussions have for the most part focused on the connection between the introduction of banana cultivation and the process of state formation. While disagreements persist regarding the precise nature of this relationship, there is a general consensus in the literature on Buganda that the banana gardens located in the kingdom's fertile cradle in the Busiro, Mawokota, and Kyaddondo heartlands constituted valuable assets worth fighting over and protecting and that the state played a critical role in this process.

There is much that is worthy in these explanations of the connection between the exceptional environmental conditions for banana farming and Buganda's emergence as the most powerful state in the region. These analyses suffer, however, from the desire to explain the rise of states. The knowledge that Buganda eventually developed into a powerful state hovers over these discussions, steering the gradual transformation of banana farmers into unwitting participants in the competitive game of royal politics. The issue of state formation, in other words, has shaped how scholars have examined the history of banana farming in Buganda.[58] The banana economy developed gradually (passing through many modes of mixed farming) and preceded the development of the Ganda state. But in focusing solely on the connections between these two processes we lose sight of momentous social and intellectual developments hidden in the formidable shadow cast by discussions of state formation. The valuable banana lands in Buganda's fertile heartland were certainly worth fighting over and protecting, but only once they were established. This process occurred gradually, involved a series of critical transformations in the realm of public healing, and drew upon the language and practices of clanship.

POLITICAL
Leaders as
PUBLIC
Healers

In this chapter I further explore the relationship between public healing and political authority through an analysis of one of the best-known episodes in the Ganda dynastic narrative: the story of Prince Kimera's triumphant journey from Bunyoro to Buganda. Most commentators have examined the narrative describing Kimera's birth in Bunyoro and his eventual assent to the Ganda throne in search of clues about Buganda's origins and its relationship with its once powerful neighbor to the northwest. Rather than probing the Kimera story for insights into Buganda's dynastic past, however, I focus the analytical lens on the narrative's circulation and reception in a predynastic context. This discursive excavation yields a new understanding of the shifting political arena in the period preceding the emergence of the northern Great Lakes region's well-known states. The Kimera narrative and the histories of the Ganda clans associated with Kimera indicate that the discourse and practices of public healing—the debates about the efficacy of a particular spirit or therapeutic procedure in combating illness, enhancing collective well-being, or ensuring fertility—stood at the heart of political activities in seventeenth-century Buganda. During this period, political leaders operated as public healers, and effective political leadership revolved to a large extent around the establishment of successful relationships with the appropriate spiritual entities. In this regard, public healing was more than a form of social criticism, a basis from which to evaluate, critique, and rebel against political leaders.[1] By illustrating how efforts to establish control over the collective conditions of health characterized the very nature of political practices in the northern Great Lakes region during the seventeenth century, this chapter highlights the need to historicize the frequently observed divide between the authority of healers and the power of royals and their chiefly representatives.

In addition to revealing the close relationship between public healing and

political authority, the Kimera narrative and the histories of the clans associated with Kimera also suggest that political endeavors in the seventeenth
century were shot through with forms of organized violence that predated
the emergence of centralized states in the Great Lakes region. This observation challenges the conventional view in Great Lakes historiography that
organized violence was largely a function of state interests. In joining morally legitimate violence to mediumship, the activities of figures like Kimera
suggest that efforts to promote public health included warfare and other
forms of violent activities. As other scholars have noted, notions of public
health in precolonial Africa encompassed activities such as rainmaking, the
control of malevolent spiritual entities, and the management of natural resources. Like these public health services, engaging in morally legitimate
violent activities informed understandings of collective well-being in the
northern Great Lakes region. The composition of healthy communities included regulating acts of political violence, and a critical component of
power and leadership flowed from the capacity to direct these acts for the
benefit of the community.

On a broader level, this chapter provides novel insights into the components of political complexity and the shifting scale of political endeavors in
seventeenth-century Buganda. During this period, practices of spirit possession, violence, the spread and treatment of disease, and struggles to control
regional trade networks together determined the contours of the broader
political arena. These findings require that we revisit some older arguments
about the concept of enlargement of scale. An earlier generation of scholarship regarded this concept as a generalized indicator of political and economic change that, in the case of the seventeenth-century East African interior, revolved around a series of small-scale migrations and the gradual
establishment of chiefly dynasties.[2] By pointing to a new set of levers for
grasping the increased scope of political undertakings in the northern Great
Lakes region during this period, this chapter revamps these earlier formulations and resuscitates enlargement of scale as a useful category of historical
analysis.

THE KIMERA NARRATIVE

As discussed in chapter 2, the opening stages of the Ganda dynastic
narrative revolve around the exploits of Kintu, the purported founder of the
Ganda dynasty. The next major episode in this royal rendering of the Ganda
past is an account of the restoration of the kingship by Kimera, the third

Ganda king and Kintu's alleged great-grandson, after a period of rule by nonroyal leaders. In characteristically royal fashion, this episode emphasizes the genealogical connection between Kintu and Kimera, whose triumphant arrival in Buganda from Bunyoro ensures the survival and perpetuation of the Ganda royal line. In this respect, the story of Kimera's ascent to the Ganda throne begins with his great-grandfather Kintu's disappearance at Magonga in Busujju:[3]

Upon realizing that their king, Kintu, would not return, the principal chiefs in his delegation chose their departed leader's son Chwa Nabakka to rule over Buganda. Chwa established his capital at Bigo,[4] where he lived for many years and produced a son named Kalemeera. When Kalemeera grew up, he learned of his grandfather Kintu's disappearance, and fearing that his father, Chwa, might suffer a similar fate, he kept a close watch over him. Chwa, however, eventually came to resent his son's constant surveillance and devised a plan to rid himself of Kalemeera's watchful eye. He instructed his prime minister, Walusimbi, the head of the Civet Cat clan, to falsely accuse Kalemeera of committing adultery with his wife. The king's council declared Kalemeera guilty and leveled a heavy fine against the wayward prince, who was sent to Bunyoro to raise funds to pay off his fine.[5]

Kalemeera eventually reached Kibulala, where Wunyi, the king of Bunyoro, had established his capital. Wunyi received Kaleemera warmly and allowed him to sleep in the same house as his chief wife, Wannyana, a woman of the Grasshopper clan. Taken by Wannyana's beauty, Kalemeera seduced his host's wife and made her pregnant. Upon hearing of Wannyana's pregnancy, Kalemeera confided his indiscretion to a royal potter named Mulegeya, who pledged to assist the young prince and approached King Wunyi with the following story: a diviner, Mulegeya told Wunyi, had instructed him to warn the king that he should not punish any of his wives found to have committed adultery. Instead, he explained, the wife should be removed from the palace and placed in a specially built house outside of the royal confines. As soon as the woman gave birth, the potter continued, the baby should be taken away from its mother and thrown in the marshes. Mulegeya concluded by informing Wunyi that he would live a long and healthy life if he followed the diviner's pronouncement.

Convinced by Mulegeya's prophesy, Wunyi agreed to follow the trusted potter's advice and permitted Kalemeera to return to Buganda despite learning of Wannyana's transgression with the Ganda prince. Two days into his homeward journey, however, Kalemeera fell ill and died. Meanwhile, Wannyana took up residence in a home on the outskirts of the royal palace, where several months later she gave birth to a child named Kimera. In accordance with the diviner's advice, Kimera was cast into one of the marshes on the banks of the river from which Mulegeya retrieved his clay. Fully aware of Kimera's fate, the royal potter lifted the child out of the pit and brought him home to be raised alongside his recently born infant son, Katumba. Eager to ensure her baby's well-being, Wannyana presented Mulegeya with some cows to provide milk for her son Kimera, as well as a beaded bracelet to distinguish him from Mulegeya's son, who wore anklets. The potter accepted Wannyana's gifts and agreed to look after Kimera, who when he grew up looked after the cattle his mother had given Mulegeya and also developed into a skilled hunter.

Meanwhile, King Chwa had disappeared in Buganda just like his father Kintu, leaving the kingdom without a ruler. Having determined that Chwa would not return and that his son Kalemeera had died on his way from Bunyoro, the chiefs chose Walusimbi, Chwa's prime minister, to rule over them. After several years had passed, however, the chiefs became dissatisfied with Walusimbi's rule, and they therefore deposed him in favor of Ssebwana, of the Pangolin clan. A few years later, a man named Nabugwamu came from Bunyoro and related to the chiefs the story of Kimera's birth to Kalemeera and Wunyi's wife Wannyana. The chiefs then dispatched Nabugwamu to Bunyoro to fetch Kimera, who set out for Buganda along with Mulegeya's son Katumba, his mother, Wannyana, Lule Kyesimba, and several other followers.

Upon his arrival at the Ganda royal compound at Gganda, Kimera received an enthusiastic welcome from Nakku—the daughter of Walusimbi, widow of King Chwa, and now Ssebwana's consort. Nakku had previously heard from a diviner that a group of people arriving from Bunyoro would bring with them the rightful heir to the throne, and after further consulting the diviner she recognized Kimera as the future king. Kimera handed Nakku a large bag of salt to offer to Ssebwana, who upon sampling the offering asked for the visitors to make an appearance at his court.[6] The following morning Kimera and his entourage appeared before Ssebwana and presented him with ten bags of salt. Ssebwana then sent out a group of servants to fetch beer and food in preparation for a feast and to collect some cattle to present to the visitors in exchange for the salt. The previous day, however, Ssebwana's consort Nakku had instructed the servants not to return to the royal palace once they had received their master's orders. Puzzled by the prolonged absence of his servants, Ssebwana sent out one messenger after another to investigate the situation. When these messengers too failed to return, the impatient ruler finally decided to leave the palace himself in order to inquire into the problem.

No sooner had Ssebwana left the palace than Nakku ordered the drummers to beat the royal drums to signify the accession of a new king. Kimera then stepped onto the royal carpet in the presence of Nakku and, after prostrating before the queen, succeeded to the kingship. Upon hearing the sounds of the royal drums, Ssebwana immediately suspected that Kimera had ascended to the throne. He sent a servant to investigate the matter, and when his suspicions were confirmed, he dropped the pot of banana beer he had been carrying and fled to the Ssese Islands. Thus began the reign of Kimera, the third king in the Ganda royal line.

NAVIGATING BETWEEN MYTH AND HISTORY: KIMERA, COLONIALISM, AND HISTORICAL ANALYSIS

Perhaps because they could not find a historical interpretation that did not point to the neighboring kingdom of Bunyoro as a central player in Ganda history, Baganda intellectuals working in the early colonial period directed considerably less attention to Kimera than they did to their much-debated founding patriarch, Kintu. Kimera, however, eventually found his way into the heart of twentieth-century Ganda historical discourse, and the manner in which this occurred has had a profound effect on Ganda historiography. The induction of this well-known figure into the historical universe presided over by professional scholars began with the works of the colonial historian John Gray, whose accomplished forays into the Ganda past established the analytical trajectory followed by several subsequent historians.

In his examination of early Ganda history as presented in Apolo Kaggwa's 1901 publication *Bakabaka b'e Buganda* (*The Kings of Buganda*), Gray argued that rather than detailing the restoration of the Ganda royal line by a foreign-born prince, the Kimera narrative creatively concealed the conquest of Buganda by the Babito rulers of Bunyoro. He contended that while Ganda dynastic narrators portrayed the returned prince as the actual descendant of Kintu, Kimera more accurately represented a historical figure from Bunyoro who had invaded Buganda and then established an independent kingdom. Kimera's successful conquest of Buganda, Gray asserted, constituted a continuation of the widespread advance of Nilotic speakers that began with the establishment of a new dynasty in Bunyoro. Wunyi—the husband of Kimera's mother, Wannyana, and king of Bunyoro at the time of Kalemeera's arrival in the kingdom—figured in this interpretation as the leader of a southward movement of Nilotic people from northern Uganda. According to Gray, these migrating Nilotes supplanted the Cwezi as the area's rulers, established a new dynasty in Bunyoro, and then extended their influence to Buganda, a development captured in the narrative recording Kimera's triumphant arrival in the Ganda heartland.[7]

The notion of an extensive Bito empire that included both Buganda and Bunyoro proved an alluring historical prospect to the first generation of literate leaders in Bunyoro, which had lost a significant amount of territory to Buganda in the political maneuverings that accompanied the establishment of colonial rule.[8] Writing in the mid-1930s under the pseudonym K.W., Tito Gafabusa Winyi, the omukama (king) of Bunyoro, published a series of articles in the Uganda Journal in which he outlined Bunyoro's dynastic history. Drawing on information obtained from his father, Kabarega, the exiled king of Bunyoro, as well as from his own research, Winyi portrayed the Babito as the inheritors of a vast Cwezi empire whose territory once included the whole of modern Uganda as well as parts of eastern Congo, western Tanzania, and western Kenya.[9] Twelve years after the publication of Winyi's first article, John Nyakatura provided a similar characterization of the early Bito period. Nyakatura served as a county chief from 1940 to 1951 and campaigned vigorously on behalf of the Banyoro to recover territory lost to Buganda. In his history of the Nyoro kingdom, originally published in Runyoro in 1947, Nyakatura described how both Buganda and Bunyoro initially constituted part of the Cwezi empire of Kitara at the time of the Bito arrival.[10] The emergence of an independent Ganda kingdom, he explained, followed the Bito takeover from the recently disappeared Cwezi rulers. According to Nyakatura, Isingoma Mpuga Rukidi, the first Bito ruler of Bunyoro, assigned control over Buganda to his twin brother, Kimera, who later rebelled against Rukidi and established Buganda as a separate domain.[11] For both Winyi and Nyakatura, the significance of Kimera's connection to the Bito court was that it served as demonstrable proof that the roots of the Ganda kingdom ultimately rested in the distant Nyoro past. And in the contentious political universe of colonial Uganda, in which control over the production of official knowledge about the past constituted an essential ingredient in any successful political recipe, this historical depiction provided Nyoro leaders with critical intellectual ammunition as they struggled to combat what they considered Buganda's illegitimate encroachment into Nyoro territories.

The work of the Verona missionary Father J. P. Crazzolara both reinforced and elaborated upon both Gray's and Nyakatura's interpretations of the Kimera figure. Crazzolara's historical writings drew upon a vast compilation of family, clan, and chiefdom traditions collected among the Nilotic-speaking Lwo of northern Uganda. As part of his examination of the Lwo migrations from southern Sudan into northern Uganda and beyond, Crazzolara credited the advancing "Lwoo hordes" with establishing both the Cwezi empire and, following a later wave of northern invasions, the kingdom of Bunyoro. He described how upon invading Bunyoro the migrating Lwo state-builders subjugated the Nyoro population, who "became, by law of conquest, the serfs and property of the Lwoo." Bewildered by the intrusion of their northern neighbors, the Banyoro submitted to the Lwo, who proceeded to occupy Bunyoro's principal centers and to incorporate their new subjects into an emerging kingdom that built upon the remnants of the defunct Cwezi empire. Crazzolara concluded that the Bito dynasty, which governed Bunyoro at the establishment of colonial rule, descended from these Lwo invaders and that Kimera's arrival in Buganda preserved the record of the Lwo's southward advance after they had conquered and occupied Bunyoro.[12]

The formative works of early commentators such as Gray, Nyakatura, and Crazzolara established the analytical framework within which professional historians later approached the Kimera narrative. Over the past five decades, historians of Buganda have put forth numerous interpretations of this well-known story of the young prince's ascent to the Ganda throne.[13] These interpretations have for the most part navigated the intellectual territory generated by two overriding analytical concerns: the question whether the Kimera narrative preserved an account of events that actually had occurred in the past or constituted a myth devoid of historical content; and the politically charged matter of Buganda's relationship with its once powerful northwesterly neighbor Bunyoro. Reacting to what they considered the ill-fated attempts of early writers to treat an essentially mythical narrative in a historical manner, some historians have focused alternative analytical lenses on the account of Kimera's rise to the pinnacle of the Ganda political ladder.[14] Most scholars, however, have elaborated upon the historically oriented interpretations forwarded during the colonial period. In recognizing that Ganda dynastic chroniclers endeavored to transform the Kimera figure into a vehicle for dynastic continuity, these historians have correctly pointed to the importance of looking beyond the restrictive historical vision offered in royal renderings of the Ganda past. Seeking to circumvent this discursive barrier, they have stripped Kimera of his ideological clothing in the hopes of exposing the missing pieces of a historical puzzle entangled in a web of royal manipulations. In most cases, their efforts have uncovered the profound influence of migrating groups of people from the northwest (Lwo Babito) or west (former inhabitants of the Cwezi realm) on the emergence of the Ganda kingdom. And by lifting these state-building migrants—encapsulated in the figure of the returning Ganda prince—from the discursive rubble generated by subsequent dynastic developments, historians have sought to accord them their rightful place in the establishment of the Ganda kingdom.[15]

Despite employing an assortment of analytical techniques and drawing a variety of conclusions, then, the numerous excavations of the Kimera story have been dominated by a singular quest for an explanation of Buganda's origins. In this respect, these interpretations have refashioned, rather than raised, the royal curtain opening onto the Ganda historical stage. In framing the debate about Kimera around the identity of migrating royal statebuilders, historians have been seduced by the very discursive strategy they sought to overcome. They have submitted to viewing the past, or at least debating it, in a manner that enhances long-standing royal efforts to shape the nature of historical discourse. Their efforts to reveal what dynastic narrators sought to conceal have themselves concealed an alternative history embedded in this royal refashioning of the Ganda past. As with Kintu, the key to grasping Kimera's predynastic import lies in probing more locally grounded epistemologies and interpretive practices.

VISUAL CUES AND VERBAL CLUES: REEVALUATING KIMERA

In order to reclothe Kimera, albeit in ideological garments of a different fashion, we shall consider why this well-known character proved an appealing figure around which royal chroniclers crafted a critical episode in the Ganda dynastic narrative. This analytical approach compels us to move beyond the limiting assumptions entrenched in the divide between myth and history and to consider instead modes of reception and interpretation more grounded in northern Great Lakes practices. The resulting shift in perspective affords precious glimpses into aspects of the past that are ordinarily buried under the weight of royalist discourse. Rather than weighing in on the origins of the Ganda royal dynasty, the interpretation of the Kimera narrative that I present below aims to paint a composite image of political authority in the period preceding the emergence of centralized states in the northern Great Lakes region. In pointing to how innovations in the practice of spirit possession, political violence, and the spread and treatment of disease determined the contours of the broader political arena during this period, this interpretation lays the groundwork for efforts to situate the Kimera story within a more specific temporal and narrative framework.

An examination of oral traditions usually associated with areas to the west of Buganda suggests that portions of the Kimera narrative once lived and circulated beyond the confines of Ganda dynastic discourse. Perhaps the most compelling clue pointing to Kimera's alternative existence lies in his biography's striking resemblance to that of the well-known Cwezi figure Ndahura. Bunyoro's dynastic narratives divide the kingdom's history into three distinct phases: Tembuzi, Cwezi, and Bito. According to these narratives, Ndahura founded the Cwezi dynasty, which presided over the kingdom of Kitara prior to the rise of the Bito, whose arrival from the north resulted in the establishment of the kingdom of Bunyoro. In explaining Ndahura's rise to power, Nyoro dynastic narratives relate how Isimbwa, son of the deposed Tembuzi king Isaza, journeyed from his birthplace in the underworld to Kitara in order to survey his father's former kingdom. Isimbwa's explorations eventually led him to the palace of his father's usurper, Bukuku, where he encountered Mugizi, the maid of Bukuku's only daughter, Nyinamwiru. At Isimbwa's request, Mugizi delivered some wildflowers to her matron and informed her of the young visitor's desire for a meeting. Eager to lay eyes on her courter, Nyinamwiru instructed her maid to arrange a rendezvous with Isimbwa, who with Mugizi's assistance managed to gain entry into Nyinamwiru's secluded room. Isimbwa remained with Bukuku's daughter for several months, after which he rejoined his companions and continued on his adventure. Shortly after his departure, however, Nyinamwiru gave birth to a baby boy, named Ndahura.

Born illegitimately in a foreign land as the result of an illicit liaison between a visiting prince and a woman of the royal palace, Ndahura's life began much the same way as Kimera's. The resemblances between the biographies of the two future kings, however, extend beyond the accounts of their conception and birth. Just as a diviner advised Wunyi to build a house for his pregnant wife Wannyana outside of the royal compound and to throw the infant (Kimera) into the marshes immediately following the birth, so too Bukuku's diviners advised him against killing Nyinamwiru's child. Minding the words of his advisers, Bukuku ordered one of his servants to cast Ndahura into a nearby river. The tiny body quickly drifted away and disappeared from sight, but at a bend in the river the young babe became entangled in some grasses and was eventually swept onto a mass of floating vegetation. The following morning a potter who had come down to the river's edge to collect some clay discovered the child and rescued him. Realizing that the boy belonged to his matron, Nyinamwiru, the potter took him to his wife, who nursed the child along with their recently born daughter. The potter then went to the royal palace and related what had happened to Nyinamwiru, who advised him to keep the matter a secret and sent him away with two cows, as well as several other gifts. Thus Ndahura, like Kimera, grew up in the home of a royal potter. And like his Ganda counterpart, he eventually ascended to the royal throne by displacing an illegitimate usurper (Bukuku), thus restoring the kingship to its rightful heir.

As other scholars have noted, the accounts of both Kimera's and Ndahura's birth, rescue from the brink of death, and subsequent rise to power follow the pattern of a cliché frequently encountered in dynastic traditions. The story of the legitimate heir who grows up away from the royal palace and then returns to claim his rightful position appears repeatedly in foundational narratives in Africa and beyond.[16] In the case of Ndahura and Kimera, the similarities in their biographies have given rise to assertions that either Baganda copied the story from Banyoro or the two stories derived from a source from which several of the region's foundational narratives were drawn.[17] In a sense, both of these explanations provide insight into how the Kimera story found its way into the Ganda dynastic narrative: critical ideas and compelling discourses circulated in the interlacustrine region along widespread intellectual networks that undoubtedly included the most commonly traveled routes between Bunyoro and Buganda. But the concepts and practices that circulated along these routes were not confined to those revolving around royal efforts to legitimate political power, and Kimera's "arrival" in Buganda encapsulated a host of developments that predated his transformation into a symbol of dynastic continuity.

A more incisive explanation for the reasons behind Kimera's striking resemblance to the Cwezi figure Ndahura provides an appropriate entry point for examining Kimera's significance beyond his place in the debates over the nature of Ganda and Nyoro relations. Nyoro dynastic traditions portray the Cwezi as the rulers of the kingdom of Kitara who peacefully ceded their ritual and political authority to Bito newcomers from the north. As Renee Tantala has suggested, however, this depiction of the Cwezi represents the outcome of their incorporation into the Bito dynastic narrative. In her superb analysis of what she labeled the Kitara epic, Tantala convincingly argued that prior to this refashioning, the Cwezi figures served as archetypical personae whose actions provided models for the spread of a specialized form of spirit possession known as *cwezi kubándwa*. Her skillful examination of the Kitara epic demonstrates that the stories about the exploits of the Cwezi developed in a pre-Bito context and circulated as narrative representations of *cwezi kubándwa* practices.[18]

Tantala's analytical insights furnish a useful guide for exploring alternative understandings of the Kimera figure.[19] Following Tantala's interpretation of the Ndahura story, we might regard the story of Kimera's being cast into a clay pit and his subsequent rescue as depicting an initiation through the "classic phases of a rite of passage."[20] In this scenario, Kimera's being taken away from his mother would represent the period of separation; his suspension above the watery clay the period of liminality; and his retrieval from the river by the potter Mulegeya the new initiate's reentry into society. The language and practices of spirit possession in the Great Lakes region further support this suggestion. As a rite of passage, *kubándwa* initiation involved the "symbolic death and rebirth of the novice, . . . [whose] old social status passed away and was replaced by a new one." In Bunyoro, for example, a senior medium (*omusegu*) selected assistants who acted as the "mother" in the ritual rebirth. Mimicking the birth of a child, "the 'mother' stood with her legs apart while the 'child' lay on the ground behind her. The 'midwife' then seized the initiate from the front, pulled her forward head first between the legs of the 'mother', who groaned like a woman in labor, and then placed the crying infant at the mother's breast." Following the "birth," the initiate behaved like a child with his or her "brothers" and "sisters," thus marking his or her entry into a new family.[21] Similarly, candidates in Ankole were taken to the bush by a group of mediums, stripped naked, and laid down as if for slaughter. After undergoing a series of rites the following day, the candidates received new names to signal their rebirth and new status. The initiated mediums then mimicked the behavior of a child: mucus dripped from their noses while they collected and played with pebbles, climbed walls, went about naked, and pretended they could not talk.[22] For audience members acquainted with these practices, descriptions of the infant Kimera being cast into a clay pit located at a river's edge—a familiar ritual model depicting symbolic death and rebirth—would have served as allusions to this aspect of the initiation rites.

Several other overlaps between the Kimera narrative's imagery and ku-bándwa initiation rituals reinforce this suggestion that Kimera's early biography would have been understood in the context of these practices. Immersion into a sacred body of water played a critical role in kubándwa initiation practices throughout the Great Lakes region. In addition, Kimera's portrayal as an infant resonated with the image of newly born novices sitting on the laps of senior initiators and mimicking the behavior of babies.[23] At the commencement of kubándwa initiation rites in Ankole, for example, initiates' bodies were smeared with ghee to make their skin smooth like a baby's. Initiates were then teased, made to sit on people's laps, and generally expected to behave like babies. A refrain in a cwezi song sung during the initiation rites in Ankole sounded: "Emandwa the baby has been shy at the rite, emandwa the baby let him be healed and prosper."[24] Finally, the use of ritual pots figured significantly in kubándwa initiation rites, as well as in the ceremonies attending a medium's funeral rites; Mulegeya's depiction as a potter therefore supports the suggestion that he represented a senior initiator.[25]

When considered in light of kubándwa initiation practices, Kimera's birth, near death, and rescue reads like a narrative depiction of the initiation of a spirit medium. Like the Cwezi figure Ndahura, then, Kimera might best be regarded as the model of an initiated kubándwa medium. According to this formulation, his mother, Wannyana, occupies the role of the ritual mother who sponsors or initiates her son's accession into the network of ordained mediums. A version of the Kimera narrative related by Henry Morton Stanley, who recorded the story from one of his porters, provides further support for this interpretation of Kimera's early biography.[26] In Stanley's version, Kimera's foster father, Mulegeya, would send him to sell pots at Wannyana's home so that his mother would have the opportunity to see him. Wannyana took much delight in witnessing the maturing of her son and offered Kimera a gift to carry home with him at the conclusion of each visit. Significantly, the gifts Wannyana gave to Kimera constituted the regalia required of a spirit medium, including leopard skins, strings of animal claws, crocodile teeth, girdles of colobus monkey skin, beads, and shells.[27]

Stanley's version of the Kimera narrative further relates that the presents the young prince received from his mother enabled him to purchase two large dogs—one black, one white—that accompanied him on his increasingly lengthy hunting expeditions. Like the black and white fur of the colobus monkey adorned by mediums throughout the region, Kimera's control over his beastly companions signaled his capacity to mediate between Life's domain on earth and Death's underworld abode. Both Stanley's and his fellow explorer Speke's informants depicted Kimera as an avid hunter who, accompanied by his two dogs, embarked upon excursions into neighboring lands.[28] Descriptions of Kimera's hunting prowess accord with the familiar motif found in many parts of sub-Saharan Africa of the hunter who wins power by distributing the spoils of his chase. Another well-known claim about hunters, however, is that they routinely transgress boundaries between safety and danger (life and death) that most people try to avoid. More specifically, in the context of kubándwa practices hunting also operated as a metaphor for the manner in which mediums pursued suitable candidates for initiation through the deployment of spirits.[29] Oral traditions from western Uganda often portrayed cwezi mediums as enthusiastic hunters, and Kimera's depiction as a hunter was an appropriate way to render his capabilities as a spirit medium.[30]

In addition to describing Kimera's prowess as a hunter, the version of the Kimera narrative recorded by Stanley also portrays the young prince as a talented flute player. Kimera's skills as a flute player were later remembered in a royal ritual in which the ssensalire, the king's chief herdsman, a titled position in the Elephant clan, took cows into the king's enclosure and asked the king to play a tune on the flute that Kimera had once played.[31] Stanley explains that Kimera carried his flute with him from Bunyoro to Buganda, where he demonstrated his musical skills to one of Queen Nakku's servants. Dazzled by Kimera's musical abilities, the servant informed the visitor that he would be more than welcome before the queen and her people, and the following day she led him to Nakku's enclosure. The queen's servant having informed her matron of Kimera's musical accomplishments, Nakku asked the visitor to play a song. Eager to oblige his host, Kimera took his flute from his girdle, kneeled on the leopard skins placed before him, and played a beautiful song. Upon hearing the sounds of Kimera's flute, Nakku "closed [her eyes] and lay down with panting breasts. . . . Her body palpitated under the influence of the emotions which swayed her; when they became more enlivened she tossed her arms about, and laughed convulsively." When Kimera stopped playing and the queen had recovered from her state, she turned to him and exclaimed, "To resist thy flute would be impossible. Again welcome to Ganda [Buganda], and we shall see if we cannot keep thee and thy flute amongst us."[32]

Stanley's well-known predilection for hyperbole would ordinarily prompt suspicions that his description of Kimera's initial encounter with Nakku represented the exaggerations of a journalist writing about Africa for a nineteenth-century European audience. Evidence drawn from other sources, however, reinforces Stanley's depiction of the interaction between Kimera and Nakku and further suggests a connection between the young prince's activities and spirit-possession practices. The root *-seegu, from which the term nseegu/nshegu, meaning "flute" or "horn whistle," derives in West Nyanza languages, for example, also yields baseegu, the term for senior officials in the kubándwa hierarchy who served as musicians at possession ceremonies.[33] Perhaps more revealingly, ethnographic descriptions point to the prominent role played by flute players at kubándwa ceremonies, during which the sounds of their instruments helped induce states of possession.[34]

In addition to exhibiting this aspect of kubándwa practices, Nakku's reaction to Kimera's flute playing and her inability to "resist [Kimera's] flute" further evoke the kubándwa context by hinting at the unrestrained sexual activities that took place at kubándwa ceremonies. Nineteenth-century missionaries and travelers often suppressed this facet of spirit-possession practices in their writings. Ethnographic descriptions of kubándwa initiation practices in Bunyoro, however, clearly indicate that participants in initiation ceremonies enjoyed unusual sexual license. According to these descriptions, on the final night of the initiation ceremonies, mediums, ntimbo drummers, and nseegu flute players "would stay in the [medium's] hut, indulging in sexual intercourse while some of them carried on the singing, dancing, and making noises in order to conceal from the . . . non-initiate what was taking place."[35] On the following day, initiates underwent a ritual known as kumara amahano, "to end ritual danger."[36] Senior mediums accompanied the initiates to the bush, where female initiates slept with a senior male medium and male initiates slept with a senior female medium in order to protect themselves from ritual danger.[37] Kimera's portrayal as a flute player, then, further evoked the scene of a kubándwa ceremony. For audiences listening to the version of the narrative presented to Stanley, the description of Kimera's skillful playing of this mystical instrument and the effect on Nakku would have signaled, at least for those familiar with these practices, Kimera's membership in a kubándwa network.

Viewed in light of the language and images of *kubándwa* practices, Kimera's "arrival" in Buganda suggests the passage into the Ganda heartland of a distinguished leader whose political prominence derived from his abilities as an initiated spirit medium. One of the most striking features of the Kimera story, however, is the relatively marginal role the young prince himself plays in his rise to prominence. As the narrative describing his exploits illustrates, Kimera's survival in Bunyoro and his successful entrance onto the Ganda historical stage depended in large measure on the assistance of those who accompanied him on his journey to Buganda. In many respects, the narrative's momentum revolves around the contrast between Kimera's father's unsuccessful return from Bunyoro to Buganda and Kimera's triumphant arrival at Ssebwana's palace. Both Kalemeera and Kimera held legitimate claims to the Ganda throne as descendants of the royal line; however, whereas Kalemeera fell ill and died on his attempted return from Bunyoro to Buganda, his son Kimera managed to complete the same journey escorted by a talented entourage of companions.

The critical contribution of Kimera's companions in ensuring the young prince's success suggests a potentially illuminating perspective from which to view the Kimera narrative. In the description of his six-month stay in Buganda in 1862, John Hanning Speke attested to the presence of harp players who recited narratives at the Ganda royal court. Speke's reference to these figures hints at royal efforts to dictate the meaning of narratives about the past. In many respects, however, the broader significance of stories such as that describing Kimera's rise to prominence was the different perspectives that various clans brought to bear on them. This lack of a discursive center, or rather the presence of multiple discursive centers, meant that tellers emphasized different aspects of the Kimera narrative depending on the public for which they crafted their particular rendition. Over the course of many discussions about Kimera in Buganda, for example, none of the individuals I spoke with related the narrative from Kimera's perspective. By examining the various inflections of these multiple tellings, we can gain further insight into the types of concerns that animated political practices in the period immediately preceding the emergence of the Ganda state. This analytical exercise provides a revealing glimpse into the nature of effective political leadership in the distant Great Lakes past.

The history of the Grasshopper clan in Buganda provides further insight into the connection between Kimera, Ndahura, and spirit-possession practices.[38] Grasshopper clan narratives establish the clan's connection to Kimera through his mother, Wannyana, whose membership in the clan renders the Ganda royal hero a Grasshopper "grandson."[39] These narratives indicate the clan's historical ties to pastoralism and situate the clan's early activities in an area southwest of Buganda, in a locality known as Mugamba Hill, in Busongola, Toro (see map 6). According to the most frequently encountered version of the clan's history, the clan's founder, a Muhima pastoralist named Kiroboozi, amassed a considerable number of cattle and served as the ruler of Busongola, in southwestern Uganda.[40] Kiroboozi fathered many children, including Buyonga, Kalibala, and their sister Nnandawula. Upon their father's death, Kiroboozi's children fought amongst themselves over their inheritance, with the result that Buyonga, Kalibala, and Nnandawula decided to leave Busongola with their herds of cattle. The two brothers and their sister headed to Bwera, in Buddu, and then moved north into Gomba, where Buyonga and Kalibala had a misunderstanding and parted ways. Buyonga and Nnandawula settled at Kisozi, in Gomba, while Kalibala journeyed to Nsiisi, in Busujju. At Kisozi, Buyonga fathered a daughter, Wannyana, who later married Wunyi, the king of Bunyoro, and eventually gave birth to Kimera. Buyonga also fathered Mugalula, who became the ruler of Kisozi and head of the Ganda Grasshopper clan.[41]

Like those of the Otter and Pangolin clans discussed in the previous chapter, the familial relationships among the Grasshopper clan's earliest ancestors undoubtedly represent the outcome of historical alliances rather than actual descent, and we should therefore refrain from treating these relationships in a literal manner. When considered in conjunction with the narratives about the Cwezi figure Ndahura, however, the historical developments embedded within this familiar descent/kinship idiom shed light on the clan's role in the dissemination of the cult of Ndahura from Busongola into neighboring areas. Oral traditions regarding Kamawenge, the first medium to occupy Ndahura's main shrine, at Mubende Hill, point to the cult's origins in western Uganda. These traditions relate the details of Kamawenge's arrival at Mubende Hill from Butiiti, in Mwenge, an area just north of Toro, suggesting that the cult of Ndahura was practiced in Mwenge prior to its dissemination into the Mubende Hill area.[42] Additional evidence for the cult's western origins appears in oral traditions from Toro and Busongola that record that the Cwezi emerged from the crater lakes of western Uganda. Furthermore, the crater lake Isaka once served as the location where high-ranking

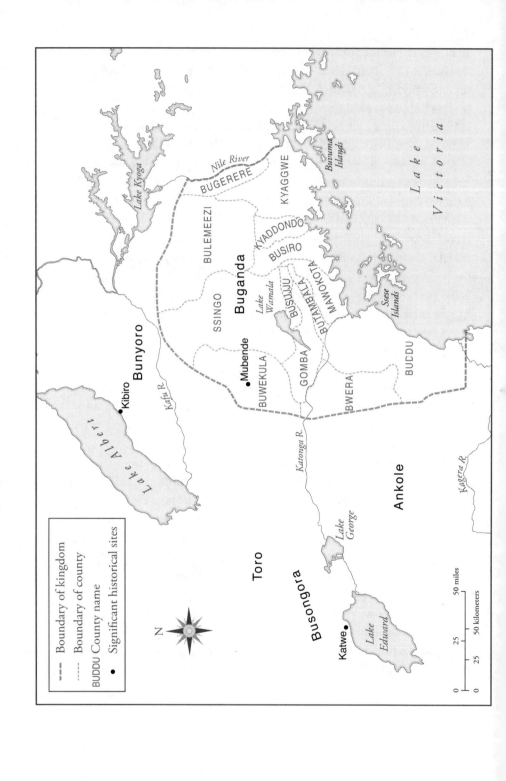

mediums were initiated into the cult of Ndahura, and Lake Kikorongo, a small salty lake located near Lake Busongola, was remembered as having been dug by Ndahura to water his cattle.[43]

Pastoralists valued the lakes of the western Rift Valley, including the crater lakes, for their medicinal salts.[44] Because these salts were critical to the continued health of both the region's human and cattle populations, the lakes from which they were obtained were important spiritual sites.[45] In western Uganda, for example, the communities living at Kibiro gathered on the occasion of each new moon to honor Nyansimbwa Abwoli, the spiritual patron of the Kibiro salt wells. The ritual acts performed on such occasions included the following praise:

Oh Nyansimbwa Abwoli
One gracious to the doves
Grant that we get riches
Grant that we get children
That we may live long
We your people
Keep and protect us always.[46]

The people of Kibiro offered Nyansimbwa Abwoli a young girl to serve as a spirit wife. The following praise was recited during the presentation of this offering:

Nyansimbwa Abwoli
We have brought you an offering
Let us get salt
Give us salt
You are gracious to the Gangaizi people
You are gracious to the Nyamwenge people
You are gracious to outsiders.[47]

Tantala remarked that the origins of the cult of Ndahura may have revolved around a local spiritual entity that was initially attached to a crater lake and later acquired mobility. The conceptual substitution of wells and springs for the crater lakes of Toro and Busongola allowed for Ndahura's transport and facilitated the cult's diffusion as pastoralists moved about in search of grazing land. While Busongola contained excellent pastures, limited space for expansion frequently forced families to leave the area, particularly in the dry season, to join pastoralist camps in Mwenge and Nkore, from where they sometimes drifted into Bwera and western Buganda. As Tantala observed, the corridor along which the cult of Ndahura diffused mirrored this northward movement of pastoralists from Busongola.[48]

The history of the Ganda Grasshopper clan illustrates how pastoralist movements facilitated the diffusion of spirit cults such as that involving Ndahura. As mentioned earlier, Grasshopper clan members recall their earliest ancestors as Bahima cattle herders from southwestern Uganda, and clan histories explain the clan's establishment in Buganda through a narrative tracing the journey of the children of the clan's founder, Kiroboozi, to western Buganda along precisely the path followed by pastoralists when they left Busongola. The name Kiroboozi hints at the nature of the authority that Grasshopper clan ancestors exercised as rulers in Busongola. A variation in a different noun class of the word *eddoboozi*, "voice," the title Kiroboozi—"The Voice"—appropriately captured its owner's ability to serve as the voice of the community's spiritual guardians.[49] As a prominent member of the Grasshopper clan suggested, however, the name also makes a poetic play on the verb *okulobola*, "to take one's share, levy (money)."[50] Busongola's location near significant sources of salt at Katwe and Kasenyi meant that the area's rulers were well-situated to levy taxes on traders passing through the region, and as the volume of the salt trade increased, there emerged a class of market masters (*abahoza*) whose primary responsibility was to collect tolls for Busongola's ruler.[51] As the person endowed with the capacity both to speak on behalf of Busongola's spirits and to levy taxes, Kiroboozi embodied, in both a literal and a figurative sense, the confluence of political and ritual authority embedded in widespread ideas regarding the components of effective leadership.

The common bestowal among Grasshopper clan members of the names Ssendawula, "Father of Ndawula," and Nandawula, "Mother of Ndawula," both of which derive from the Ganda pronunciation of Ndahura, suggests that Kiroboozi's efforts to exercise control over Busongola involved a close association with the spirit Ndahura.[52] Tantala observed that the prominence of these names in the Grasshopper clan indicates that its members once included Ndahura among their spiritual patrons. In this respect, Grasshopper clan narratives that recount the journey from Busongola taken by Kiroboozi's daughter Nandawula (Mother of Ndawula/Ndahura) and her two brothers might be regarded as an allusion to the commencement of the spirit Ndahura's journey northward from Busongola.[53] These narratives suggest that in addition to traveling with their cattle and valuable supplies of salt, pastoralists moving from Busongola into Mwenge, Bwera, and western Buganda also transported spiritual entities, such as Ndahura, which played an equally significant role in ensuring the success of their endeavors.

As discussed earlier, Grasshopper clan narratives recount how Kiroboozi's son Buyonga left Busongola with his herds of cattle following a dispute over his father's inheritance. Buyonga eventually settled at Kisozi, in Gomba, where he fathered Mugalula, who established himself as the ruler of a prominent polity in the western grasslands and achieved the position of head of the Grasshopper clan. The name of Mugalula's father, Buyonga (Land of Ashes), provides a compelling clue regarding the nature of his son's authority. As Tantala observed, according to Cwezi narratives, the Land of Ancestral Ghosts (Okuzimu), located beneath the earth, was presided over by Nyamiyonga (Owner of the Burnt Pastures). These narratives consistently describe Nyamiyonga's domain as a black, smoky abode covered in soot and ashes.[54] In the version of Cwezi and Nyoro traditions recorded by the Church Missionary Society missionary Ruth Fisher, for example, the deposed Tembuzi king Isaza enters a guest room in the underworld, "which was strewn with singed grass and charcoal; over this were spread black hides, and the couch and feeding utensils were all covered with soot. The food given him was smoked, and the milk of a black cow was offered him."[55] The name Buyonga, then, evoked a common image of the Land of Ancestral Ghosts, and Mugalula's status as a son of the Land of Ashes points to his role as an ancestral spirit or a medium who had the ability to possess ancestral spirits.

The portrayal of Mugarra—the Nyoro equivalent of Mugalula—in the dynastic narratives of western Uganda further supports the suggestion that Mugalula's responsibilities as head of the Grasshopper clan included engaging in acts of spirit possession. Mugarra appears in these narratives as a Cwezi born to the archetypical *cwezi* itinerant medium, Isimbwa (Isaza's son who managed to escape the underworld), at Kisozi, the principal estate of the Grasshopper clan.[56] This depiction of Mugarra indicates the assimilation of a Grasshopper clan ancestral spirit into the more efficacious category of *cwezi*, whose ability to return from the underworld when called upon by an initiated medium distinguished them from ancestral ghosts. Perhaps prior to this ontological transformation, the capacity to speak for the spirit Mugalula constituted an essential component informing the authority of Grasshopper clan leaders named Mugalula, who maintained and perpetuated their status by drawing upon, both literally and figuratively, the exalted status of their predecessors.

Grasshopper clan leaders who occupied the position of Mugalula, however, relied on more than their skills as spirit mediums to sustain and enforce their authority. The multiple meanings of the Grasshopper clan head's title point to the complex, often violent nature of political activities condensed in seemingly straightforward narratives such as those relating the journey of the clan's earliest ancestors from Busongola. The name Mugalula represents a deverbative from the verb *okugalula*, which carries the meaning "to bring back, to return, to come back" in many Great Lakes languages. In the languages spoken in western Uganda, the term frequently appears with this meaning in the context of healing and spirit-possession practices in reference to the process of bringing a spirit back from the Land of Ancestral Ghosts.[57] In Buganda, however, *okugalula* also carries the meaning "to brandish a weapon in order to strike."[58] The relationship between these two meanings hinges on the notion that the moral authority to endorse violent activity was inextricably connected to the capacity to confer with the appropriate spiritual entities through acts of spirit possession.

This association of violence with mediumship and healing also appears in descriptions of initiation ceremonies in Bunyoro. Female mediums in Bunyoro anticipated the appearance of spirits by dressing like warriors and "strolling up and down, holding and shaking their spears and shields like men of war."[59] Senior mediums then accompanied initiates to the *akasaka* (small bush) for instruction, part of which included extensive exposure to threats of violence and possibly even death. When an initiate arrived in the *akasaka*, for example, an initiated medium threatened to push a spear down his or her throat, and the initiate endured similarly aggressive threats following this initial act of intimidation.[60] This violent element of *kubándwa* practices further surfaces in narratives relating the activities of well-known Cwezi figures. In examining these narratives, we perceive the critical role that militant aspects of *cwezi kubándwa* played in the establishment of *kubándwa* networks. The narratives describing the expansion of Ndahura's realm of authority, for instance, reveal that Ndahura's ability to protect his clients from dangers and ensure their prosperity included the capacity to wage successful military campaigns, plunder neighboring areas for cattle, and execute potential challengers.[61]

The violent establishment of *kubándwa* networks suggests the extent to which public healing and collective violence together informed large-scale political developments in the northern Great Lakes region during the period preceding the emergence of a more centralized Ganda polity. This joining of morally legitimate violent activity to mediumship highlights the practical reason at the heart of public healing and also requires that we think about public health as involving warfare. The success of public healers, in other words, depended in part upon their capacity to wield the means of violence through the coordination of activities related to raiding and warfare. The violent components of public healing ceremonies also meant that these gatherings had the potential to function as military rallies (see chapter 5). In drawing upon their skills as spirit mediums, leaders such as Grasshopper clan heads named Mugalula may have inspired communities to engage in collective violence as a means of ensuring their collective well-being. As both public healers and wielders of weapons, these figures drew upon their moral authority as representatives of their communities' spiritual guardians to channel the collective energies of public healing practices toward the sometimes violent fulfillment of political ambitions.

While Grasshopper clan members maintain a particularly strong connection to the Kimera figure owing to the fact that the young king's mother, Wannyana, was a member of their clan, the Kimera figure and the narratives of his exploits by no means are the exclusive discursive property of the Grasshopper clan. As part of their efforts to situate themselves within the Ganda political milieu, several other clans draw upon the Kimera narrative by pointing to the roles of their respective leaders in enabling Kimera's successful journey from Bunyoro to Buganda. The histories of the Grey Monkey, Colobus Monkey, and Buffalo clans, whose earliest ancestors played a prominent role in securing Kimera's safety, offer tantalizing clues regarding the types of knowledge that accompanied Kimera's "arrival" in Buganda.

The Grey Monkey clan recognizes Mulegeya, the potter who persuaded the Nyoro king Wunyi to spare Kimera's life, as one of its founding ancestors. Narratives relating the clan's early history place particular emphasis on the contributions of Mulegeya and his son Katumba to Kimera's success. According to these narratives, Mulegeya's wife, Namujumbi, had given birth to a boy, Katumba, just prior to Kimera's rescue from the clay pit. When Mulegeya recovered Kimera and took him to his home, Namujumbi breastfed the infant as if he were her own son. Kimera grew up in the potter's household, and when the time arrived for him to depart for Buganda, Mulegeya's son Katumba accompanied Kimera on his eastward journey. In appreciation of Katumba's role in protecting him and ensuring that he did not suffer the same fate as his father, Kalemeera, Kimera bestowed upon his companion the name Mugema (The Inoculator), which became the title for the head of the Grey Monkey clan.[62]

Like the Grey Monkey clan, the Colobus Monkey clan traces its prominence in Buganda to the services its principal ancestor rendered Kimera on his passage to Buganda. According to Colobus Monkey histories, Kimera suffered from a terrible fever (omusujja) on his journey from Bunyoro to Buganda. Desperately in need of assistance, the young prince sought relief for his condition from a talented medicine man (musawo) named Lule Kyesimba, who managed to cure the future king's illness. Lule Kyesimba's medical talents endeared him to Kimera, who as a sign of appreciation offered the doctor the estate of Busujja, located just to the west of the ancient ritual center at Bakka, in Busiro, as a base from which to practice his medical skills. In addition, Kimera bestowed upon Lule Kyesimba the title Kasujja (The Curer of Fevers, from omusujja, "fever") and confirmed him as head of the Colobus Monkey clan.[63]

The Buffalo clan, which like the Grey Monkey clan locates its origins in the grasslands of western Uganda, also achieved distinction in the Ganda political milieu for services its early ancestors rendered Kimera on his eastward journey. According to Buffalo clan histories, Wavuuvuumira, the son of the clan's founder, Makumbi, carried his weary sister Namagembe as they traveled alongside Kimera from Bunyoro to Buganda. When Kimera noticed Namagembe on the shoulders of her brother Wavuuvuumira, he asked Makumbi to assign another one of his sons to perform the same task for him. Makumbi complied with the young leader's request, and as a result the Buffalo clan acquired the honor of serving as the royal bakongozzi (s. mukongozzi), the king's carriers. In its broader application, however, the term mukongozzi refers to a person who served as a vehicle through whom spirits spoke, suggesting that the early leaders of the Buffalo clan parlayed their skills as the carriers of spirits into the honorable task of carrying the king.[64] The name of the Buffalo clan ancestor who attracted Kimera's attention, Wavuuvuumira, reinforces this proposition. A deverbative from the verb okuvuuvuuma, "to mutter, murmur, speak in a confused way," the name Wavuuvuumira evokes the grumbling and often indistinct manner in which mediums speak while in a state of possession.[65]

Viewed through the lens of Grasshopper, Grey Monkey, Colobus Monkey, and Buffalo clan histories, Kimera's journey from Bunyoro to Buganda offers the image of an initiated medium (Kimera) surrounded by a skilled inoculator (Mugema), a talented doctor (Kasujja), and a fellow specialist in the art of spirit possession (Wavuuvuumira). This image illustrates that the capacity to protect communities from illness and disease, which included the effective deployment of spirits, constituted a critical component of political leadership. Kimera succeeded because he surrounded himself with people who were capable of providing such protection, a leadership strategy that drew upon deeply embedded ideas regarding the relationship between public healing and political authority. That Kimera's companions managed to channel their skills into positions as heads of clans illustrates the integral role the politics of clanship played in determining the character of Buganda's political development and the expansion of political scale in the period preceding the emergence of a state apparatus. We saw in chapter 3 that the politics of clanship revolved around the compilation of dispersed networks of knowledge into communities of collective well-being. As the vehicle for social relations joining people who served as the repositories of intellectual and material wealth, the clan concept proved essential for the promotion of leaders whose authority drew upon their capacity to bring together different bodies of knowledge for the benefit of the community. Kimera represented just such a leader, and in many respects his success resulted from his ability to draw together the networks of knowledge presided over by his companions. Mugema, Kasujja, and Wavuuvuumira stood at the apex of clan networks, which, along with Kimera's skills as a spirit medium, made him an effective political leader. Their successors built upon these achievements by using the stores of wealth embedded in the communities over which they presided to create and maintain a healthy political center, a topic to which I turn in the following chapter.

LOCATING KIMERA: VIOLENCE, DISEASE, AND THE SALT TRADE IN THE NORTHERN GREAT LAKES REGION

We now turn to the question of how to locate historically the activities embedded in the Kimera narrative and the histories of the clans associated with Kimera. Our discussion to this point has presented a composite picture of political authority in the predynastic Ganda past. This discussion revealed that the components of effective political leadership revolved around practices of public healing and included the capacity to direct collective violence for the benefit of the community. The prominent roles played by Mugema (The Inoculator) and Kasujja (The Curer of Fevers) in the Kimera narrative also suggests that the spread of disease and the attendant ability to both protect people and offer treatment contributed to the rising fortunes of leaders such as Kimera and his companions. The proliferation of disease posed significant threats to a community's collective well-being and propelled those who had the ability to alleviate such threats to the forefront of the political arena. An examination of the potential channels through which diseases disseminated in the northern Great Lakes region therefore offers the possibility of situating the developments hinted at in the Kimera story within a regional historical narrative. In this regard, two related explanations deserve consideration: the connection between violence and the spread of disease; and the connection between the establishment of trade routes and the emergence of disease vectors.

Oral traditions relating the expansion of the polity presided over by the Cwezi figure Ndahura, whose early biography bears a striking resemblance to Kimera's, indicate the violent nature of these political developments. Because of the conflation of the *cwezi* spirit Ndahura with the mediums who personified him, the traditions describing his campaigns most likely refer to the activities of more than one historical figure. According to these traditions, upon unseating the usurper king Bukuku, Ndahura set out to subdue all neighboring areas that had resisted Bukuku's rule. His imperial efforts involved violent campaigns into the regions surrounding Kisengwe (including an excursion into the ancient Ganda ritual center at Bakka, in Busiro), during which his followers executed rival chiefs, extracted tribute by force, and plundered the countryside.[66] The descriptions of these campaigns suggest that the militant aspects of *cwezi kubándwa* were an important element in the dissemination of innovative spirit-possession practices. These descriptions also indicate that the realm of public healing included acts of collective violence directed by prominent mediums.

While Ndahura's armies procured considerable prizes, such as cattle and women, in their expeditions into neighboring territories, they also acquired some undesirable spoils of war. According to oral traditions from western Uganda, Ndahura's soldiers contracted various skin diseases during their excursions into foreign lands. These diseases followed Ndahura's armies as they moved from one campaign to the next, with the result that the entire region became afflicted with one scourge or another.[67] A *kubándwa* song performed for Ndahura reflects these developments:

Eyi . . . eyi . . . you went far away to wage war,
To crush them.
Eyi . . . eyi . . . Welcome my master.
From Tonyoka's place you brought yaws,
From Nyamuhangara's the Kokoro disease,
Smallpox from Junjura's.[68]

The widely held association between the Ndahura figure, warfare, and disease exemplified in this song raises the question which diseases might have been prevalent in the region prior to the eighteenth century, when increased long-distance trade with the coast resulted in the introduction of various new diseases into the interior. The reference to smallpox in this song most likely represents an anachronism that drew upon the *cwezi* Ndahura's conversion into the national spirit (*lubaale*) of smallpox following the spread of the disease in the region beginning in the second half of the eighteenth century and the early nineteenth century.[69] Most scholars attribute the introduction of smallpox into the East African interior to the extension of the Indian Ocean trade in the nineteenth century.[70] While ample evidence exists to support this claim, we cannot completely discount the possibility that an ancient strain of the disease existed in the region prior to this period. Until the mid-1970s, physicians distinguished only two clinical forms of smallpox: *variola major*, the most fatal form, which predominated until just before smallpox was eradicated; and *variola minor*, a milder strain identified in the nineteenth century in southern Africa and the West Indies.[71] In the 1960s and 1970s, however, studies by British virologists and smallpox-eradication workers identified a third strain, *variola intermedius*, in samples isolated from East and West Africa.[72] These studies, along with evidence of widespread practices of inoculation in sub-Saharan Africa prior to the nineteenth century, have led some scholars to argue that smallpox was an ancient disease in Africa whose proliferation in the late nineteenth and early twentieth centuries resulted from the socioeconomic changes that accompanied the establishment of colonial rule.[73]

While an intermediate strain of smallpox may have existed in the Great Lakes region prior to the eighteenth century, the outbreak of smallpox epidemics throughout the region in the nineteenth century suggests a more recent introduction of *variola major* via long-distance trade routes between the region and the coast.[74] The establishment of the well-known connection between Ndahura and smallpox therefore most likely coincided with the intensification of the coastal caravan trade during this period. This connection, however, built upon an existing association between Ndahura and the spread of diseases with a longer history in the region. As indicated in the song performed in honor of Ndahura, Ndahura's military campaigns may have resulted in an epidemic outbreak of yaws, a disease with ancient roots in East Africa.[75] Those infected with the disease initially develop a macular lesion (the mother yaw) followed by smaller, widespread papules (the daughter yaws) and possibly severe skin ulcers. These symptoms may account for the descriptions of the sores and various skin diseases contracted and spread by Ndahura's armies during their campaigns.[76] While additional research, particularly in the area of historical linguistics, on the history of diseases in the Great Lakes region prior to the eighteenth century will likely shed further light on these issues, oral traditions point to a long-standing connection between the Ndahura figure and both the spread and the treatment of diseases. This connection surfaced at Ndahura's main shrine, at Mubende Hill, which in the eighteenth and nineteenth centuries was an important pilgrimage site and inspired the respect of both Ganda and Nyoro kings seeking to protect the health of their followers.[77]

In addition to serving as Ndahura's capitol and most important shrine site, Mubende Hill also was a focal point in the region's trading complex.[78] The hill stood at the convergence of a network of trade routes that passed through Kyaka and Mwenge and extended as far as Katwe, in Busongola (see map 6). One of these regional trade routes was the most well traveled path between Bunyoro and Buganda, along which traders carried bark cloth, fish, salt, and various metals. Differences in environmental conditions and the uneven distribution of natural resources largely determined the nature of this trade. For instance, the areas along the western shores of Lake Victoria lacked natural sources of the high-quality salt found on the edges of the crater lakes of western Uganda. The communities living in this fertile crescent therefore acquired salt from western Uganda in exchange for bark cloths made from the giant fig trees (Ficus) that thrived near the shores of Lake Victoria. Buganda and Buhaya in particular were known for the high quality of their bark cloths, which people used as clothing and burial shrouds and also as gifts to initiate patron-client relationships.

The trade in metals probably equaled that in salt and bark cloth in terms of its contribution to regional political developments. The honor accorded to ironworkers and the role played by these skilled professionals in many of the region's royal installation ceremonies point to ironworking as a significant element in Great Lakes political culture. Efforts to control both the sources of iron and the routes along which iron goods were traded were critical to the emergence and expansion of the region's well-known kingdoms.[79] The discontiguous distribution of iron-bearing ores in the Great Lakes region meant that areas such as Buganda, which lacked significant deposits, relied upon regional trade networks to obtain iron tools, weapons, and jewelry. This reliance may have encouraged early Ganda communities to generate surpluses of desired goods to exchange for both iron and salt. In addition to the area's famed red bark cloths, these communities would have offered dried fish and other foodstuffs produced in the fertile lands along the northwestern shores of Lake Victoria.[80] In this manner, differences in environmental conditions and the availability of natural resources combined to draw dispersed centers of specialized production into a series of vibrant and lucrative regional trade networks.

The geographical focus of Ndahura and his "son" Kiro's military campaigns suggests an awareness of the importance of securing strategic trade routes for the success of their political undertakings.[81] Their military endeavors seem to have been particularly concerned with obtaining access to the critical salt-producing centers at Kibiro and Katwe (see map 6): Ndahura led a successful expedition into Bugoma, a locality strategically positioned between the Cwezi heartland in Kisengwe, which included Mubende Hill, and the salt-producing center at Kibiro, on the eastern shore of Lake Mwitanzige (Albert); and Ndahura and Kiro together commanded a campaign in Busongola close to the salt-producing center at Lake Katwe. Similarly, Ndahura's "step-brother," Kyomya, led a military campaign into the Ganda heartland in Busiro, and his efforts resulted in the composition of a song performed by cwezi adherents that describes their spiritual patron as a trader in salt.[82] These as well as other campaigns, such as those undertaken in the Lake Kyoga basin, point to the concerted efforts of cwezi mediums and their followers to control the region's trading networks connecting lake and land routes.[83]

The participation of mediums and their followers in regional trading endeavors drew upon the intersection of public healing and material prosperity at the heart of northern Great Lakes political culture. The establishment of kubándwa networks, whether through military or other means, both facilitated and enhanced regional trade. Travel along the region's far-flung trade routes posed serious dangers, and the authority commanded by itinerant mediums proved beneficial in overcoming potential hazards.[84] Mediums enjoyed greater protection from both spiritual and other dangers than did non-initiates, and their status also provided them with access to local networks of assistance and hospitality made up of fellow initiates and supplicants.[85] They therefore moved relatively freely over long distances and engaged in trade as they traveled between communities. This connection between the protection enjoyed by mediums and their ability to engage in regional trade surfaces in oral traditions that depict many Cwezi figures as prominent traders.[86]

In Buganda, the ability to engage in regional trade may also have depended upon the networks of knowledge and collective well-being cemented by the clan concept. The growing long-distance trade in Buganda from the eighteenth century on built upon much older local trade networks in which clans played an important role.[87] Clans specialized in the production of particular goods that were traded along regional trade routes. For example, segments of the Otter, Genet Cat, and Crow clans were renowned for their manufacture of bark cloth, while clans associated with the maritime culture surrounding Lake Victoria and those located close to the forests of Kyaggwe provided dried fish and skins in exchange for goods produced outside the area. Clan networks would therefore have offered those itinerant traders willing to work with clan leaders a ready supply of goods.[88] In addition, the therapeutic networks presided over by these leaders would have provided protection from spiritual danger, allowing itinerant traders—who might also have functioned as mediums—to engage in peaceful trading endeavors in exchange for the periodic redistribution of their accumulated wealth through offerings presented at local shrines.

The connection between the establishment of kubándwa networks, the circulation of trade goods, and the spread of diseases provides an appropriate context in which to view the Kimera figure.[89] In addition to pointing to Kimera's role as an initiated spirit medium, several of the earliest published versions of the narrative relating his rise to power indicate a link between the Kimera figure and regional trading activities. Both R. P. Le Veux and Stanley described the journey of Kimera's father, Kalemeera, to Bunyoro in order to exchange cattle for salt and hoes. Nsimbi likewise described Kalemeera as a prominent trader in hoes whose activities warranted his nickname Mutikkizankumbi (One Who Carries Hoes on His Head). In addition, both Le Veux and Nsimbi depicted Kimera himself as a prominent trader. Le Veux noted that Kimera and his companions traveled to Buganda with large bags of salt, while Nsimbi remarked that Kimera and his cohort arrived in Buganda with both salt and hoes, desirable products that the Baganda had previously lacked.[90] Finally, the inclusion in Kimera's entourage of specialists in the prevention and treatment of illnesses suggests that the trade routes along which these goods traveled also guided the circulation of curative measures. As traders journeyed along these paths with goods such as salt and hoes, they also carried novel forms of ritual protection and innovative therapeutic techniques whose dissemination influenced regional political developments.

Given the depictions of Kimera and Kalemeera as traders in salt, the history of salt production and the salt trade in the northern Great Lakes region provides an opportunity to situate the story of Kimera's journey from western Uganda to Buganda within a regional historical framework. The production and trade in salt played a critical role in the social history of western Uganda, whose pockets of supply of this much-sought-after commodity facilitated the development of complex political communities.[91] The significance of the salt industry was certainly apparent at the time of the first European contact, in the second half of the nineteenth century. The two most important salt deposits in western Uganda were located at Kibiro, on the southeastern shores of Lake Albert, and at Katwe, on the northern fringes of Lake Edward (see map 6). The frequency with which early European travelers and officials visited Kibiro indicates the importance of this salt-producing center in the region's political economy. Their firsthand accounts describe a thriving industry and provide a sense of the scale of the salt trade in the late nineteenth century. The scientist and administrator Emin Pasha visited Kibiro in 1885 and observed that

all the energies of the native population . . . are devoted to the extract and preparation of salt. This constitutes an important industry in Kibiro, which supplies with salt not only all the northern parts of Unyoro [Bunyoro] as far as Mrûli, but also most districts of Uganda [Buganda] and the Lúr [Alur] and Shúli [Acholi] countries. The salt deposits of Kibiro, therefore, constitute one of the most valuable portions of [the king of Bunyoro] Kabaréga's dominions.[92]

Major Arthur Thruston, who accompanied Colonel Henry Colville on his expedition to Kibiro in 1894, similarly described the site as "the great salt field of the country [Bunyoro]" and noted that large quantities of the salt produced there were sold in both Buganda and Bunyoro.[93] In addition to supplying Buganda, salt from Kibiro was also distributed across Lake Albert by dugout canoe to populations in the Lendu area of northeastern Congo and, as alluded to in Emin Pasha's observation, the trade extended beyond the Victoria Nile.[94]

The scale of the salt trade at Katwe at least equaled and more than likely surpassed that surrounding Kibiro. Piecing together the records of early European travelers, Charles Good noted that Katwe's sphere of influence in 1890 "extended northeast into Bunyoro, north to the Amba country west of Ruwenzori, occasionally perhaps as far east as Lake Victoria in southern Buganda, south into Rwanda and Tanzania, and westward in the eastern Congo."[95] By the second half of the nineteenth century, then, large quantities of salt produced at Kibiro and Katwe were being traded over a considerable area according to a well-defined infrastructure of routes and distribution points, several of which, including Mubende, were located on the border between Bunyoro and Buganda.[96] These routes extended over land and waterways connected by a network of marketplaces, linking widely separated communities to the region's major salt-producing centers.

Graham Connah's excavations at Kibiro, which served as the major source of salt for Ganda communities, offer insight into the long history of the thriving salt industry at this site. The unusually deep, extensive, and well-stratified archaeological deposits at Kibiro indicate that people have occupied the area and its immediate environs since the first part of the second millennium AD. The presence of such a remarkable accumulation of deposits at an otherwise unremarkable site led Connah to attribute the antiquity of Kibiro's occupation to the concentration of activity brought about by the production of salt. Despite its antiquity, the material excavated at Kibiro suggested that long-distance trade had not infiltrated the area until about the seventeenth century and that it had remained very limited until the nineteenth century. The presence of ironwork and an abundance of pottery, however, clearly indicated the significance of regional trade. As Connah has argued, the very existence of Kibiro, which produced more salt than could be consumed in the immediate locality, implied the existence of an organized regional trading network as well as a form of authority capable of protecting and controlling such a trade.[97]

Connah's analysis of the material excavated at Kibiro indicates that the development of a substantial regional trade in salt preceded the spread of cwezi kubándwa practices. As discussed in chapter 3, about the fifteenth century historical actors speaking North Nyanza and Rutara dialects invented an entirely new category of spirits that they called cwezi.[98] Paleoenvironmental evidence from western Uganda indicates that cwezi kubándwa practices developed during an extended period of aridity in the region. Viewed in conjunction with the archaeological record from western Uganda and oral traditions that talk about *cwezi*, this evidence suggests that *cwezi kubándwa* practices may have emerged in response to protracted challenges to social health in the region.[99] As communities struggled to meet their food needs, contests over access to productive land in communities characterized by increasing social and political hierarchies most likely provided the "context in which *cwezi* mediums claimed they could unblock the flow of social life better than the custodians of lineage spirits." These contests unfolded over the course of the fifteenth and sixteenth centuries, during which *cwezi* mediums asserted that their spirits were superior to ancestral ghosts in promoting prosperity, fecundity, and collective well-being.[100]

The emergence of *cwezi kubándwa* practices offered politically ambitious mediums the opportunity to extend the reach of their authority to larger communities. By the seventeenth century the spirits in whose name these leaders spoke included departed people of royal status, the well-known royal Cwezi figures, such as Ndahura, whose exploits constitute the earliest portions of oral dynastic traditions in western Uganda. Archaeological evidence pointing to the existence of a regional trade in salt prior to this period lends further support to the argument that the military campaigns attributed in oral traditions to Ndahura and his son Kiro sought, in part, to gain control over well-established trade routes connected to the major salt-producing centers in western Uganda. The association between Ndahura's campaigns and the spread of diseases also suggests that the raiding activities and population movements that accompanied these campaigns may have provided an opportunity for endemic diseases such as yaws to become epidemic. For ambitious political leaders such as Ndahura, however, such a development represented as much a potentially advantageous political opening as a source of vulnerability.

The widespread recognition of Ndahura as a benevolent *cwezi* spirit and the emergence of his shrine at Mubende Hill as a site where people sought protection and prosperity are illustrations of such a process. Communities seeking to escape the consequences of military incursions and ensure their collective well-being pledged their allegiance to figures such as Ndahura at public sites such as his principal shrine at Mubende. The shrine's location at the convergence of trade routes leading to both Katwe and Kibiro also offered adherents the opportunity to acquire salt and other goods traded between western Uganda and the areas along the western shores of Lake

Victoria. Thus, the ability to establish control over regional trade networks, to direct morally legitimate forms of violence, and to provide protection from disease constituted the components of effective political leadership. These factors both shaped the political universe in which aspiring leaders operated and informed the formation of publics within which communities sought to ensure their collective well-being in the northern Great Lakes region during the seventeenth century. The Kimera figure emerged from this complex configuration of historical processes, and situating him within the context of these regional developments allows us to better understand the historical significance of the story of his momentous journey from Bunyoro to Buganda.

CONCLUSION

When one considers its circulation and reception in a predynastic context, the Kimera narrative provides novel insights into the expansion of political scale in seventeenth-century Buganda. Kimera's role as a trader in salt and hoes, his abilities as a spirit medium, and the inoculatory and curative skills of his devoted companions together rendered him a capable wielder of political authority. His compositional talents, in other words, rendered him sufficiently prominent to claim leadership over large numbers of people and to have his claims accepted. Kimera's portrayal as both a trader and a medium also reveals that mediums drew upon their authority in the ritual arena to engage in the distribution of the material sources of livelihood.

The Kimera figure provides a striking illustration of the confluence of public healing and political authority in the period preceding the development of the Ganda state apparatus. Far from constituting separate domains of experience, creative and instrumental forms of power fused together in figures such as Kimera, who in their capacities as spirit mediums sought to establish the basic conditions under which people could survive and prosper. Public healing and politics, in other words, constituted a single domain of experience in seventeenth-century Buganda. The institutionalization of the divide between these two forms of authority occurred later as part of the gradual development of an instrumentally powerful kingship and a state apparatus.

CLANSHIP, STATE FORMATION, AND THE SHIFTING CONTOURS OF PUBLIC HEALING

The convergence of public healing and political authority discussed in chapters 2–4 compels us to reconsider the process of state formation in Buganda. The gradual emergence of a bureaucratic state apparatus and the militaristic nature of territorial expansion from the late seventeenth to the early nineteenth century transformed deeply embedded concepts of collective well-being. Rather than effacing previous conceptions and practices, however, the state-formation process directed efforts to ensure collective well-being toward the maintenance of a more muscular political center. These undertakings prompted transformations in clan practices, involved innovations in the relationship between public healing and military endeavors, and resulted in the emergence of distinct forms of organized violence designed to meet the needs of shifting realities. During this period, clan formation served as a means of engaging an emerging state apparatus in a political environment characterized by escalating violence and increasing vulnerability for large segments of the population.

The observation that clans and clan formation played a central role in the state-building process introduces a new set of historical actors into a discussion ordinarily dominated by kings and their royal representatives. Highlighting the contribution of clans to Buganda's territorial expansion, however, hardly effaces the manner in which the developments emanating from the kingdom's mobile royal centers affected community-building processes in outlying areas. The success of royal ideology was dependent on its capacity to persuade the communities who came to constitute Buganda's clans to conceive of their collective well-being as intimately connected to the health and prosperity of the kingdom itself. This gradual process involved the creation of royal medicines, the nationalization of clan-based spiritual entities, and the transformation of dispersed groups of occupational specialists and their followers into clan networks. By focusing on the shifting contours of clanship and the interactions between multiple forms of authority from the late seventeenth to the early nineteenth century, this chapter examines how the struggles that characterized the emergence of the Ganda state both drew upon older notions of public healing and inspired momentous changes in long-standing efforts to compose healthy and prosperous communities.

TERRITORIAL EXPANSION AND THE
DEVELOPMENT OF A STATE APPARATUS

At the beginning of the seventeenth century, Buganda remained a tiny kingdom whose royal center was at Bakka, in Busiro, about fifteen miles northwest of Kampala. By the beginning of the nineteenth century the kingdom included territories stretching from the Katonga River to the Nile and deep into the interior (see map 7).[1] Scholars have long recognized the mid-seventeenth-century reigns of Kabaka Kateregga and his successor, Mutebi, as inaugurating the period of military development and territorial expansion that would "eventually transform an obscure little kingdom, one of dozens in the forest lands fringing the Lake, into the formidable state 'discovered' by Speke and Grant in 1862" (see table 1).[2] In a militaristic period that most commentators point to as initiating the practice of appointing royal nominees to replace local rulers, Kateregga oversaw the incorporation of the territories of Butambala and Gomba into the emerging Ganda state.[3] Mutebi's rise to the throne involved an unprecedented level of force and fatalities, an indication that violence had become a prominent feature of Ganda politics and that "ambitious politicians could raise armed followings." Upon securing the throne, Mutebi launched a series of attacks in the areas just beyond Buganda's western and northern borders. These attacks resulted in the acquisition of valuable cattle-grazing lands in the territories of Busujju and Ssingo and, as in the case of Kateregga's conquests, the replacement of the local rulers with the generals who had led the military campaigns.[4]

The next major period of territorial expansion occurred during the reign of the mid-eighteenth-century kabaka Mawanda. Historians of Buganda have pointed to the reign of Mawanda as the most significant period in the development of the Ganda state.[5] Mawanda established chiefships for the territories of Kyaddondo, Bulemeezi, and Kyaggwe, whose inclusion in the kingdom shifted Buganda's orientation eastward. Kyaggwe represented a particularly valuable addition to the kingdom. Noted for its rich fishing reserves and renowned for its markets dotting the northern shores of Lake

TABLE 1. THE KINGS OF BUGANDA

1. Kintu	19. Ndawula (c. 1700–1730)
2. Cwa	20. Kagulu (c. 1730–1760)
3. Kimera	21. Kikulwe (c. 1730–1760)
4. Ttembo	22. Mawanda (c. 1730–1760)
5. Kiggala	23. Mwanga (c. 1760–1790)
6. Kiyimba	24. Namugala (c. 1760–1790)
7. Kayima	25. Kyabaggu (c. 1760–1790)
8. Nakibinge[a]	26. Jjunju (c. 1790–1800)
9. Mulondo	27. Ssemakookiro (c. 1800–1812)
10. Jemba	28. Kamaanya (c. 1812–1830)
11. Ssuna	29. Ssuuna (c. 1830–1856/7)
12. Ssekamaanya	30. Muteesa (c. 1856/7–1884)
13. Kimbugwe	31. Mwanga (1884–1899)
14. Kateregga (c. 1640–1670)	32. Kiweewa (1889)
15. Mutebi (c. 1670–1700)	33. Kalema (1889–1890)
16. Juuko (c. 1670–1700)	34. Daudi Cwa (1897–1939)
17. Kayemba (c. 1670–1700)	35. Edward Muteesa (1939–1966)
18. Tebandeke (c. 1700–1730)	36. Ronald Mutebi (1993–present)

Source: Médard, Le royaume du Buganda au XIX siècle, 570–71.
Note: Dates are provided for the reigns of kings beginning only in the mid-seventeenth century. Dates for reigns prior to this period are unreliable.
[a]In Kingship and State: The Buganda Dynasty, Christopher Wrigley argues that despite his appearance in the early sections of the Ganda king list as the eighth Ganda king, Nakibinge more properly belongs with the generation of eighteenth-century Ganda kings that includes Mawanda and Namuggala.

Victoria, the territory also included the river port of Bulondoganyi, whose location at the intersection of several regional trade networks reaching Buganda, Bunyoro, and Busoga attracted traders from throughout the region. As Richard Reid has pointed out, whoever controlled Bulondoganyi could monitor the Nile trade, and the port also functioned as a strategic military

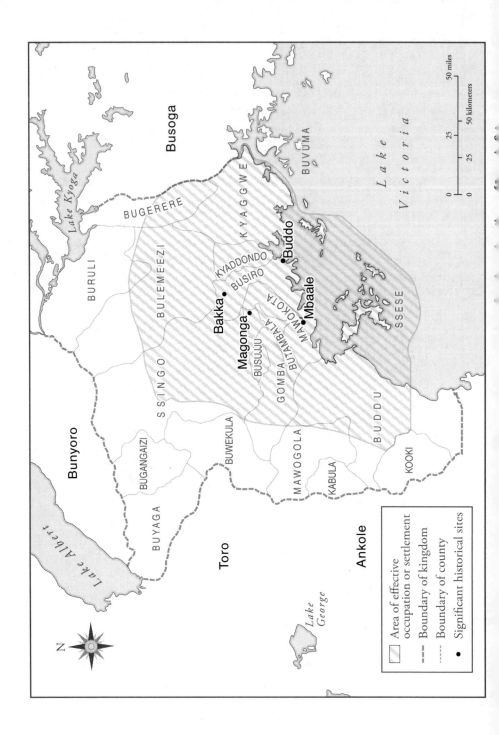

outpost.[6] Mawanda's reign has also been noted for the emergence of the "king's men," a group of chiefs appointed by the king who swore allegiance solely to him. Unlike the hereditary chiefships established during the reigns of Kateregga and Mutebi, the chiefships created by Mawanda were controlled directly by the king, who designated the successor upon a chief's death or removal from office. As part of his efforts to establish a civil administration capable of utilizing the resources available in newly incorporated territories, Mawanda also introduced ebitongole. Captives of war in the employ of a royally appointed representative, ebitongole represented a new form of chiefship designed to settle recently conquered areas or perform a particular productive activity, such as clearing forests, making drums, or growing food for the king's attendants.[7]

The last major phase of Buganda's territorial expansion occurred during the reigns of kings Jjunju and Ssemakookiro, the late eighteenth- and early nineteenth-century rulers who conquered and established control over the resource-rich territory of Buddu, to the south of the Ganda heartland. The most obvious motivation behind Jjunju's annexation of Buddu was his desire to control the area's fertile banana plantations and rich supplies of iron and timber. Buddu also served as a base from which to conduct raids into the surrounding cattle-grazing areas. Perhaps equally important, however, was Buddu's location at the center of a series of lucrative regional trade networks. The territory was particularly noted for its production of the high-quality bark cloths produced in southern Buddu and favored by Ganda royalty, and the potential lucrativeness of the bark cloth trade in this territory may have motivated the entire expansionist endeavor.[8] Control of Buddu also provided Buganda with access to the large market in Karagwe by way of the kingdom of Kooki, with which Buganda's leaders established a tributary relationship. Finally, with Buddu, Buganda gained control over the only land route for trade goods from Zanzibar and other coastal locations to northern Uganda, a commercial link that became increasingly significant in the second half of the nineteenth century.[9]

THE BUDDO RITES

About 1760, shortly after an assassin brought an end to the brief reign of Mwanga, his brother Prince Namuggala, a nephew of Kabaka Mawanda and son of Prince Musanje, of the Leopard clan, assumed the Ganda throne. In an effort to solidify the kingdom after several tumultuous decades that had witnessed the killing of numerous kings, Namuggala and his advisers devised an elaborate ceremony of installation that took place close to the shores of Lake Victoria, at Buddo Hill, in southern Busiro. All subsequent Ganda kings would undergo the ceremony initially instituted at the commencement of Namuggala's reign, and several published descriptions, most notably that of Apolo Kaggwa, furnish the details of this new royal rite.[10]

The royal installation ceremony began with the arrival of the kabaka-elect and his entourage at the foot of Buddo Hill, after which they were escorted to the shrine of Sserutega, which guarded the hill and contained the umbilical cord (twin) of the lubaale Kibuuka.[11] There the royal party was met by the hill's guardian, the Lungfish clan member Ssemanobe, who along with his fellow clanmate Makamba served as a priest at the hill. Ssemanobe blocked the king-elect from entering the compound and, along with his representatives, engaged the kabaka's men in a mock battle (ebirembirembi, "battle of reeds") fought with sugarcane reeds and plantain-leaf shields. The ebirembirembi, which commemorated Kintu's defeat of Bemba (see chapter 2), illustrated how closely Buddo Hill was guarded and marked the impossibility of an imposter's gaining admission. The combat ended when Ssemanobe and his men backed away from the royal party, at which point the kabaka-elect advanced and, in a symbolic gesture indicating the founding of an estate, touched a bark-cloth tree at the gate.[12]

Upon the completion of the kabaka-elect's victory in the "battle of the reeds," Ssemanobe led him to the shrine of Lumansi, which contained the umbilical cord of the diviner, Buddo, who had facilitated Namuggala's ascent to the kingship. There the prince was endowed with the strength of Buddo, after which he was taken to the shrine that housed the famous diviner's jawbone. The king-elect next went to the House of Buganda, the place regarded as the former residence of Bemba and his predecessors. Ssemanobe took the king-elect's right hand, Makamba took his left, and together they led the prince into the dwelling and seated him on a bark cloth. The prince spent the night in the House of Buganda along with his queen sister (lubuga), while the prime minister (katikkiro) and his retinue built their houses in the surrounding compound in order to guard the king-elect from danger.

The following morning, Ssemanobe ordered the prime minister to rouse the king-elect and the queen sister. He then led the royal couple once again to the shrine of Buddo, where he presented the king-elect with Buddo's skull and umbilical cord and declared: "I have given Buddo to you to hold and this is his cord. He is the one who gave your ancestors the Kingdom and he has bidden you go and eat the Kingdom, and may you live longer than your ancestors and may nobody speak you evil."[13] Ssemanobe next led the king-elect to the investiture mound, an anthill called Nakibuuka, or "Mother of Kibuuku," on which was placed the *jjembe* Namulondo. The royal couple crawled to the mound on their knees, while the prime minister and the county chief Kasujju held aside the bark cloth that blocked the entrance of the surrounding reed fence. Once inside the enclosure, the king-elect stood up and ascended the anthill Nakibuuka, whereupon Ssemanobe presented him with the royal spear Kanuna and invested both him and the queen sister with a new bark cloth knotted on each shoulder. Ssemanobe then exhorted the king-elect to behave in a kingly fashion, to conquer his enemies, and to quell any rebellions in the kingdom, thus marking the climax of the investiture ceremonies.

THE BUDDO RITES REVISITED:
CREATIVE PATHWAYS TO POLITICAL COMPLEXITY

As Christopher Wrigley and others have aptly noted, the original nucleus of the Ganda kingdom was most likely located about fifteen miles northwest of Kampala, in the land lying between the two branches of the upper Mayanja River. At the heart of this area stands Bakka Hill, the highest point for miles around and the oldest center of kingship. Bakka served as the principal estate for Walusimbi, the head of the Civet Cat clan, who may once have also occupied the position of king. The hill and its immediate environs also provided the setting for the ceremony called *okukula kwa kabaka*, "the king's growing up," which prior to the establishment of the Buddo rites in the mid-eighteenth century was the most important royal ritual in Buganda.[14]

Most commentators have regarded the Buddo rites instituted by Kabaka Namuggala in the mid-eighteenth century as signaling "the beginning of the modern [Ganda] kingdom," an indication that the kingship had grown more powerful than the clan confederacy that had characterized the Ganda polity in the previous century. They have argued that the advent of these newly created royal rites represented the culmination of a perhaps century-long period during which kings gradually established the autonomy of the kingship by extracting royal ideology from the restrictive bonds of clanship. According to this formulation, the Buddo rites represented a completely new process of sanctification, distinguished from previous rites by the exclusion of the clan heads, who up until Namuggala's reign had presided over the royal ceremonies undertaken at the clan estates surrounding the Civet Cat clan leader Walusimbi's estate at Bakka, in northern Busiro. An essential component of the recently consolidated Ganda state, the Buddo rites provided the kingship with its own territorial foundation, thus marking the ascendance of royal authority and the concomitant diminishment of the authority of clan heads.[15]

Upon initial examination, the Buddo rites appear to support the prevailing interpretations sketched above. The heads of the four clans that held estates in the areas neighboring Bakka—the Civet Cat, Frog, Colobus Monkey, and Mushroom clans—were excluded from the rites instituted during Namugala's reign. Their absence from the Buddo rites, however, need not necessarily indicate the emergence of an increasingly potent royal apparatus at the expense of nonroyal forms of authority. Such an interpretation privileges the perspective of those situated at the center of the rites—the king and his royal representatives—and fails to account for the history of the intellectual innovations that generated the central images and discourses associated with the installation ceremonies. Most Baganda recognize the Buddo rites as reinforcing and reproducing two essential components of Buganda's past: the founder-king Kintu's defeat of the tyrannical ruler Bemba; and the kingdom's indebtedness to the lubaale Kibuuka, upon whose mound—Nakibuuka —the king-elect and his queen sister were invested. An examination of how these two figures achieved such prominent positions in the Buddo rites reveals a complex relationship between clan formation, royal authority, and the shifting contours of public healing in eighteenth-century Buganda.

KINTU AND MAWANDA

As discussed in chapter 2, when viewed from the perspective of an audience seated at a healer's shrine, the Kintu figure appears as a territorial spirit converted into a regional, portable spirit through the work of itinerant mediums. In the discourse and practices associated with the Buddo rites, Kintu emerges as the first Ganda monarch and founder of the Ganda kingdom. The differences between these two depictions reveal the opening stages of a momentous intellectual transformation in which the politics of the practical world became increasingly focused on an instrumentally powerful kingship. The emergence of a more robust and muscular kingship, however, did not efface the work of the healer's shrine. Scholars often draw upon the distinction between creative and instrumental forms of power in order to explain how royals and their representatives negotiated with competing sources of authority embodied by healers.[16] But the fact that creative and instrumental power may be distinguishable by scholars often serves to obscure the manner in which they appear in the historical record as mutually implicated in political undertakings. As the previous chapters illustrate, we must consider both creative and instrumental modes of power in order to grasp the ideology of clanship and the practical reasoning behind healing. In the following discussion I consider the extent to which the royal/instrumental and medium/creative binaries were disputed, ideological claims in eighteenth-century Buganda that only later achieved hegemonic status.

The intellectual and political transformations that would characterize eighteenth-century Buganda first appear in the narratives describing the early eighteenth-century reign of Kabaka Mawanda, the grandson of a Leopard clan member (Ssegirinya) whose lineage maintained important duties in connection with the Kintu cult at Magonga. Ganda dynastic narratives relate that Mawanda was confronted by a healer (musawo) while living at Lulumba Hill. The healer approached the king and relayed the following message: "While I was in the bush gathering firewood, I saw a man who said to me, 'Go and tell the king that if he wants to see Kintu, his great ancestor [jjaja], he should go to Magonga. Once the king has seen Kintu, he will live for a very long time.' "[17] Eager to court Kintu's patronage, Mawanda immediately appointed a representative to pay a visit to the Leopard clan leader, Mwanje, who served as the priest at Kintu's shrine at Magonga. The king provided his messenger with cows and goats and instructed him to tell Mwanje to slaughter the animals and prepare a large feast. After presenting the offerings to Mwanje, Mawanda's messenger informed the priest that the king wanted to visit his ancestor Kintu. Mwanje told the messenger that he would communicate with Kintu that night and contact the king the following morning. The royal messenger then returned to the capital, and that evening the priest visited Kintu's shrine to communicate Mawanda's proposal. Later that night, Kintu emerged from his shrine and told Mwanje that he would receive Mawanda after eight days. Kintu insisted, however, that Mawanda come only with his queen sister, Ndege.

The following morning Mwanje went to Lulumba Hill and delivered Kintu's message to Mawanda. Despite welcoming Mwanje's announcement that Kintu had agreed to grant him an audience, Mawanda refused to accept his great ancestor's request that he wait eight days before journeying to Magonga. Mwanje then reported the king's response to Kintu, who instructed the priest to return to Mawanda's capital and tell the king to visit

Magonga after four days. Mwanje delivered Kintu's message to Mawanda and advised the king to arrive at Magonga during the night. When four days had passed, Mawanda gathered his important chiefs and informed them that Kintu had invited him to Magonga on the condition that he appears only with his queen sister. The king's chiefs agreed to abide by Kintu's request, and that night Mawanda set off for Magonga with Ndege.

When the couple reached the edge of the forest in which Kintu dwelt, the great ancestor called to the king and instructed him to enter through the front door.[18] Mawanda passed through a hall and entered the shrine, where he saw Kintu seated upon an earthen platform.[19] At that moment, however, a man named Ssenkoma appeared behind Mawanda, prompting Kintu to admonish the king for not following his order to come only with his queen sister.[20] Mawanda turned his head and, much to his surprise, noticed the figure of Ssenkoma standing behind him. He then directed his eyes back toward Kintu to explain that the visitor had come uninvited, but Kintu had already disappeared. Stricken with grief, Mawanda departed Kintu's shrine to return to his capital. Thus ended Mawanda's ill-fated encounter with his great ancestor Kintu.

Mawanda's endeavor to secure the support of the ritual complex at Kintu's shrine at Magonga ultimately ended in failure. Yet just one generation later the Kintu figure became an integral component of royal ideology when Kabaka Namuggala instituted the Buddo rites to commemorate the founder-king Kintu's defeat of the python-ruler Bemba. In devising the Buddo rites and their discursive justification, Namuggala and his advisers bestowed an additional interpretation upon "Kintu and Bemba the Snake" that portrayed Kintu as a conquering king whose defeat of the tyrannical ruler Bemba had established the Ganda dynasty.[21] This interpretation would be reinforced at each performance of the royal installation rites at Buddo Hill and became part of the charter for the expanding Ganda state. Just as Kintu defeated Bemba, so too all Ganda kings from Namuggala's reign on would overcome competing forms of authority by taking part in the elaborate ceremony described at the outset of this chapter. The pivotal issue in examining the centrality of the Kintu figure in the Buddo rites, then, is why Namuggala and his immediate predecessors sought to harness Kintu to the interests of the recently emerged Ganda state. What, in other words, would have compelled Mawanda and his nephew Namuggala to seek the support of their "great ancestor" and situate him at the center of the kingdom's most important royal rites?

The key to understanding Kintu's emergence in the mid-eighteenth century as the founder of the Ganda kingdom lies in locating this momentous development within the preexisting conception of the Kintu figure as a spiritual entity (see chapter 2). Viewed in light of this understanding of Kintu, Mawanda's visit to Kintu's principal shrine at Magonga and Namuggala's establishment of the Buddo rites in commemoration of Kabaka Kintu's defeat of Bemba reveal the efforts of two of Buganda's best-known state-builders to draw upon deeply embedded ideas regarding the relationship between public healing and political order. In their endeavors to transform Kintu from a prominent spiritual entity into the founder of the Ganda dynasty, Buganda's eighteenth-century royal leaders sought to direct the collective energies embedded in rituals performed for Kintu toward royal ends. Their success in doing so—evidenced in the prominent role accorded to Kabaka Kintu in the Buddo rites, as well as the widely held perception of Kintu as the first Ganda king—necessarily involved the concerted undertakings of the priests, mediums, and diviners who attended to the rituals directed toward Kintu at shrine sites throughout the area that would become Buganda.[22]

The contribution of these often overlooked historical actors to both Kintu's transformation and the broader process of state formation stemmed in large measure from their occupying strategic positions of semantic creativity. As the voices—both literal and figurative—of authority on the local level, public healers had the potential to initiate intellectual transformations such as those involving Kintu, and the impetus to do so came from their desire to stake a claim in the instrumentally powerful kingship emerging in Buganda in the first half of the eighteenth century. Thus it was Buddo, the famous diviner from the Ssese Islands, who recounted to Kabaka Namuggala the story of his ancestor Kintu's victory at Buddo (Naggalabi) Hill, "where evil and danger are shut out."[23] In Buganda as elsewhere in the region, the delineation of the boundaries between good and evil—the identification of sources of both well-being and misfortune—fell to political authorities such as the diviner Buddo and the shrine priest Mwanje, whose abilities to direct the flow of moral discourse played a critical role in Kintu's momentous transformation.

In overseeing and sanctioning intellectual developments such as Kintu's transition from a regional spirit to Buganda's founding king, the contribution of wielders of authority at local shrines to Buganda's political development was far more significant than most historians have recognized. Their capacity to shape the boundaries of collective prosperity and to steer the current of collective energies compels us to reconsider prevailing characterizations of such state-building kings as Mawanda. As mentioned earlier, most commentators have recognized Mawanda's reign in the early eighteenth century as the most significant period in the history of Ganda state formation. Characterized by significant territorial expansion, Mawanda's reign witnessed an increase in state-directed violence and, according to prevailing narratives of Ganda state formation, the rise to prominence of "the king's men," royal representatives whose political fortunes rested in the hands of the *kabaka*.[24] I discuss the consequences of Mawanda's reign in greater detail later in the chapter, but the pertinent point for the current discussion is that following the advice of a healer, Mawanda sought an audience with the prominent spirit Kintu, as well as his legitimizing sanction. Mawanda's efforts to garner Kintu's support may ultimately have ended in failure and prompted the ambitious king to ignore the prohibition issued by the country's healers against beating the war drums.[25] But the story of Mawanda's encounter with Kintu illustrates the continued significance of historical actors who policed the boundary between collective well-being and political order in shaping the nature of political endeavors.

The story of Mawanda's visit to Kintu's shrine at Magonga also reveals a critical shift in the character of political practices in eighteenth-century Buganda. Whereas the previous three chapters demonstrated the confluence of public healing and political authority in the distant Ganda past, the story of Mawanda's encounter with Kintu's medium discloses an emerging division between the power of kings and the capacities of mediums. The negotiations about the timing of their meeting also illustrates the sorts of tensions that characterized this divide. The period of eight days that Kintu insisted Mawanda wait before visiting his shrine is suspiciously similar to the length of time, plus one day, of New Moon–related work stoppages and festivities overseen by mediums throughout the region. This demand represented the efforts of Kintu's medium to force the king to abide by the rhythms and cycles established by public healers, and Mawanda's refusal to obey Kintu's demand was the response of a king determined to dictate the flow of political life on royal terms. In this regard, the figure of Mawanda presents a striking contrast to political leaders such as the Colobus Monkey clan leader Kawooya Ssemandwa (Father of the Mediums), the Otter clan founder Kisolo Muwanga (medium for the spirit Muwanga), and the initiated medium Kimera, all of whose authority rested on their roles in the realm of spirit possession.[26] Unlike these figures, Mawanda did not engage in spirit possession. His authority rested elsewhere, most significantly in his control over the means of violence. Yet as illustrated in the history of Kibuuka, the other central figure in the Buddo rites, garnering support for military campaigns required that kings recognize forms of authority and political practices in which they were not necessarily the central actors and over which they could never assume complete control.

KIBUUKA AND NAKIBINGE

Kibuuka is one of the most prominent Ganda lubaale, a distinction reserved for those spiritual entities whose efficacy reaches beyond a particular territory or clan network and ensures the well-being of the entire kingdom. An examination of the formation of this national spirit, indeed of the emergence of the notion of a national spirit, therefore provides an opportunity for exploring transformations in the scale of public healing in eighteenth-century Buganda. Kibuuka's contributions to the historical developments that culminated in the establishment of the Buddo rites began during the reign of Kabaka Nakibinge, in the mid-eighteenth century.[27] According to Ganda dynastic narratives, Nakibinge assumed the throne during a period of increasing hostility between the Baganda and their Banyoro neighbors, whose support for a rival claimant to the Ganda kingship meant that Nakibinge maintained an exceedingly precarious hold on his kingdom.[28] Distressed that their leader had failed to gain a swift victory against his rival, Nakibinge's advisers brought a diviner before the king to advise him on how to secure his throne against Nyoro aspirations. The diviner counseled Nakibinge to travel to Magonga to consult Kintu, who would tell him what actions to take. Thus, like Mawanda, Nakibinge traveled to Magonga to seek an audience with the revered Kintu. Upon reaching Kintu's shrine site, the king relayed the diviner's message to a ritual attendant named Bwoya, who advised the king to spend the night at Magonga. That evening Kintu appeared to Bwoya and instructed him to tell Nakibinge to journey to the home of Kibuuka's father, Wannema, in the Ssese Islands, in order to enlist the support of Kibuuka, who would assist the king in his endeavors against the Banyoro.[29]

Following Kintu's advice as relayed through Bwoya, Nakibinge set out for Wannema's place, on Bukasa Island. He was guided in his journey by Kalyesubula, the son of Wannema's elderly attendant, Bbosa. Kalyesubula led the king to Bukasa Island, where Nakibinge greeted Wannema and presented him with nine women, nine servants, nine heads of cattle, nine loads of cowrie shells, nine goats, and nine bundles of bark cloth. The king then told Wannema of the threat posed by the Banyoro and requested his assistance in defeating them. Wannema sympathized with Nakibinge's predicament and offered him the services of his son Mukasa. Nakibinge, however, refused Wannema's offer and, following Kintu's suggestion, asked instead for Kibuuka. After careful consideration, Wannema met Nakibinge's request on the condition that the king leave him a princess as well as his umbilical cord as a guarantee for Kibuuka's safety.

When the bargain had been struck, Nakibinge returned to the mainland, and Wannema's son Kibuuka followed shortly thereafter. A few days after Nakibinge's arrival, the king attacked and defeated the Banyoro with the assistance of his leading fighters. Kibuuka, meanwhile, had journeyed a bit further inland to Mbaale in Mawokota, where he enlisted the support of Buvi, Nakatandagira, and Kituuma in a series of successful battles against the Banyoro living in the area. Despite these initial triumphs, however, the tide began to turn in favor of the Banyoro following the capture of a beautiful Munyoro woman by Kibuuka's man Nakatandagira. When news of the eye-catching captive reached Kibuuka, he ordered the returning Baganda fighters to release the woman from her stocks so that he might see her. Kibuuka then took her to his place and revealed the secret of how he defeated his enemies: by flying in the air and fighting them from this advantageous vantage point. Several days later the woman escaped from Kibuuka's place and informed her people of Kibuuka's secret fighting strategy. A Nyoro force then invaded the area and, armed with their newly acquired knowledge, aimed their arrows upwards, fatally wounding Kibuuka and ensuring their victory against Nakibinge.

Kibuuka's body did not fall to the ground following his death but instead remained caught in the branches of a *mvule* tree from which he had been fighting. Kibuuka's man Kituuma noticed the body of his slain leader, and his companion Nakatandagira climbed the tree in order to retrieve it. Unaware that Nakibinge had been killed on the battlefield, the two men sent messengers to inform the king of Kibuuka's death. As Kibuuka's men were preparing for their leader's burial, a wise man from the Lungfish clan named Muzingu declared that Kibuuka had come to him the previous night and commanded that he not be buried. Muzingu also told the heads of the community that Kibuuka had ordered him to speak in his voice and fight the people who had killed him. The following morning, Muzingu became possessed by the fallen leader's spirit and spoke before the community to prepare them for battle. When the fighting had subsided, the leaders at Mbaale wrapped Kibuuka's corpse in leopard, hyena, and lion skins, placed it in a specially constructed house, and sent Ssematimba, of the Lungfish clan, to inform Wannema of his son's death.[30]

Wannema was extremely grieved upon receiving the news of his son Kibuuka's death. He immediately sent a message to his attendant Bbosa reminding him that it was he who had facilitated Kibuuka's journey to the mainland by offering his son Kalyesubula to guide Kabaka Nakibinge to Bukasa Island. At Wannema's request, Bbosa took Kalyesubula to Bukasa Island, where Wannema instructed him to take his son to Kibuuka's resting place at Mbaale to be killed. So Bbosa took his son to Mbaale and handed him over to the area's leaders. Meanwhile, a dispute had emerged among the community leaders at Mbaale concerning who would serve as the principal priest and guardian at Kibuuka's tomb: Buvi claimed the post on account of being the eldest; Nakatandagira maintained that he deserved it for having fetched Kibuuka's body from the *mvule* tree; and Kituuma asserted that his having noticed Kibuuka's body in the tree branches entitled him to the position.[31] Unable to settle the dispute, the three men sought assistance from those who had gathered for Kibuuka's funeral rites, but they too could not reach a resolution. Just as the conflict threatened to devolve into a physical confrontation, the prisoner Kalyesubula (Bbosa's son) inquired into the nature of the dispute. The three men explained the matter to Kalyesubula, who proposed the following solution: Buvi would serve as the *ssaabaganzi*, or chief of the household;[32] Natandagira would occupy the position of Kibuuka's principal priest; and Kituuma would operate as the secondary priest, whose responsibilities would include receiving those who attended Kibuuka's funeral rites. All three men found Kalyesubula's proposition satisfactory, and when those who had assembled for the funeral rites heard what the prisoner had done, they pardoned him and then appointed him as one of Kibuuka's priests.

The narratives about the activities of Kabaka Nakibinge and Kibuuka offer a precious glimpse into the social processes involved in the composition of a *lubaale*, a national spirit of Buganda. Like the story of Kimera discussed in the previous chapter, the account of Kibuuka's entrance onto Buganda's historical stage might best be regarded from the perspective of those who supported him in his well-known endeavors. Perhaps the most striking observation in this regard is that Buvi, Nakatandagira, and Kituuma all belonged to the Sheep clan. The early history of this clan shows how historical actors living on the Ssese Islands and the Mawokota shorelines channeled their creative energies directed toward the spiritual entity Kibuuka into the formation of a clan.

Members of the Sheep clan trace the origins of their community to Ssekoba, who left his home at Bumogera and traveled to the Ssese Islands.[33] Upon arriving in Ssese, Ssekoba pledged himself to Wannema, who provided him with the village of Busanga, on Kkoome Island. Like many of the spiritual entities discussed in the previous three chapters, Wannema surfaces in narratives such as those describing the history of the Sheep clan as a historical figure not unlike a king or a prominent chief. Throughout Buganda, however, Wannema was regarded as one of the principal lubaale of Lake Victoria and the father of the lubaale Mukasa and Kibuuka. That the Sheep clan's founding ancestor, Ssekoba, offered himself as a client to Wannema therefore indicated his inclusion in the healing complex associated with this revered spirit.[34]

While living at Busanga, Ssekoba fathered a son named Bbosa, who in his role as a servant of Wannema's offered his son Kalyesubula to guide Kabaka Nakibinge to Bukasa Island. As discussed above, Wannema, upon learning of his son Kibuuka's death, demanded that Bbosa hand Kalyesubula over to the community leaders at Mbaale. The leaders at Mbaale, however, decided to release Kalyesubula and to appoint him as one of Kibuuka's priests as a reward for settling the dispute among Kibuuka's men Buvi, Nakatandagira, and Kituuma. During Kalyesubula's time in captivity his hair had grown long (a sign of a liminal figure). The prison guards therefore shaved his head and told him, "Lw'owona obusibe, lw'omwa" (You are free, you are shaved). Because of this, the leaders at Mbaale bestowed upon Kalyesubula the name Lwomwa (from lw'omwa, "you are shaved"). He became the head of the Sheep clan and presided over the clan's main estate, surrounding Kibuuka's shrine at Mbaale, in Mawokota.

Shortly after his release, Kalyesubula Lwomwa married Nakitabajja, the daughter of the Lungfish clan member Muzingu, who had served as Kibuuka's medium immediately after his death. The couple produced two sons, Kiguli and Nakabaale. Kiguli carried Kibuuka's umbilical cord when Kibuuka engaged in battle with the Banyoro and also looked after the Sheep clan's two most important wells (Kaddumya and Kyogabakyala), from which both Kibuuka and his brother Mukasa drew water for cleansing patients.

Nakabaale, for his part, looked after the mortar in which Kibuuka ground herbs used for treating illnesses, and both he and Kiguli served as pages at the shrines of Kibuuka and Mukasa. Thus, Kalyesubula Lwomwa and his fellow clanmates, including Buvi, Nakatandagira, and Kituuma, acquired the critical duty of maintaining Kibuuka's shrine at Mbaale.[35]

As I have stressed several times, we cannot regard the familial relationships that are embedded in narratives such as those recounting the Sheep clan's early history literally. The literal mapping of familial relationships on a kinship grid, however, can provide insight into the development of the hierarchical relations that undergirded the process of clan formation. The roles of the Sheep clan's earliest remembered ancestors, Ssekoma and Bbosa, reveal the clan's general connection to the ancient ritual and political complexes in the Ssese Islands and a particular association with the lubaale Wannema. Despite these links to the more distant history of the communities inhabiting Lake Victoria's numerous islands and vast shorelines, however, the clan's histories clearly state that there had never been a head of clan—and therefore a clan itself—before Kalyesubula Lwomwa's rise to prominence during the reign of Kabaka Nakibinge.[36] In order to understand the connection between the development of Kibuuka as a lubaale and the Sheep clan's emergence during this period, we need to consider the Sheep clan's early history in terms of the relationship between clanship, public healing, and the effective composition of knowledge.

The narratives relating the initial composition of the Sheep clan suggest that the clan emerged from the collaborative efforts of communities living along the lakeshores of Mawokota and ritual specialists from the Ssese Islands in response to a military threat from intruders associated with the kingdom of Bunyoro. Buvi, Nakatandagira, and Kituuma appear in these narratives as the three main community leaders living in Mbaale when Kibuuka arrived in Mawokota. These three leaders—and by extension the communities over which they presided—pledged their support to the recently arrived spirit and to ritual specialists such as Kalyesubula, who facilitated Kibuuka's journey from the Ssese Islands to the mainland. Their enterprising efforts to get support for their campaign against the Banyoro revolved around the emergence of Kibuuka as a spiritual entity whose effectiveness was based on his ability to harness the collective energies of the communities living around Mbaale. By assigning responsibility for carrying out the various tasks involved in the maintenance of Kibuuka's well-being to officials residing in a number of communities around Mbaale and beyond, the area's leaders assembled a large political body whose members perceived a compelling connection between their collective health and the fate of their spiritual patron. In the process of establishing this connection, these various communities came to regard themselves as clanmates who observed a common totem, descended from a common principal ancestor, and, as illustrated in the narratives about the Sheep clan's founder and earliest ancestors, shared a common history that connected the clan's origins to the Ssese ritual complex.

While Kibuuka's movement from the Ssese Islands and his subsequent establishment on the mainland, in coastal Mawokota, was intimately entwined with the formation of the Sheep clan, the ritual activities undertaken at Mbaale involved the participation of a host of individuals from a variety of clans. Kaggwa's and Roscoe's early twentieth-century descriptions of Kibuuka's shrine and the numerous attendants who participated in the ceremonies performed there at each new moon offer a vivid image of the ritual setting in which these practices occurred.[37] According to Kaggwa, Kibuuka appeared in public once a month, at the appearance of the new moon. At that time the shrine's curtains were lifted and all the covers of Kibuuka's relics were removed save the leopard, lion, and hyena skins, after which the entire assemblage was invited into the courtyard. Kibuuka's officials then took their prescribed seats. First, Kalyesubula Lwomwa, the head of the Sheep clan and the principal caretaker (*mutaka*) of Mbaale, assumed his position on the shrine's righthand side. Then, Nansumbi, Kibuuka's *ssabaddu* (head of servants) from the Civet Cat clan, sat in the middle of the assembly surrounded by Kibuuka's ten wives, who were drawn from the Lungfish, Buffalo, Colobus Monkey, and Seed clans. When these women had taken their places, nine officials, including the priest Buvi, of the Sheep clan, seated themselves beside Kibuuka's wives. To the left of Kibuuka's shrine were seated twelve more officials, each of whom performed a specific task connected to ensuring Kibuuka's well-being.[38] When all of these officials had taken their places, the crowds who had assembled outside were invited in and took seats toward the back of the courtyard until the entire compound was filled. Kibuuka's fourteen mediums, who belonged to ten different clans, then entered the compound and were seated in a single row behind the other officials.[39] The mediums were distinguished from the rest of the crowd by their attire, which consisted of a bark cloth fastened with two knots, a goat skin wrapped around the waist, and a leopard skin slung over the back. Each medium also carried a fly whisk (nkinga), an emblem of office throughout the region.

In addition to offering a sense of the nature and scale of the activities undertaken at Mbaale, Kaggwa's and Roscoe's detailed descriptions of Kibuuka's shrine site and its officials also provide an important hint as to how Kibuuka, a spiritual entity intimately connected to the formation and preservation of the Sheep clan, became a prominent lubaale. The large number of officials and attendants who resided near Mbaale and presided over the ceremonies there conveys something of the strategy that Ganda kings, their royal representatives, and Kibuuka's local guardians may have adopted in order to direct Kibuuka's effective capacities toward the well-being of a larger political body. In addition to the ritual officers mentioned above, Kibuuka's compound also housed a prince, whose official duty was to tend to the fire that burned continuously in Kibuuka's shrine, as well as two princesses. The presence at Kibuuka's shrine of these royal representatives, as well as numerous other officials drawn from a variety of clans and selected from lineages occupying widely dispersed localities, suggests that Ganda royal rulers (or nonroyals working in conjunction with royal officials) sought to transform Kibuuka from a localized spirit into a lubaale through the strategic deployment of ritual specialists to Kibuuka's shrine at Mbaale. Kibuuka's local Sheep clan guardians may have welcomed and even sanctioned the broadening of their spiritual patron's social and ritual networks, as such a development would have brought them increased prestige as well as material benefits in the form of the obligatory offerings presented to shrine guardians by both royals and commoners. But they would only have supported such an endeavor as long as they managed to maintain their authority over the shrine's activities, which, judging from the Sheep clan leader Kalyesubula Lwomwa's position as the principal priest at Mbaale, they did. Thus, Sheep clan members living around Mbaale came to perceive their collective fate as connected to that of the larger Ganda polity, specifically in relation to military affairs.

PUBLIC HEALING AND POLITICAL VIOLENCE

Kibuuka was the principal lubaale of warfare in Buganda; his main responsibilities thus revolved around ensuring the success of Ganda military endeavors. Like their predecessor Nakibinge, subsequent Ganda rulers conferred with Kibuuka prior to engaging in battle. Whenever the kabaka wished to consult the lubaale, he sent a messenger and several other representatives to Mbaale with offerings of slaves, cattle, and other goods. The messenger was met at Kibuuka's compound by an assistant priest, who received the gifts and then entered the shrine to announce the royal representative to the principal priests, Lwomwa, Kituuma, and Nakatandagira. The priests then invited the messenger into the shrine and, with the assistance of a medium, requested Kibuuka's presence at a public gathering.

After completing the arrangements, the royal messenger resided in a nearby house until the day of assembly, appointed by Kibuuka. On that day all of Kibuuka's priests, mediums, officials, and wives gathered in the courtyard along with the kabaka's representatives and other members of the surrounding communities in the manner described above for the new-moon ceremonies.[40] The critical moment in the proceedings was when Kibuuka's mediums called upon their spiritual patron. With the battery of drums sounding in the background, Kibuuka possessed his earthly representatives and informed them of the plans for the impending military campaign. The following morning, Kibuuka visited the kabaka's military general and outlined the campaign strategy to him. When the war party set out, a priest and a medium from Kibuuka's estate accompanied the leader of the expedition; they carried with them the drum Kibuuka had acquired on Bugala Island prior to embarking on his battles against the Banyoro. Kibuuka's representatives had a hut built near the general's headquarters and provided him with advice whenever they were called upon to do so.[41]

While Kibuuka served as the guardian of Buganda's western frontier, the lubaale Nende performed a similar though less exalted role on the kingdom's eastern frontier. Nende's principal shrine stood at Bukeerere, in Kyaggwe, and was looked after by the priest Kajugujwe, of the Mushroom clan. Like that of his western counterpart Kibuuka, Nende's compound housed an impressive entourage of priests, mediums, and spirit wives (some of whom were princesses dedicated to him by the kabaka) and served as a site where the king's military generals sought counsel. According to Kaggwa, Nende appeared in public every two to three years. On these occasions people from many parts of Buganda flocked to Bukeerere. Nende's guardians would bring him out from his shrine and place him on fresh bark cloths and lion and leopard skins. His body was wound with several types of beads, and parrot feathers and colobus monkey furs adorned his head. The festivities lasted for nine days, during which Nende, accompanied by the beating of his battery of drums, appeared in the courtyard every other day before a crowd that included the king's military generals.[42]

Accounts of the activities undertaken at Kibuuka's and Nende's shrines point to an intriguing practice alluded to in the previous chapter: the operation of public healing ceremonies as military rallies. These accounts suggest that successful military campaigns relied on more than superior technological resources and a well-trained fighting force.[43] Large-scale rituals—and the capacity of these acts to influence military activities—served as technologies of warfare. In their capacities to shape the moral economies of the widespread social networks over which they presided, political authorities such as the priests and mediums at Kibuuka's and Nende's shrines played a critical role in both amassing support for and determining the character of military endeavors. Their pronouncements at large public gatherings designated particular communities for possible attack and protected others from the wrath of Ganda military expeditions, which may have contributed to the formation of ethnic identities.[44] Moreover, the attendants at these shrines often acted as spies, so that shrine sites frequently doubled as intelligence-gathering centers. The princesses who served as spirit wives were particularly adept in this capacity, as their distinctive place in the Ganda social milieu allowed them to roam freely about the countryside. Princesses in Buganda were treated socially as males, did not officially marry, and enjoyed an unusually free sexual license, all of which made them perfectly suited to act as either spies for royal authorities or sources of support for ambitious princes seeking the throne.[45]

Highlighting the contributions of priests, mediums, princesses, and other shrine attendants to Ganda military affairs allows us to include a group of often overlooked historical actors in a discussion ordinarily dominated by kings, chiefs, and military generals. While it deepens our understanding of the connections between public healing practices and military campaigns, pointing to the roles of these alternative authority figures in a sense offers yet another elitist perspective from which to view such endeavors. This perspective reveals little about the people who constituted the bulk of the fighting forces, the crowd who, according to Kaggwa's and Roscoe's descriptions, filed into Kibuuka's courtyard on important occasions after the principal dignitaries had taken their places. Specific details regarding the lives of such actors rarely, if ever, surface in the historical record. Yet if we think critically about the types of people most likely to seek relief at shrine centers such as

Kibuuka's, we can gain insight into the social makeup of Buganda's fighting forces and the types of motivations that may have prompted them to participate in military expeditions.

The most common explanation cited in early written accounts for both women's and men's visiting mediums residing at shrine sites such as Kibuuka's had to do with infertility. In this context, however, their concern may have been not only the biological production of children; it was quite likely also the ability to bear socially recognized offspring. In his examination of healing as a form of social criticism, Steven Feierman suggested that public healing ceremonies be regarded as rituals of "personal reproduction and group survival" and that mediums' prescriptions be understood as "medicine for achieving the social purposes of natality." For Feierman, the "social purposes of natality" referred to "the ability to conceive children, to bear living children, and to have them survive into maturity—to reproduce the social group."[46] From this perspective, one of the main reasons for visiting mediums when experiencing "infertility" was to ensure that one's children survived and became socially recognized individuals. This understanding of infertility provides insight into the types of people most likely to be attracted to public gatherings at shrine centers such as Kibuuka's and to engage in the activities undertaken there. Participation in public healing complexes would have presented socially marginalized individuals and communities with a way to overcome the formidable social barriers attached to their status as outsiders, an observation that brings us to the critical but underexplored topic of slavery and dependence in Buganda.

As Reid has noted, "it is impossible to assess . . . the extent of slave ownership in nineteenth-century Buganda." Written accounts from the second half of the century, however, suggest the presence of a substantial population of various types of nonfree people, a status characterized most of all by a denial of both freedom of movement and full acceptance in a recognized social group.[47] Baganda, for example, distinguished between those stolen or pillaged in war (abanyage) and those bought (abagule), all of whom fell under the general category "reviled people" (abenvumu). There also existed a category of nonfree persons, including those pawned during times of emergency, who could not be sold out of the country. The presence in nineteenth-century Buganda of large numbers of nonfree people, who constituted what Reid has called a "social hierarchy of slaves," undoubtedly reflects the effects of the increased intensity and scale of the Indian Ocean slave trade in nineteenth-century East Africa. Yet recent research on the history of violence and vulnerability in the distant Great Lakes past, along with scholarly attention to the consequences of the massive influx of war captives that accompanied Buganda's eighteenth-century territorial expansion, indicates that the commodified forms of slavery observed in the nineteenth century emerged from older, sometimes ancient forms of dependence and servitude. This scholarship suggests that capturing people was a long-established feature of warfare and raiding in Buganda as well as in the wider Great Lakes region. The dramatic transformations that accompanied the increasingly large Indian Ocean slave trade, then, revolved around the narrowing of the terms of vulnerability attached to these older forms of dependency. This process rendered a stolen person in the mid-nineteenth century much more likely to be ejected utterly from the region than a person stolen in warfare only a generation earlier.[48]

Nineteenth-century observers noted that Baganda employed captives in subsequent military expeditions and that chiefs' servants accompanied their patrons on these excursions.[49] Given the violent character of Buganda's eighteenth-century territorial expansion (see below), this practice more than likely developed before the second half of the nineteenth century. The eighteenth century, for example, witnessed the emergence of a new type of chiefship known as *ebitongole*, made up of an appointed leader and a group of followers who were mostly war captives. In addition to performing such tasks as clearing forests and growing food for the king's enclosure, these groups were also employed on military expeditions that often resulted in the acquisition of additional captives.[50] Precisely these and other types of socially marginalized individuals would have been most attracted to the curative prescriptions offered by public healers and would have had the most to gain from participating in military campaigns.

In the context of increasing violence in eighteenth-century Buganda, participation in military expeditions sanctioned by *lubaale* such as Kibuuka would have been a possible way for infertile individuals to produce socially recognized progeny. Socially marginalized people who served in Ganda military parties might partake in the spoils of war and employ their newly acquired material wealth to gain acceptance into established social networks. Perhaps more significantly, these individuals could themselves acquire both male and female dependents drawn from the captives acquired in military expeditions. By so doing, they could establish themselves as heads of networks of dependents whose members often conceived their relationships to one another in terms of descent, a source of prestige that could eventually result in their acceptance as members of the larger social networks to which their patrons belonged. In this respect, we might regard military endeavors endorsed by shrine officials as a form of public healing through which participants sought cures for their social marginalization, an ailment often attributed to an inability to produce children.

In many respects, the notion that participation in public healing complexes offered a remedy for the social illnesses of marginalized individuals represents a relatively well-rehearsed theme in Great Lakes historiography. Scholars of the Great Lakes region have long recognized the relationship between efforts to provide remedies for infertility, broadly defined, and the emergence of new forms of public healing. For example, several scholars have pointed out that infertility, including the sort defined by Feierman as hinging on the "social purposes of natality," might have led to the demotion of ancestral ghosts and the emergence of a new form of spirit possession known as *cwezi kubándwa*. They have also noted that membership in a healing network provided those experiencing infertility with a place in a social network comprising a family of ritual mothers, fathers, and siblings, as well as the opportunity to serve as parents to future initiates.[51] The novelty of the argument presented here revolves around violence and the narrowing terms under which socially marginalized people could negotiate better lives for themselves. The increase in violence and the massive influx of war captives in eighteenth-century Buganda provided a willing constituency of people seeking to reduce their vulnerability through participation in the public activities at shrines such as Kibuuka's. In this context, large-scale public healing practices, which could generate support for military campaigns, came to be a crucial component of Buganda's eighteenth-century expansionist endeavors. In other words, public healing and politically inspired violence, two seemingly contradictory and irreconcilable practices, together informed large-scale political developments in Buganda's past.

PUBLIC HEALING, PRINCESSES, AND THE LIMITS OF ROYAL AUTHORITY

The contribution of shrine centers such as Kibuuka's and Nende's to the organization and implementation of military expeditions illustrates how public healing practices informed political endeavors in eighteenth-century Buganda. Public healers presided over dense social and tribute networks, and continued royal interest in these leaders and their healing capacities throughout the eighteenth century may have stemmed in part from the pressures such institutions could bring to bear on a king's principal challenge, namely, maintaining flows of goods. The significant influence of priests and mediums in the political realm, however, also derived to a certain extent from the fact that the practices related to military as well as other sorts of affairs undertaken at *lubaale* shrines represented a form of authority over which Ganda kings and their royal representatives could never claim complete command.

Ganda clan and dynastic narratives provide numerous examples of healers defying the efforts of kings and other royal figures to exercise control over them. Members of the Kkobe clan, for instance, recall that the early nineteenth-century *kabaka* Ssemakookiro placed one of their clanmates, Ssebuliba, in a house and set it on fire, only to see the powerful figure emerge alive and unharmed.[52] Similar types of stories also cropped up in my discussions with practicing mediums. In an effort to explain the nature of his power, for example, one medium pointed to the fact that he could place a metal rod in the fire, get it red-hot, and then lick it until it became black again. He further related that he was able to dress in his medium's robe, step into a fire, and emerge unharmed.[53] The accounts of conflicts between Ganda kings and healers also show that Ganda kings often struggled in their efforts to successfully contend with the type of authority held by spirit mediums and priests on behalf of their spiritual patrons. In the mid-nineteenth century, for instance, Kabaka Ssuuna's men arrested Kigemuzi, a prominent medium for the *lubaale* Kiwanuka, and branded his entire body with red-hot pieces of iron. Kigemuzi responded by proclaiming that the king would suffer a similar punishment, and later that evening a bolt of lightening struck the king, scorching his leg, shoulder, and cheek.[54] These sorts of stories, which surface regularly in dynastic and clan traditions, highlight the difficulties involved in trying to control healers by force and the dire consequences often suffered by rulers who made such attempts. As Feierman has noted, the medium's drum "beat a rhythm of [its] own, not at all like the rhythm of the royal drums," and was located "in a domain which is beyond violence, where power is unstable and yet in some sense beyond the control of elders, chiefs, and kings."[55] Perhaps for this reason, the shrine sites at which mediums and priests operated often lay beyond the bounds of plundering Ganda war parties and served as centers of refuge where villagers sought protection during violent campaigns.[56]

As illustrated in both Mawanda's and Nakibinge's encounters with prominent spirits and their earthly representatives, eighteenth-century Ganda kings understood the significance of this alternative form of authority and actively courted the support of esteemed priests and mediums, who themselves recognized the benefits of cooperating with the royal center. One of the ways that kings sought to direct the authority held by the priests and mediums at shrine centers toward royal ends, or at least to maintain a watchful eye on the developments at these centers, was to dedicate princesses to particular spirits. As noted earlier, princesses were among the attendants residing at the compounds surrounding both Kibuuka's and Nende's principal shrines.[57] The dedication of princesses to lubaale in fact occurred throughout Buganda.[58] As also mentioned earlier, princesses dedicated to lubaale shrines often served as networks of spies, in part because of the unusual position princesses occupied in the Ganda social milieu. The writings of late nineteenth- and early twentieth-century travelers, missionaries, and ethnographers describe Ganda princesses engaged in or subject to practices conventionally restricted to men: princesses were addressed as "Sir" and bowed down to during greeting rituals; they could use obscene language, usually considered a male prerogative; and they were free to move about the countryside at their will. In addition, while they were free to initiate liaisons with any man they fancied and were consistently described as sexually aggressive, princesses were not permitted to marry in the sense of participating in a union cemented by the offering of bridewealth and characterized by a woman's moving to her husband's residence.[59] These characteristics afforded princesses an unusual independence and allowed them to travel around the countryside in relative freedom.

Most commentators have regarded the unusual cultural construction of Ganda princesses and their dedication to lubaale shrines as either an example of "state-controlled sexual reproductive constraint and repression" or an expression of Ganda kings' continuing debt to the country's spirits and their earthly representatives.[60] These scholars note that by gendering princesses as male and preventing them from producing socially recognized offspring, royal men sought to gain control over a possibly dangerous segment of the population that had the potential to spearhead rebellions against reigning monarchs.[61] Such explanations offer insight into some of the intentions and motivations undergirding the Ganda state's interventions into gender relations. Yet they fail to account for the specific nature of these interventions and their relationship to long-standing practices related to both spirit possession and the dedication of spirit wives to important shrine centers. Significantly, the cultural and social distinctions associated with Ganda princesses bear a striking resemblance to those recorded for female mediums throughout the region.[62] The question why Ganda kings dedicated princesses to *lubaale* shrines, then, might best be approached through an examination of the relationship between this political strategy and the role of women in public healing complexes.

In assigning to Ganda princesses cultural characteristics usually reserved for men and, more importantly, for female spirit mediums and ritual specialists, Ganda royal actors sought to imbue them with a type of authority that was widely associated with the practitioners of public healing. The practice of dedicating these women to *lubaale* shrines, however, also represented a creative innovation stemming from the far older practice of offering young girls and women to important spiritual entities as spirit wives. As discussed in chapter 2, the power associated with spirit wives related to the general connection between women, fertility, and the continuity of life, the idea being that a spirit wife's fecundity could be redirected to benefit a particular individual or community.[63] Ganda chiefs sought to increase their authority through an innovation in this deeply rooted practice. Roscoe reported that the compounds of important Ganda chiefs housed girls who had been dedicated to a particular spirit at their birth. Known as *kajjabuwonga* (from the verb *okuwonga*, "to dedicate to a *lubaale*"), these girls lived with their patrons and attended to their ritual needs, such as handing them fetishes and bringing them the butter or medicine with which they smeared their bodies. They also accompanied their chiefly patrons on war expeditions, during which they carried protective fetishes, and were prohibited from coming into contact with boys. When these consecrated girls attained puberty, the particular spirit to whom they had been dedicated ordered their marriage, often to the chiefs they had been serving.[64] The strategy adopted by Ganda royals was a variation of these chiefly practices. By dedicating princesses to *lubaale* and restricting their ability to marry officially or produce socially recognized offspring, Ganda kings sought to direct the collective energies and authority associated with shrine complexes toward the royal center.[65]

Returning to the Buddo rites with which we began this examination of some of the intellectual and social innovations in eighteenth-century Buganda, we can now perceive something of the political strategy employed by Kabaka Namuggala and his advisers in devising these royal ceremonies intended to ensure the king's well-being. In situating Kintu and Kibuuka at the heart of the newly devised rites, Namuggala and his advisers sought to build upon their predecessors' endeavors to direct the authority embedded in public healing networks toward the support of an increasingly ambitious royal center. Rather than seeking to exclude influential leaders such as the priests and mediums who presided over prominent shrine centers throughout the country, Ganda kings recognized their significance—as well as the potential threats they posed—and sought to channel their authority toward royal ends. As described above, their efforts revolved around the transformation of certain locally grounded or regional spiritual entities into national spirits and of Kintu into the first ruler of Buganda. These momentous developments, however, could not have occurred without the support of the priests, mediums, and clan leaders who were at the center of semantic and ritual creativity.

The integration of this critical set of historical actors into our understanding of political developments in eighteenth-century Buganda challenges conventional interpretations of the Buddo rites established by Kabaka Namuggala and his advisers. Most commentators have regarded these rites as representing the consolidation of royal authority following several tumultuous decades that witnessed increasing competition for the kingship and the consequent rise and fall of numerous monarchs.[66] While such interpretations properly identify the establishment of the Buddo rites as part of the efforts of a late eighteenth-century king and his royal representatives to stabilize the kingship, they fail to properly account for the political strategy undergirding these efforts. By the time Namuggala ascended to the throne in the late eighteenth century, Ganda royals recognized both the potential threat posed by public healers and their own inability to assume control over the form of authority embedded in the social and tribute networks connected to the maintenance of spiritual entities. The Buddo rites devised by Namuggala and his advisers were a royal endeavor to direct the authority held by public healers to the maintenance of a healthy royal center. They sought to incorporate into an emerging state apparatus a group of historical actors whose contributions to Buganda's development both deserve greater recognition and add considerable complexity to the state formation process in Buganda.

CLANSHIP, GOVERNANCE, AND TERRITORIAL EXPANSION

The early history of the Sheep clan hints at the fact that the clan concept and the contours of Ganda clans continued to develop during the primary period of state formation in the latter seventeenth and eighteenth centuries.

While this period undoubtedly witnessed an increase in the coercive powers of Ganda kings and their royal representatives, the notion that clans and the ideology of clanship wilted in the face of an increasingly militarized royal center simply does not hold up when viewed from the perspective of Ganda clan histories. This observation calls into question some of the fundamental tenets supporting conventional explanations of Ganda state formation, many of which bear the residue of evolutionary models of state development. According to this literature, the kingdom of Buganda emerged as a result of the gradual unification of once autonomous clans in the fourteenth and fifteenth centuries. The kingdom then underwent a process of territorial expansion and administrative consolidation in the seventeenth and eighteenth centuries, during which royalty and kingship gradually replaced lineage authority as the focus of political maneuverings. This increase in royal authority occurred at the expense of other forms of authority, such as those associated with clans, which ceased to function as viable political units and ceded control of communal resources to the royal center. According to this formulation, the end result of this process was a centralized state equipped with a bureaucratic apparatus dominated by royal representatives who united people in the service of the *kabaka*.[67]

Recent studies have to a certain extent challenged this conventional narrative of Buganda's development. Reid's examination of the Ganda economy points to a "marked degree of decentralization in terms of organization," while Hanson's analysis of the social disorder and political conflict stemming from Buganda's violent territorial expansion presents an important critique of the triumphalist vision of Ganda state formation.[68] These studies, however, do not fully account for the manner in which royal authority built upon and transformed well-established forms of authority. We have already discussed some of the innovations in public healing involved in the development of large-scale shrine centers as well as in royal efforts to draw these sites into the expanding political arena. This section further explores the relationship between an emerging royal apparatus and preexisting political practices. An examination of the reigns of the Ganda kings most closely associated with the formative period of expansion reveals both continuities and critical shifts in the clan concept and the process of consolidating large-scale political communities.

As noted earlier, Buganda's territorial expansion began during the late seventeenth-century reign of Kabaka Kateregga, which witnessed the capture of the territories of Butambula and Gomba (see map 7). Most scholars

have characterized his reign as inaugurating a period of military development in which Ganda kings began to collect tribute from wealthy chiefs and
appoint royal nominees to replace clan heads as the dominant force in
Ganda politics. As discussed earlier, however, successful military campaigns
relied on more than simply physical force, and an examination of how
Kateregga crafted the alliances that allowed him to both conquer these
territories and appoint chiefs there provides new insights into the nature of
these political developments.

The period of territorial expansion initiated during Kateregga's reign
opened with the annexation of Butambala and the establishment of the
position of *katambala*, chief of Butambala.[69] Although generally highlighted
as the first of what would become a series of Ganda military conquests in the
late seventeenth and early eighteenth centuries, Kateregga's incursion into
Butambala also provides a valuable glimpse of the creative capacities of
Ganda leaders, both royal and nonroyal, to both muster support for their
military campaigns and consolidate their victories. According to a less frequently recounted, nondynastic version of Kateregga's conquest of Butambala, the king's victory resulted from a successful alliance with Maganyi, of
the Lungfish clan, and Mpungu, of the Sheep clan. In this version, Maganyi
maintained control over a powerful charm (*jjembe*) named Mbajjwe. Maganyi left his home during the reign of Kabaka Kateregga and pledged
himself as a client of Mpungu, at Makuku, an area in the vicinity of the Sheep
clan's principal estate at Mbaale, Mawokota. Upon learning of Maganyi's
charm, the king immediately requested that he appear at the royal palace along with his *jjembe*. Mpungu instructed his client to take the charm
Mbajjwe to the king, but Maganyi insisted that Mpungu accompany him to
the palace. When they reached Kateregga's enclosure, the *jjembe* spoke to the
king and instructed him to request Mpungu to carry it (the charm) to Bweya,
in Butambula, where it would defeat a Munyoro named Kizunga, who lived
in the caves there.[70] Following the charm's advice, Kateregga appointed
Mpungu to lead the expedition into Bweya, where the Sheep clan member
defeated Kizunga's forces and killed their leader. The charm Mbajjwe then
asked Mpungu to remain in Bweya, a request to which the king assented.
Thus Mpungu became the first *katambala*, chief of Butambala, a position
that remained hereditary in the Sheep clan until the last decade of the nineteenth century.[71]

As chief of Butambala, one of the *katambala*'s principal duties consisted
in tending to the *jjembe* Mbajjwe, whose rope body and clay head were

fashioned to resemble a serpent.[72] The *katambala* served as the guardian of Mbajjwe's principal shrine in Butambula, where he placed the charm's head on a stool in imitation of a resting serpent. Hanson has observed that representatives from several clans assisted the *katambala* in Mbajjwe's operation and maintenance: a man from the Seed clan carried the charm; the stool bearer belonged to the Yam clan; the female medium was drawn from the Leopard clan; two men from the Bushbuck clan beat the *jjembe*'s drum on ceremonial occasions; a woman from the Grasshopper clan served as Mbajjwe's wife and looked after the leopard-skin rug upon which the serpent-like charm reclined; and a representative from the Bird clan had the task of thatching the shrine's roof. As Hanson notes, the cumulative contributions of these representatives resulted in the creation of the "strongest medicine" in the kingdom, whose continued efficacy was critical to the kingdom's well-being.[73]

The case of Mbajjwe illustrates that *mayembe* required the participation of extended networks of individuals in order to be effective. In this they were similar to *minkisi* in the central Congo basin, whose potency Wyatt MacGaffey describes as deriving from their participation in social relations and their ability to mediate between persons. The efficacy of *mayembe* stemmed from their ability to distill and harness the collective energies of dispersed communities around a common purpose. These objects became powerful when people attributed power to them, and the compositional process involved in their creation served to designate figures such as the *katambala* as necessary catalysts in the mobilization of the effective capacities of *mayembe*. Moreover, the agency attributed to *mayembe* "fit[ted] them for political functions" that were gradually incorporated into the expanding political realm in eighteenth-century Buganda.[74]

The creation of royal *mayembe* marked a notable innovation in the use of public healing practices to assert political rule. Whereas the power of *misambwa* and, to a lesser extent, *lubaale* was connected to the firstcomer status of the officials who oversaw the activities at the shrines dedicated to these spirits and focused on the specific territories in which their shrines were located, the work of *mayembe* was not bound by this restraint. Thus, actors in the employ of the state could carry these spirits to new territories and place them wherever necessary in order to consolidate political rule. Like the creation of *lubaale* spirits discussed in the previous section, *mayembe* such as Mbajjwe served as a means for composing communities, generating support for military endeavors, and consolidating military victories. Roscoe recorded that six royal *mayembe*, along with their mediums and entourage of attendants, accompanied Ganda military generals into battle. These *mayembe* were placed in the ground in front of the general's residence, where all the chiefs participating in the expedition took an oath before entering battle.[75] An innovation based on the widespread and ancient practice of using horned charms for protective purposes, royal *mayembe* aimed to direct these protective capacities toward an expanded notion of community. The presence of these powerful objects in the Ganda administrative apparatus highlights the impact of shifting notions of collective well-being on the state-formation process.[76] Like national spirits, royal medicines both facilitated territorial expansion and preserved the continued health of the kingdom, and their development beginning in the late seventeenth century is further testament to how ideas concerning public healing informed the emergence of the Ganda state.

While Mbajjwe is the most notable example of how the creation of royal *mayembe* informed the process of territorial expansion, Kabaka Kateregga drew upon two additional *mayembe* to strengthen his hold on newly acquired territories in Busujju. Dog clan histories relate that the clan's head, Gguluddene Mutasingwa, accompanied Kateregga's forces in their westward endeavors. Skilled in both the art of forging weapons and the composition of *mayembe*, Gguludene Mutasingwa carried with him a *jjembe* named Musisi. The leader's son Ssebakiggye also joined the expedition and brought with him the *jjembe* Mulindwa. Upon the defeat of the Banyoro in Busujju, the king asked Gguluddene Mutasingwa to transport his *jjembe* to the westernmost point in the country in order to protect Buganda from future Nyoro attacks. Kateregga presented Gguluddene Mutasingwa with Kititu Hill, in Busujju, where the clan head constructed a shrine for Musisi. This hill became the Dog clan's principal estate following the construction of Musisi's shrine, replacing the clan's previous *butaka* at Kitugga, in Busiro.[77] Gguluddene Mutasingwa's son Ssebakiggye constructed a shrine for his *jjembe*, Mulindwa, on Jjaawo Hill, in Gomba, which became known as Bulindwa. The *jjembe* Mulindwa further guarded Buganda's western borders against enemy incursions.[78]

In addition to further illustrating how ritual specialists employed *mayembe* in the service of the Ganda kingdom, the Dog clan's participation in Kateregga's westward expansion also was an early example of a significant process that would occur repeatedly over the next century: the development of clans and the clan concept as a means of both facilitating military conquests and consolidating control over newly acquired territories. Kateregga's expansion into Gomba, for example, inspired the emergence of the Duiker clan, whose ancestor, Balamaga Wasswa, led the area's residents in the defeat of a Munyoro chief on behalf of the Ganda king. In return for his services, Balamaga Wasswa received the newly created post of kitunzi, chief of Gomba, a position that remained hereditary in the Duiker clan until the reign of Kabaka Ssemakookiro in the early nineteenth century. The area in which Balamaga Wasswa defeated his Nyoro enemy, however, also became the principal estate for the Duiker clan, whose members presented Kateregga with a drum called Nakawanguzi as a symbol of their allegiance to him.[79] This overlap between clan formation and territorial expansion provides an early illustration of how eighteenth-century Ganda kings, as well as those seeking to reap the benefits and protection of an expanding royal complex, sought to harness the ideology of clanship to the emerging Ganda state.

The rise to the throne of Mutebi, Kateregga's successor, involved an unprecedented level of violence, and the military campaigns conducted during his reign resulted in the addition of the territories of Busujju and Ssingo to the Ganda administrative realm (see map 7). Like Kateregga's conquests, these campaigns led to the replacement of local rulers by the generals who had led the campaigns. Kalali, of the Pangolin clan, defeated Kajubi, of the Grasshopper clan, and was rewarded with the post of kasujju, chief of Busujju, a position that remained hereditary until the twentieth century. Meanwhile, Lubulwa, of the Oribi Antelope clan, received the post of mukwenda, chief of Ssingo, as a reward for leading Mutebi's military into the territory. Mutebi's annexation of the short grasslands of Busujju and Ssingo added valuable cattle-grazing pastures to the Ganda state and temporarily shifted the kingdom's focus to the northwest, where Mutebi established his first capital at Butebi, in Ssingo. Dynastic narratives also reveal that during his stay at Butebi, Mutebi increased his wealth by controlling the trade route along which cattle were brought from Mityana (an area even further to the northwest) to central Buganda and engaged in further cattle raids in the area surrounding Lake Wamala.[80] Most commentators have therefore regarded the manner in which Mutebi annexed Busujju and Ssingo, installed his military generals as rulers, and directed the wealth generated through control of these territories toward the royal capitol as evidence of the further increase in royal authority at the expense of hereditary rulers and other sorts of authorities. Summing up this viewpoint, M. S. M. Kiwanuka noted that "by the end of [Mutebi's] reign, the balance of political power had shifted more into the royal hands than it had ever done before."[81]

Mutebi's reign was undoubtedly characterized by an increase in the authority of the Ganda monarch and his representatives. Several examples of Mutebi's vulnerability drawn from nondynastic sources, however, suggest that forms of authority over which the king could not assume control exerted more influence on his reign than previously acknowledged. These examples also demonstrate that Mutebi's success resulted in part from his ability to accommodate and transform nonroyal forms of authority by providing their bearers with a stake in the royal apparatus.[82] The continued influence of nonroyal authorities during Mutebi's reign is evident in narratives that describe the monarch's suffering from an affliction whose cure required cooperation with a particular spirit and its representatives. These sorts of stories appear repeatedly in dynastic as well as other types of narratives describing the reigns of several Ganda kings. Rather than indicating a personal illness, the ailments suffered by kings in these narratives might better be understood as a more general threat to royal authority.

In the case of Mutebi, Oribi Antelope clan histories recount that in his efforts to recover from a serious illness, the ailing king followed the advice of his diviners and offered several princesses, as well as a deputyship, to a monsterlike ritual specialist named Kkungu.[83] A narrative relating how Lubinga, of the Pangolin clan, acquired the duty of looking after the princes and princesses, however, suggests that Mutebi's interactions with Kkungu did not represent the first time the king had suffered from a condition that required recourse to the area's spiritual authorities. After Mutebi assumed the throne, one by one his children died shortly after birth. The king's misfortune apparently resulted from the violation of his blood-brotherhood with Jumba, of the Monkey clan, the guardian of the lubaale Mukasa on Bunjako Island. Mutebi's fortunes eventually changed when, following instructions provided by Mukasa's medium, the Pangolin clan member Lubinga carried the necessary medicines to the king in return for offerings of women, servants, bark cloth, and beer. When Mutebi's children grew up in a healthy manner, the king appointed Lubinga to look after the princes and princesses and to settle their grievances. This office remained hereditary in Lubinga's family and placed its holder in an advantageous position from which to influence royal political developments.[84]

As caretaker of the king's children, Lubinga brought considerable prestige to the Pangolin clan, which increased both the scope and diversity of its social networks through the acquisition of several significant royal duties during Mutebi's reign. The history of the Oribi Antelope clan, which like the Pangolin clan rose to prominence during Mutebi's expansionist endeavors, provides another illustration that the extension of clan networks often coincided with the rise of royal authority. Oribi Antelope clan histories recall that Mutebi provided the clan with its principal estate in Bubiro and created the hereditary position of *kibaale*, whose occupant was to voice objections to any of the king's actions deemed unacceptable by members of the *lukiiko* and also served as the head of the clan.[85] Perhaps the most revealing examples of the role of clans and the ideology of clanship in the state-formation process, however, are from the reign of Kabaka Mawanda in the first half of the eighteenth century, the most significant period of Buganda's territorial expansion.

As mentioned earlier, historians have long recognized the reign of Mawanda as the main formative period in the history of the Ganda state. Mawanda established royally appointed chiefships for the territories of Kyaddondo, Bulemeezi, and Kyaggwe (see map 7), and his reign inaugurated the development of the administrative apparatus that greatly impressed the first foreign visitors to Buganda in the second half of the nineteenth century. Most historians have therefore portrayed his rule as a period of increasing royal power at the expense of clans and other forms of local authority. A closer inspection of Buganda's eastward expansion during this period, however, reveals that rather than resulting in the demise of clanship as an organizing principle, Mawanda's campaigns actually resulted in both the formation of new clans and the extension of existing clan networks. Prior to embarking on his campaign in Kyaggwe, for example, Mawanda formed an alliance with Nkutu, of Lwaje Island, a well-known canoe craftsman who managed a fleet of canoes employed by his followers for fishing and commerce along the Kyaggwe shoreline in Bukunja. When Mawanda began his campaign in Kyaggwe, Nkutu and his followers used their skills to build a formidable naval force that contributed significantly to Mawanda's success. In recognition of Nkutu's accomplishments, Mawanda bestowed upon him the name Kikwata (The Capturer), a reference to the many captives taken by Nkutu's forces. The king also appointed Nkutu head of the Eastern Fleet, provided him with a copper paddle, and gave to him the area around Namukuma, which became the principal estate for the Sprat Fish clan, headed by Nkutu Kikwata.[86]

The formation of the Sprat Fish clan during Mawanda's reign illustrates that the state-building process provided the context for the emergence of new clans and a modified ideology of clanship. By parlaying their maritime skills into a formidable naval force that assisted Ganda war parties in crossing the Nile, the inhabitants of Kyaggwe's shorelines and islands who came to constitute the Sprat Fish clan both connected the well-being of their community to the success of the Ganda state and also played a significant role in ensuring that success.[87] The clan's formation, in other words, facilitated the integration of its members into the Ganda kingdom and provided them with a means of partaking in the benefits of citizenship. Perhaps more importantly, however, membership in the clan also offered protection from the predations of Ganda war parties and may have helped to ensure that individuals and communities did not fall prey to "The Capturer," Kikwata.

The history of the Reedbuck clan offers another example of a network of occupational specialists who transformed themselves into a clan and whose members linked their livelihood to the Ganda state apparatus by performing critical services for the kingdom's rulers. Kyaggwe, in particular the areas surrounding the Mabira Forest, was noted for its large game population and contained the largest concentration of professional hunters in Buganda. Members of what would become the Reedbuck clan inhabited the northeastern part of Kyaggwe, which fell mostly in the Mabira Forest and in Bulondoganyi, where they managed the principal shrine of Ddungu, the spirit of the chase. Prior to their incorporation into Buganda, the most prominent inhabitants of this area constituted a well-established network of hunting specialists who initially offered their services to the rulers of Bunyoro, from where they claim to have migrated. Following Mawanda's conquest of Kyaggwe and the raiding of Busoga initiated by Kabaka Kyabaggu in the second half of the eighteenth century, however, these hunting specialists drew upon their well-established social networks to assume the critical responsibility of monitoring the flow of trade goods through the territory on behalf of the *kabaka*. Beginning in the mid-eighteenth century, clan members levied taxes on goods flowing through strategically located markets at Kirungu, Bulondoganyi, and Bugungu, all of which were situated at the intersection of trade routes reaching central Buganda, Busoga, and Bunyoro. The clan's acquisition of this lucrative task resulted from the support it offered to Buganda's leaders in their efforts to extend the kingdom's eastern frontier, a further illustration of how the social networks cemented by the ideology of clanship facilitated both the expansion and governance of the Ganda state.[88]

In addition to the Sprat Fish and Reedbuck clans, several other Kyaggwe communities sought to attach themselves to the Ganda state in the mid-eighteenth century and were incorporated into the kingdom as the Bird, Fox, Hippopotamus, and Marsh Antelope clans. But Buganda's eastward expansion also presented opportunities for clans from outside the region to enhance their prestige and further extend their networks of wealth through participation in the kingdom's military endeavors. For example, a member of the Bean clan named Mugalu led Mawanda's forces in Bukunja, the area along the northern shores of Lake Victoria where Ganda troops had established an alliance with Kikwata, of the Sprat Fish clan. In recognition of the bravery Mugalu had displayed in Bukunja's conquest, Mawanda awarded his general the estate of Nambeta and permitted him to wear copper bracelets, a privilege ordinarily reserved for those of royal status. Mugalu's clanmate Kawenyera, who had accompanied the general during the campaign, also received an estate in Bukunja and represented Mugalu at the king's enclosure. In a telling illustration of the manner in which Baganda employed the ideology of clanship as a means of appending newly acquired prestige and sources of wealth to already established social networks, both Mugalu and Kawenyera appear in Bean clan histories as the heads of maximal patrilineages and sons of the clan head.[89] A further example of this process appears in the history of the Sheep clan, whose principal area of concentration lay along the Mawokota shorelines. A member of the clan named Kibeevu assisted Mugalu in the Bukunja campaign and received the estate of Ssi as a reward for his efforts. Like his military superior Mugalu's, Kibeevu's newly acquired status resulted in his insertion into the upper echelon's of the Sheep clan's genealogy, in which he appears as the head of a maximal patrilineage and grandson of the clan's founder, Mbaale.[90]

Having secured control of Kyaggwe and enriched the kingdom's wealth through several plundering campaigns in Busoga, Mawanda turned his attention to the northeastern territory of Bulemeezi. While Bulemeezi was not particularly noted for its rich soils, its large tracts of land suited to raising cattle made it attractive to Mawanda. A general named Lutale Sikyaya Matumpaggwa directed the conquest of the territory, after which the king transferred his capital to an area located close to the scene of the final battle. Mawanda also appointed his successful general as the *kangawo*, chief of Bulemeezi. Like the other chiefships created by Mawanda, and in contrast to those established by his predecessors, the *kangawo* became an appointed position whose occupant served at the behest of the reigning monarch. Most commentators have therefore pointed to the establishment of such royally appointed chiefships as an indication of the increased capacity of eighteenth-century Ganda kings and their representatives to dictate the course of political developments in the kingdom.

While prevailing analyses of Mawanda's reign contain many trenchant observations, the enduring emphasis in Ganda historiography on the increased royal authority that accompanied Buganda's territorial expansion in some respects reflects the nature of the sources at hand. As discussed previously, many of these sources bear the dual imprint of royal efforts to shape the character of historical discourse and the emergence of a royally inflected understanding of historical writing during the early colonial period. The success of these efforts has made the uncovering of alternative perspectives —an understanding, for example, of how communities who did not directly participate in the expansionist process responded to the incursions of the Ganda state apparatus—extremely difficult. However, a precious description of the ceremonies undertaken by the *kangawo* prior to assuming his post offers a rare glimpse into how the success of royally appointed officials in many respects depended on their capacity to effectively engage with and participate in the locally grounded moral economies operating in the communities over which they presided.[91]

Upon his appointment by the *kabaka*, the *kangawo* received a set of drums and a trumpet from the king and was guided to Bulemeezi by a royal messenger. He spent the first night after leaving the capital at the home of a local leader named Bwamikitimba in the village of Kakusubula, where he made an offering of a goat, a bark cloth, and ninety cowrie shells at a specially designated shrine.[92] Bwamikitimba then led the appointee to a large rock called Kungu, where the caretaker Nadibanga led the *kangawo* and his entourage into a cave to meet an assemblage of the area's residents. There the *kangawo* made an offering of a bark cloth and some cowrie shells to the caretaker of the cave, after which the assemblage journeyed to Kungu's shrine at Sindo. After being denied entrance by the shrine's doorkeeper, the *kangawo* presented him with a goat and some bark cloth and then entered the shrine, where he and Nadibanga sat before Kungu's medium. As Kungu's three drums sounded, the chief presented the spirit with a large number of cowrie shells, two bark cloths, and two hens.

Nadibanga, the *kangawo*, and the chief's entourage next set out for the home of the local leader Kalyankolo, in Buzinde, where the *kangawo* once again presented an offering at a prominent and revered rock. The priest for the *lubaale* Nagawonye, to whom the area's residents turned in times of drought, then led the *kangawo* to the spirit's shrine. After presenting an offering to the shrine's priest, the party continued on their journey until they reached a well called Katonga. There the Kangawo drew some water and drank it from a ladle, which he then passed to a woman named Nabalemezi, "Mother of the People of Bulemeezi." Nabalemezi then passed the ladle to the *kangawo*'s men, each of whom drank the sacred water.

Upon leaving Buzinde the party headed to the home of the medium for the spirit Bowa, who appeared in the form of a leopard and whose name also belonged to the area in which he resided. Accompanied by two of his men and carrying two spears, the chief slowly approached Bowa's medium, who smoked his pipe while the Kangawo was paraded before him to the sound of the spirit's drum. The medium then touched the adorned spears, after which the *kangawo* presented some cowrie shells, two bark cloths, and a goat to the spirit. The *kangawo* next entered Bowa's shrine and sat before a "wife" of the spirit named Nakundi, who brought out a three-pronged pipe and filled it with tobacco and burning charcoal. Nakundi gave the pipe to the chief, who smoked twice and then handed it to Nabalemezi. The *kangawo*'s men then smoked in the same order that they had drawn water from the well Katonga.

From Bowa's shrine the *kangawo* and his entourage journeyed to the home of the local leader Mutongole, who took the chief to the shrine of Matumpaggwa, the first *kangawo* appointed by Kabaka Mawanda. The *kangawo* announced himself to Matumpaggwa's spirit, after which he and his men entered the shrine and offered two heads of cattle for slaughter. The *kangawo*'s drums, which Kabaka Mawanda had given to the first *kangawo*, Matumpaggwa, were sounded throughout the night as the area's leaders introduced themselves to the new appointee. Each leader took a piece of roasted liver from one of the slaughtered bulls and then introduced himself to the *kangawo*, who rested with Nabalemezi next to Matumpaggwa's shrine. The following morning the newly installed chief offered six cattle, thus completing the ceremonies designed to ensure the success of his reign.

This detailed description of the ceremonies that the *kangawo* underwent in Bulemeezi prior to assuming his post illustrates that territorial spirits and the associated firstcomer authority of those who presided over the activities involving them remained crucial to the legitimization of rule during Buganda's territorial expansion. The sequence of approvals the *kangawo* endured in Bulemeezi also shows that the holders of authority at the local level continued to exert their influence in the face of an increasingly prominent state apparatus.[93] By extending deeply embedded notions of collective well-being to include the maintenance of the success of royal appointees, the local leaders who presided over an area's spiritual sites compelled the "king's men" to engage in political practices over which they could never assume complete control.

In the case of the *kangawo* described above, one of the ways that Bulemeezi's local leaders sought to anchor their authority in the developing Ganda state structure was to establish control over the ancestral ghost of Matumpaggwa, the first *kangawo* appointed by Kabaka Mawanda. By establishing a shrine dedicated to Matumpaggwa's spirit and assigning the various duties involved in the shrine's maintenance to a group of local authorities, Bulemeezi's leaders managed to ensure their participation in the political endeavors orchestrated by the royally appointed territorial chief. The leaders of local communities, in other words, responded to the challenges presented by the representatives of an encroaching state apparatus by refashioning the boundaries of collective well-being to include royally appointed officials assigned to their territories. This process both helped ensure the continued significance of these leaders and also shaped the contours of the Ganda state itself. Royal appointees could never succeed in their endeavors without the participation of the members of the communities residing in their assigned territories, and in the absence of a permanent and centralized standing army as a means of enforcing that participation, the "king's men" necessarily relied on the organizing capacities of local leaders.[94]

The last major phase of Buganda's territorial expansion occurred in the late eighteenth and early nineteenth centuries. During this period, the *bakabaka* Jjunju and Ssemakookiro conquered the resource-rich territory of Buddu, to the south of Gomba, Butambala, and Mawokota (see map 7). As mentioned earlier, Jjunju's immediate motivation for annexing Buddu was to acquire control over the territory's fertile banana plantations and rich supplies of both iron and timber. Buddu's location at the center of a series of lucrative regional trade networks further added to its potential value for Ganda kings, and the southern part of the territory was also particularly noted for its production of the high-quality bark cloths favored by Ganda royalty. Control of Buddu also provided Buganda with more direct access to the large market in Karagwe and allowed the kingdom to gain control over the only land route for trade goods from the coast to northern Uganda.

Like the earlier phases of territorial expansion, the appropriation of Buddu involved military conquest as well as local political alliances. As was the case with Mawanda's excursions to the east and north, Jjunju's expansionist endeavors resulted in both the extension of clan networks based in the Ganda heartland and the consolidation of clans whose members resided predominantly in the newly acquired territory. Shortly after assuming the throne, for example, Jjunju entered into a blood-brotherhood with Kiganda (also known as Kajabaga), of Birongo, a member of the well-established Otter clan who maintained authority over a strategic crossing point of the Katonga River. The assistance Kiganda provided Jjunju's war party endeared him to the kabaka as well as to his fellow clanmates, and Kiganda eventually acquired a prestigious position as the head of a prominent lineage within the Otter clan.[95] Similarly, the Lion clan managed to augment its existing networks of wealth and knowledge during this period by acquiring the estate of Bukkakata. The clan incorporated this fertile area and its residents into its organizational infrastructure by bestowing upon the community's leader the status of head of a maximal patrilineage and working him into the clan's history as a son of the clan's founder, Namuguzi.[96]

While Jjunju's and Ssemakookiro's expansionist endeavors in Buddu provided the opportunity to extend existing clan networks based in the Ganda heartland, the consolidation of local communities into officially recognized clans played an even greater role in Buddu's successful incorporation into the kingdom. The villages surrounding the resource-rich area of Kasaka, for instance, witnessed the emergence of the principal and secondary estates for several clans, including the Crow, Porch Water, and Heart clans.[97] The integration of the Buddu clans provided the kingdom with a network of skilled individuals, most notably in the areas of bark-cloth making and ironworking. Members of the Crow and Porch Water clans specialized in bark-cloth production, while prominent Cow clan leaders in the territory included a network of well-known blacksmiths. These artisans drew upon their talents to acquire prestigious royal duties in the service of the kabaka.[98] In this regard, the clan concept served as a vehicle for the addition of networks of skilled individuals to the Ganda state. Buganda's rulers recognized Buddu's regional commerce as a significant source of potential wealth, and their efforts to gain control over this resource-rich region included the incorpora-tion of the territory's communities into the kingdom as clans with a stake in the Ganda state apparatus.

The reconfiguration of existing clan networks and the emergence of new clans in eighteenth-century Buganda also enabled communities to insulate themselves from the considerable threats posed by an increase in state-sponsored violence. In her reconsideration of the momentous changes in Ganda political culture that accompanied the kingdom's territorial expan-sion, Hanson describes the eighteenth century as a profoundly destabilizing period characterized by an escalation in violence and the substantial influx on nonfree persons.[99] As mentioned earlier, Hanson's focus on the social disorder and political crisis stemming from the escalating violence that accompanied Buganda's territorial expansion offers an important revision of the triumphalist version of eighteenth-century Ganda history found in most scholarly accounts. Her insights also provide an appropriate frame-work within which to consider the question why a significant number of Ganda clans seem to have emerged during this tumultuous period.

While Hanson correctly notes that state-sponsored violence destabilized older concepts and practices of obligation, I have demonstrated throughout this chapter that these violent campaigns also inspired the development of new forms of community building as well as creative innovations to deeply embedded practices. The emergence of new clans and the reconfiguration of existing clan networks in eighteenth-century Buganda represented just such an effort. While drawing on the discourse and practices of older forms of clanship, these new clans differed from earlier ones in their focus on estab-lishing connections to the royal center. As Buganda expanded, clanship was a means by which communities could plug into the state structure by mak-ing the collective efforts of clan members indispensable to the kingdom's well-being. In a sense, however, the process of clan formation during this period both served as a form of protection from state-sponsored violence for vulnerable communities and also facilitated its continuation. For while membership in a clan located individuals within social networks that helped guard against the possibility of becoming war captives, the inability to gain membership exposed the vulnerabilities of particular individuals or commu-nities and may have singled them out for possible attack. The securing of captives in Buganda during the kingdom's territorial expansion in the eigh-teenth and early nineteenth centuries involved establishing the boundaries separating insiders from outsiders, a process in which the ideology and practices of clanship played a crucial role.

CONCLUSION

The process of state formation in Buganda reinforced and transformed existing community-building practices. The creation of royal medicines such as Mbajjwe and Musisi, the nationalization of clan-based spiritual entities, and the incorporation of preexisting forms of knowledge and practices into more recently devised royal rituals all allowed communities to participate in increasingly ambitious royal undertakings from the late seventeenth to the early nineteenth century. The emergence of new clans and the broadening of existing clan networks during this period facilitated Buganda's growth and contributed to the extension of deeply embedded notions of collective well-being toward an increasingly larger and more complex political body. The clan concept served as a powerful tool for organizing societies, creating alliances, and promoting collective health, and Buganda's aspiring leaders drew upon this coordinating principle in their efforts to craft the Ganda state. Throughout this process, some of the core concepts and practices of public healing—the significance of territorial spirits, the authority associated with firstcomer status, and the capacity of mediums to steer the content of a community's moral economy—remained critical for the legitimization of rule during Buganda's territorial expansion.

conclusion

In January 2007 I had the unexpected opportunity to return to Uganda for a quick, three-week visit. At the top of my list of people I wanted to contact during this short stay was Morris Ssekintu, a man who had been instrumental in the construction and curation of the Uganda Museum in the mid-1950s. An artist by training, Ssekintu designed and built many of the models that fill the museum's interior to this day. I had actually met Ssekintu five years earlier while conducting my dissertation research, when I had spoken with him at length about the history of the Lion clan. Upon rereading the transcript of our conversation several years later, I noticed that Ssekintu had mentioned in passing that he had worked as a research assistant for Michael Nsimbi in the early 1950s. In addition to serving as an inspector of schools, Nsimbi conducted extensive research on Ganda history and culture. His efforts culminated in the 1956 publication of *Amannya Amaganda N'Ennono Zaago* (Ganda names and their origins), in which Nsimbi presents a wealth of information on the origins and meanings of Ganda names as well as on the histories of Buganda's clans. Ssekintu's casual reference to his role as Nsimbi's assistant, which as mentioned earlier caught my attention only several years after our conversation, led me to reconsider the circumstances surrounding the production of historical knowledge contained in the works composed by the second and third generation of literate Baganda intellectuals. Despite drawing quite extensively upon *Amannya Amaganda* in my work, I had not considered the process of its production nearly as closely as I had the works produced by the first generation of literate Baganda, such as Apolo Kaggwa and James Miti (see chapter 2). I therefore contacted Ssekintu in the hope that he might provide some insights into the motivation behind his and Nsimbi's endeavors, the research process itself, and the reception of Nsimbi's work in Ganda communities.

Ever the gracious host, Ssekintu suggested that we meet at the Uganda Museum, a place in which he continues to take obvious pride given his contribution to its design and construction. After we exchanged greetings and renewed our acquaintance, I explained to Ssekintu that I was interested in learning about how he had come to assist Nsimbi in his research and about his experiences in this capacity. Ssekintu began by describing how as a young man he had honed his natural artistic talents at Makerere College, where his gifts drew the attention of Buganda's officials and eventually resulted in their commissioning him to design Buganda's flag.[1] A few years later he received a commission to design a display at the Uganda Museum, which at that time was located on Makerere Hill. After working for a couple of years at the East African Literature Bureau and the Coryndon Museum in Nairobi, Ssekintu returned to Uganda in 1953 to help move the Uganda Museum from Makerere Hill to its current location in a suburb of Kampala. The knowledge of early Ugandan history and culture that he displayed in constructing the models for the new museum drew the attention of Nsimbi, who eventually asked Ssekintu to assist him in his ongoing research.

Ssekintu explained that he respected Nsimbi's research methods because Nsimbi insisted on visiting a place before he spoke or wrote about it. He said that when they visited a site, "I would collect the material artifacts and Nsimbi would collect the words—the stories. The material artifacts were very important as far as the museum was concerned and the words— the information—made them even richer. They were complementary—what I did and what he did. So we joined forces." Ssekintu cited as an example their visit to the Ssese Islands. A young man named Ssebaduka, who was knowledgeable in the techniques of conservation, accompanied Ssekintu and Nsimbi on this outing, during which they collected information related to the many shrine centers located on the islands. "I was of the opinion that when we found a cult still active," Ssekintu recalled, "we should not take things away but rather advise people if we saw them engaging in practices that were ruining the regalia." Ssekintu recollected that he, Nsimbi, and Ssebaduka found themselves in an interesting position: that of Baganda fully literate in Ganda culture who did not engage in many of the practices they were interested in documenting. In a revealing statement about how they situated themselves as researchers of Ganda culture and history, Ssekintu explained that "we did not take away their regalia because we thought that if there was a drought we would be blamed. Instead, we advised them how to preserve the materials."

Intellectuals such as Nsimbi and Ssekintu did more, however, than simply "collect the words" and advise shrine keepers on how to "preserve the materials." Like the first generation of literate Baganda scholars, they occupied the position of "middle figures" who served as translators, both literally and figuratively, of Ganda culture and history for an audience that extended beyond the boundaries of Buganda.[2] But in the process of presenting their findings (whether in written form or, in the case of Ssekintu, in the form of models created for the Uganda Museum to educate the viewing public on early Ugandan history), figures such as Ssekintu struggled, in a more self-conscious manner than such predecessors as Kaggwa and Miti, to reconcile their personal upbringing as members of the educated elite (and often as practicing Christians or Muslims) with their understanding of Ganda cultural practices. When I asked him what sorts of information he had gathered during his visits to shrine centers in the early 1950s, Ssekintu explained that he had discovered that "a bit of information had been presented wrongly, though not necessarily deliberately." He then pointed to the example of the *lubaale* Kibuuka, whose history and connection to the Sheep clan I discussed in chapter 5:

> At Mbaale—Kibuuka's home—we found out that Kibuuka was a man, not a god. Even his relics are here [in the museum]—the bones. . . . People like Kibuuka, Mukasa, Kawumpuli, and Nende [some of the principal *lubaale* in Buganda] were people who were gifted in a particular area. All of these were people who once lived on earth. They ate food. Kibuuka was a warrior and when he died a cult was left in his name to assist people in the field of warfare. There are all sorts of misunderstanding [on these matters], whether intended or a genuine ignorance. Kibuuka is not a god. He is a *lubaale*.

Ssekintu's insistence that Kibuuka, Mukasa, Kawumpuli, and Nende are *lubaale* rather than gods points to the difficulties involved in translating Ganda ideas about health and the manner in which most commentators, both Baganda and foreigners, have sought to interpret healing practices within a religious—frequently Christian—idiom. When asked to further explain what he meant by insisting that Kibuuka was a *lubaale* rather than a god, Ssekintu responded:

> Many people who go to church also visit these places [*lubaale* shrines] because they may be connected with relatives. The two seem not to conflict, especially when you look at things in the real way—not to call Kibuuka a god but as a man who lived, had a brother, and so on and had particular skills. The people at these places often give advice similar to what you hear from a social worker or psychologist or something like that. Sometimes things are shrouded in things that someone from a different culture might not understand. . . . For example, a healer would give someone a bundle of beans as medicine and tell them to rub a tablet on the stone, mix it with water, put one bean in the mixture, and then

drink. In the morning the healer said to throw the bean away toward the sun. This prevented overdoses since when the bundle of beans was finished you had to get a new supply. And as you come back the healer checks on you to see if there was some improvement and if you need a new medication. These were controls. But many people don't recognize this. They say, "what does this stone have to do with that medicine, with malaria?" All of these things were somehow misinterpreted.

By pointing to the fact that the practices endorsed by officials at *lubaale* shrines served as "controls," Ssekintu sought to highlight the practical aspects of activities that have often been "misinterpreted" as irrational or superstitious when viewed within a religious framework. The misinterpretation that Ssekintu referred to stems in large measure from the use of analogies to describe Ganda healing practices, an interpretive strategy that Ssekintu himself had difficulty avoiding or overcoming. In the excerpt of our conversation quoted above, for instance, Ssekintu compared the *lubaale* shrine to a church and noted that "the people at these places [*lubaale* shrines] often give advice similar to what you hear from a social worker or psychologist or something like that." He may have made these comparisons because he was speaking in English to a foreigner. Yet by this point in our conversation Ssekintu was well aware that I had visited many shrines and was familiar with their practices. Moreover, I have on many occasions heard Baganda employ similar comparisons when speaking to each other in Luganda. These sorts of discussions illustrate the extent to which ideas about Ganda healing rarely surface in and of themselves in conversations between nonpractitioners, as well as that practitioners consistently draw upon analogies to explain their practices to nonpractitioners. In these conversations there is usually a reference point, whether religious or, more increasingly, biomedical. As one healer explained to me when describing the types of healers who diagnose through spirit possession, "Then there are those who say that before I treat you I have to first consult with the spirits. This is another way of treating, just like the modern x-ray, for he has to know what lies beyond."[3]

I ended my conversation with Ssekintu by asking him about the reception Nsimbi's most well-known publication, *Amannya Amaganda*, has received in Buganda. He answered, "It is respected. Even now people still know who Nsimbi is." This response confirmed the impression I had received several years earlier when more than a few people expressed their admiration for Nsimbi and drew upon his work as a reference point during our conversations about clan histories. Yet despite this continued respect and the wealth of information contained within it, *Amannya Amaganda* has never been translated into English. For most foreign scholars, as well as many Baganda, *The Kings of Buganda*, M. S. M. Kiwanuka's 1971 English translation of Apolo Kaggwa's *Bakabaka b'e Buganda*, continues to serve as the principal source for early Ganda history. Kiwanuka undertook this project at the suggestion of Roland Oliver, his supervisor at the School of Oriental and African Studies. His translation of Kaggwa's dynastic history constituted part of a broader research project on Ganda history conducted during a period when scholars felt the urgency, in Kiwanuka's words, "to collect and record all traditions before they are lost or become too contaminated." The collection and transcription of these traditions, however, did not automatically solve the problem of the dearth of sources for writing precolonial African histories. As Kiwanuka noted in the preface to his translation,

> The main barrier in the studying of tribal histories is linguistic. It is a problem which affects Africans as well as non-Africans. Given that most researchers have no time to learn the vernacular languages, the only obvious and practical alternative is to translate the oral traditions in the languages of learning such as English and French and make them available to the world of learning. Translations must be followed by critical studies, otherwise the study of the pre-colonial history of Africa will continue to lend itself to easy generalization.[4]

The process of translation, then, often served as the first step in the use of oral traditions to compose histories of precolonial Africa. Far from a value-free exercise, however, translation often involves acts of interpretation that have consequences for the ways scholars employ a translated text. Kiwanuka acknowledged these difficulties:

> It is possible [either] to translate a text word for word, or to give it a free interpretation. Free translations, however, tend to obliterate the form of thinking and character of the original writer, while the only danger of a word for word translation is that it reads clumsily. I have tried to strike a balance between the two, because I believe that translations of learned texts should still bear the imprint of the original writer.[5]

Striking the appropriate balance between "free interpretation" and "word for word" translation is a difficulty that I imagine every translator confronts. For the purposes of the current discussion, however, the significance of this process lies in the decisions regarding which English terms to employ for Luganda terms that have no direct or obvious translation. In Kiwanuka's translation, for example, *lubaale* become "gods." Such translations have the potential to result in the sorts of "misunderstandings" to which Ssekintu referred in our conversation, and they also have broader ramifications with respect to subsequent historical analysis. The religion-state dichotomy, for instance, pervades analyses of the relationship between Ganda kings and "religious officials" in most scholarship on early Ganda history. This analytical approach stems in part from the translation decisions made by intermediary figures such as Kiwanuka and, as should be clear by now, often results in misleading historical interpretations.

In an effort to learn more about the translation of Apolo Kaggwa's *Bakabaka b'e Buganda*, I scheduled an appointment to meet with Kiwanuka shortly after my conversation with Ssekintu. Kiwanuka left the academy many years ago and at the time of our meeting was the minister of state for finance, planning, and economic development. When we met in his government office, Kiwanuka proved reluctant (or perhaps too busy, given his demanding schedule) to discuss the translation process other than to offer the tantalizing comment that dissatisfaction with his initial translation had led him to scrap the entire first draft. He did, however, express an interest, or at least a mild curiosity, in my research. I explained that I was writing a book on early Ganda history, specifically on the history of clanship and healing, and had spent considerable time speaking to various people about these matters. After listening to the brief description of my project, Kiwanuka responded, "There are no traditions remaining in the villages. You might speak to an old man in the village and he will tell you what he has read in a book or maybe even pull out a book and read from it."[6]

In many respects, Kiwanuka's response was similar to the reactions I had often received from skeptical or sometimes inquisitive academics, both Ugandans and outsiders. A typical reaction from Ugandan historians upon learning about my research interests might be, "But what else can we learn about Buganda? So many others have already studied the kingdom's history. The traditions have been collected. What else is out there?" Non-Ugandan historians, in particular non-Africanist historians, often react by posing probing—and entirely appropriate—questions about the use of oral material collected in the early twenty-first century to write a history of the seventeenth and eighteenth centuries. Like Kiwanuka, many historians with whom I have discussed my work have expressed concerns regarding the infiltration of oral traditions by widely circulated written accounts of Buganda's past.

These are all legitimate and well-founded concerns. On several occasions I listened patiently while people living in rural villages, as well as those residing in more urban areas surrounding Kampala, read to me from books or pamphlets—most often Kaggwa's *Bakabaka* or one of Nsimbi's Luganda-language publications—in response to my inquiries about the history of their clan, a particular spirit, or a shrine site. Even more people referred over the course of our conversations to written texts not in their possession. Rather than reading or referencing these texts as definitive sources for the particular topic under discussion, however, some people used them to initiate conversations about misunderstandings or oversights in the best-known and most widely circulating written accounts of Buganda's past. In some instances these sorts of responses were in answer to probing questions from me about either the text under discussion or why a particular issue was absent from the text. These discussions revealed the ways in which local intellectuals in contemporary Buganda sometimes disagreed with their predecessors' portrayals of the kingdom's past. Written accounts of Buganda's history, in other words, served as a reference or starting point for productive discussions. In this manner, the intertwining of the oral and the written, along with my searching and sometimes suggestive questions, contributed in crucial ways to the production of knowledge and the uncovering of alternative perspectives onto Buganda's past.

As stressed throughout this book, one of the alternative perspectives that emerged over the course of my inquiries into the history of clanship concerned the role of public healers and the concept of public healing—the idea that groups of individuals perceive the pursuit of well-being as a collective endeavor—in determining Buganda's contours and character. As illustrated in chapters 2–4, focusing the analytical lens on the connected histories of clanship and public healing opens the door for a more thorough examination of historical periods that preceded the development of the Ganda state. Because of the emphasis on the role of kings and their royal representatives in the existing literature, a sense of inevitability often pervades discussions of the more distant Ganda past. Because Buganda eventually emerged as a centralized state, scholars have been tempted to treat prestate developments from the restrictive perspective of their contribution to this centralizing process.

I have sought to overcome this teleology by examining the relationship between changes in deeply rooted notions of collective well-being and the enlargement of political communities. Beginning about the sixteenth century, the transformation of previously territorial spirits into portable spiritual entities enlarged the range and effectiveness of healing networks. This process allowed for the extension of the power and authority associated with specific shrines and territories and facilitated the development of complex communities in the areas surrounding the northwestern shores of Lake Victoria. By mobilizing various kinds of knowledge into therapeutic networks whose range extended well beyond the territories in which their principal shrines were located, portable spirits and their earthly representatives drew together dispersed communities in an effort to ensure the collective well-being of increasingly larger publics. This reconfiguration of the boundaries of public healing occurred during a period of gradual yet ultimately dramatic social and economic change that coincided with the development of land-intensive banana farming. The gradual transition to intensive banana farming presented opportunities for permanent settlement and the accumulation of wealth in the form of perennially fruiting banana trees. These opportunities, which rendered bananas a potentially lucrative long-term investment, were accompanied by increasing social tensions revolving around property inheritance and succession. The effective arrangement of various forms of knowledge distributed over wide geographical areas served as a way for communities living along the northwestern shores of Lake Victoria to meet these challenges. The establishment of these networks of knowledge resulted in the formation of more efficacious social and productive networks and offered a means of alleviating the pressures generated by increasing competition for the best banana-bearing lands.

At the core of this process stood the language and practices of clanship, which allowed increasingly larger groups of people to conceive of their relationships to one another in unprecedented ways. The activities undertaken at shrines located on discontiguous estates facilitated the forging of relationships between groups of people who did not necessarily share face-to-face interactions, and the composition of clan histories cemented these widespread therapeutic networks into social collectivities. Rather than accounts of reified institutions, these histories constituted part and parcel of the clan-formation process. By mobilizing various bodies of knowledge in an effort to ensure social health, the webs of shrines situated on what would become clan lands—and the creation of narratives to describe the relationship between these shrines—forged a powerful connection between clan-ship, collective health, and the effective composition of knowledge.

The intimate relationship between public healing and politics evident in the earliest processes of clan formation in Buganda continued to inform political practices in the seventeenth century, which witnessed a further increase in the scale of political action. During this period, the social composition of knowledge situated at the heart of the earliest processes of clan formation shaped the contours of the increasingly larger publics for which political leaders sought to provide collective well-being. Efforts to establish control over expanding regional trade networks, direct morally legitimate forms of violence, and provide protection from disease together determined the contours of the broader political arena in seventeenth-century Buganda. These undertakings were led by those initiated spirit mediums whose compositional talents—their ability to draw together the various skills required to ensure the collective health of potential followers—and expertise in establishing successful relationships with the appropriate spiritual entities rendered them effective political leaders. Their efforts drew together and combined the networks of knowledge embedded within a number of clans, a compositional process that resulted in the development of an increasingly larger and more sophisticated political arena.

In addition to directing attention to the relatively understudied periods preceding the emergence of the Ganda state, an examination of clanship and public healing also provides new insights into the process of state formation from the late seventeenth to the early nineteenth century. This process reinforced and transformed existing community-building practices by directing efforts to promote collective well-being toward a more muscular political center. The creation of royal medicines, the nationalization of clan-based spiritual entities, and the incorporation of preexisting forms of knowledge and practices into more recently devised royal rituals all enabled communities to participate in increasingly ambitious royal undertakings. Rather than succumbing to royal ambitions, however, clans directly participated in and shaped the kingdom's development. The emergence of new clans and the extension of existing clan networks coincided with Buganda's territorial expansion, and clans took new forms as communities adapted familiar practices to new circumstances. As Buganda expanded, the process of clan formation provided a way for communities to plug themselves into the state structure by making the collective efforts of their members indispensable to the kingdom's well-being.

Despite displaying continuities with previous practices of community building, however, the eighteenth century also witnessed a momentous change in the character of political practices in Buganda. Unlike political leaders in the sixteenth and seventeenth centuries, the kings who reigned in the eighteenth century did not exercise their authority through the practice of spirit possession. Their authority rested elsewhere, most significantly in their control over the means of violence. The gradual institutionalization of the divide between the power of kings and the capacities of public healers, however, did not result in the frequently observed process of royal domination. As Ganda kings and their representatives sought to direct deeply embedded practices of public healing toward royal ends, they were forced to contend with forms of authority and political practices in which they were not necessarily the central actors and over which they could never assume complete control. The state-building efforts of Ganda kings and royal officials necessarily relied in part on the efforts of the mediums, priests, and diviners who occupied strategic positions of semantic creativity, directed the flow of moral discourse, and shaped the boundaries of collective prosperity. These figures drew upon their authority in the realm of public healing to both shape and claim a stake in the instrumentally powerful kingship that emerged over the course of the eighteenth century. In so doing, they contributed to Buganda's political development in a far more significant manner than most historians have recognized.

The focus on the relationship between public healing and political complexity discussed in this book provides some new possibilities for researching and writing histories of precolonial Africa. Many of the core images and symbolic referents related to the history of public healing in Buganda appear throughout much of Bantu-speaking Africa. In chapter 5, for example, I examined the royal-installation rites that took place at Buddo Hill beginning in the second half of the eighteenth century. These rites culminated with the king-elect ascending the anthill Nakibuuka, where he received the royal spear and was exhorted to behave in a kingly fashion. As Kairn Klieman describes in her eloquent study of what she terms the "Ideology of the Primordial Batwa," historical actors in West Central Africa employed termite hills in a variety of ritual contexts, including initiation rites for fertility cults, practices designed to placate lineage ancestors, and ceremonies performed by rain specialists. These hills serve for West Central Africans as "receptacles for ancestral first-comer spirits who control the fecundity and fertility of people and land," an association that, as Klieman notes, reaches beyond

West Central Africa and appears among Bantu-speaking peoples living in areas stretching from the southern Central African Republic to Zambia.[7]

In addition to termite hills, several other key concepts and symbolic referents—the importance of twins, conical shrines with eternally burning sacred fires, physical abnormality as a sign of enhanced spiritual status—of public healing practices in Buganda appear among Bantu-speaking populations in West Central Africa and beyond. To cite just one example, West Central Africans, like Baganda and other Great Lakes communities, associated the continued well-being of both people and land with the supplication of territorial spirits that resided in particular locales such as caves and, most often, bodies of water. The more specific conceptual overlap between territorial spirits, pythons, and sacred bodies of water found in Buganda also is found well beyond the Great Lakes region. In *River of Blood*, his important study of the Mbona cult, in the Shire Valley of contemporary Malawi, for instance, Matthew Schoffeleers states that the site of the cult's ritual center originally housed an influential rain shrine dedicated to the High God Chiuta in his python manifestation. Many Bantu-speaking communities throughout south-central Africa make similar associations between pythons, rain, and territorial spirits.[8] As public arenas that provided—and in some cases continue to provide—a forum for debates about issues of communal importance, the territorial cults of south-central Africa, like those in the Great Lakes region and West Central Africa, played a vital role in shaping public consciousness by stressing the connection between a community's moral economy and conditions in the material world.

These brief examples represent just a few of the many conceptual and symbolic overlaps between public healing practices in Buganda (and the Great Lakes region more generally) and elsewhere in Bantu-speaking Africa. Far from coincidence, these overlaps suggest a wider history of public healing—and of the relationship between public healing and political complexity—originating deep in Africa's ancient past. By focusing on the practices of public healing and their supporting institutions, which ranged across the ethnically infused spatial boundaries that dominate our perceptions of contemporary Africa, we gain a revealing vision of the political and social landscape of earlier periods. Drawing on his observation about the symbolic, conceptual, and institutional connections between territorial cults in south-central Africa, Schoffeleers presented a bold vision of "an interlocking complex, relating neighboring societies with one another in a manner which in theory at least knows no boundaries." He compared this complex to "a net cast over the Central African landscape," which "may be torn and rent in places but which somehow hangs together."[9] The conceptual and practical threads that shaped this net, as well as similar ones in other parts of the continent, deserve careful historical examination, for their textures and patterns provide critical insights into the motivations behind much political activity in the distant African past.

Focusing the analytical lens on public healing moves us away from what T. C. McCaskie has described as the "kings and princes" approach, which dominated the studies of precolonial Africa produced by many in the pioneering generation of African historians in the 1960s. Guided in part by the imperatives of reconstructing the historical legacies of newly independent nations, these "barebones political histor[ies]" cast ruling elites and the polities over which they presided at the heart of narratives about the past. These histories "distanced themselves from and substantially abandoned the concerns of anthropology—belief and religion, language and discourse, kinship and culture, and all the rest," a "fatal error" that resulted, in McCaskie's words, in "a curiously disembodied and superficial form of knowledge that lacked any resonant depth." The task of transforming "barebones political history" into social history requires that historians of precolonial Africa examine the activities of historical actors who were often overlooked in what McCaskie described as "ideologically simple and unproblematic tale[s] of great empires, states and government."[10]

As McCaskie has noted in a more recent article, one consequence of the relative lack of attention to precolonial African history over the past two decades or so is that "what might yet be possible in researching this period remains indeterminate."[11] Examining transformations in public healing allows historians of precolonial Africa to view the development of the moral communities, such as those grounded in the social philosophy of health discussed in this study, which lay at the heart of political undertakings. In directing attention to transformations in these communities over extended periods of time, we shift attention away from the usual culprits in discussions of politics in precolonial Africa—powerful kings and chiefs—and instead highlight the importance of diffuse forms of power, as well as ritual and other types of knowledge, in achieving political complexity. This analytical shift illustrates, for example, that the notion of firstcomer status and the various types of spirits associated with the authority of firstcomers remained a crucial component in establishing political legitimacy even in places such as Buganda, where political centralization occurred. We must now incorporate what in the nineteenth century scholars called "superstition" and in the twentieth century became "religion" into our examinations of politics and the history of political complexity in precolonial Africa. As Wyatt MacGaffey has recently commented, if we restrict our sense of the political to "the use of material resources and secular or 'real' powers by leaders, officials, pressure groups, and armed forces," we lose sight of the extent to which factors such as the concept and practices of public healing discussed in this book were central to the experience of politics in many parts of Africa, both today and in the distant past.[12]

In 1900 the kingdom of Buganda signed a treaty with the British colonial government that laid the groundwork for the events of the next several decades. The Uganda Agreement was significant in that it accorded Buganda a privileged position in the Uganda Protectorate and allowed the kingdom to maintain a semi-autonomous status. In addition, the agreement marked the political victory of a particular group of Ganda leaders, the Protestant chiefs. For although the chiefs who benefited from the agreement included members of the Protestant, Catholic, and Muslim factions of chiefly authority, the dominant position within the ruling elite belonged to Apolo Kaggwa and his Protestant cohorts.

The roots of the Protestant ascent to power lay in the Buganda succession war of 1888–92, an extended battle between Protestant, Catholic, and Muslim aspirants for control of the kingship. The war culminated with the Battle of Mengo in 1892, in which the Protestants, led by Kaggwa and supported by British colonial forces headed by the eminent Frederick Lugard, took control of the kingdom. In the aftermath of the civil war, the Protestants—the smallest of the parties—secured the dominant position in the Uganda Protectorate declared by the British in 1893. The ascent of the Protestants resulted in the confinement of Muslim influence to a remote section of the country and forced the Catholics, the party with the largest number of adherents, to accept a minority position in the political system. After an unsuccessful rebellion in 1897 by Kabaka Mwanga, who was at that point little more than a puppet leader, Kaggwa led the Christian chiefs in the installation of the one-year-old Daudi Chwa to the throne. Supported by colonial officials, Kaggwa then appointed himself as one of the *kabaka*'s regents, along with the Protestant Zakaria Kisingiri and the Catholic Stanislas Mugwanya.[13]

Kaggwa had risen to the forefront of Ganda politics, and the Uganda Agreement of 1900 reinforced his position as the primary wielder of authority in the kingdom. Under the terms of the agreement, Kaggwa and the other leading chiefs transformed the Lukiiko, the assembly of chiefs that prior to this period had gathered to attend to the whims of the *kabaka*, into a legislative body from which they dictated the kingdom's policies. Perhaps most importantly, these chiefs used their newly acquired positions of authority to redistribute land in the kingdom. The Uganda Agreement called for the distribution of freehold estates (*mailo*, literally "miles") and placed Buganda's leading chiefs in charge of the allocation of these plots. In a process that would have enduring and often unintended consequences, these chiefs and their followers received eight thousand square miles of some of the best land in the kingdom, drawn from the areas designated for Ganda use.[14]

Almost twenty years after the signing of the Uganda Agreement of 1900 and the allotment of freehold *mailo* estates, those left out of this redistribution process or displeased with its consequences mounted a challenge against the newly empowered chiefly elite. The case against *mailo* culminated with the establishment of the Protectorate Commission of Inquiry into Butaka Clan Lands in 1924. Those who protested what they viewed as the injustices committed by Buganda's political leaders presented themselves as disgruntled clan leaders and called themselves *bataka*, the owners of clan estates (*butaka*). As Holly Hanson has illustrated, however, the complainants were "not only *bataka* (clan elders), but also royal women and royal men, spirit mediums" and other wielders of authority who had lost influence during the first two decades of colonial rule, and their decision to portray themselves as the legitimate owners of confiscated clan lands was a strategic decision designed to make their arguments understandable to British officials. In her illuminating analysis of the case against *mailo*, Hanson describes the result of this process as a "complex conflict over power with diverse participants" that "became, in terms that made sense to colonial observers, a fight between clan elders who had lost land and appointed chiefs who had taken land." Yet behind this simplified presentation of their grievances, Hanson incisively observes, the *bataka* protesters mounted a "sustained and penetrating critique of colonial modernity" that extended beyond the issue of property rights and sought to reconcile individual land tenure with the notion that land as property should be attached to social concerns.[15]

Hanson's examination of the case against *mailo* convincingly demonstrates that the complaints voiced by the *bataka* protesters encompassed far more than the loss of clan lands and a call for the restoration of clan leaders to positions of political authority. The manner in which the *bataka* presented their arguments, however, nevertheless had an enduring impact on the character of clanship in Buganda. The distribution of freehold plots in the early twentieth century and the ensuing public protests in the 1920s led to significant shifts in the meaning of clanship and the nature of the possibilities embedded in the clan concept in twentieth-century Buganda. At the same time that members of the *bataka* movement were mounting a challenge to the newly empowered chiefly elite in the name of clanship, Ganda clans became embroiled in a series of internal disputes. The language and form of argumentation employed in these disputes capture the manner in which clanship became implicated in a broader set of transformations affecting Buganda in the first three decades of the twentieth century. A case concerning the origin and leadership of the Oribi Antelope clan serves to illustrate this point.

In January 1915 Eriya Sekamwa brought a case against Zakayo Naduli before Buganda's parliament, the Lukiiko. Sekamwa accused Zakayo Naduli of falsely attributing the clan's origins to Kayimbyobutega, of Kiwawu in Busujju, and also of fraudulently claiming that he, as the successor to Kayimbyobutega, was the head of the clan. Sekamwa countered these assertions, which Naduli presented in a book he had written about the clan's history, by explaining that the Oribi Antelope clan had originated on Bubiro Hill, in Kyaggwe, and had been founded by Kiggye. After listening to testimony from both sides, the Lukiiko court ruled in favor of Sekamwa and provided a series of explanatory points supporting its judgment.

In the eyes of the court's members, the case turned on the quality and nature of the evidence presented by Sekamwa and Naduli in support of their respective ancestries. While both men discussed their places of origin, only Sekamwa introduced to the court his forefather (*jjajja*), who lived at the founding estate at Bubiro Hill and claimed Sekamwa as his child. In addition, Sekamwa described in detail his predecessors' place of birth and the areas they had passed through before settling on Bubiro Hill, which several witnesses testified was the site for the performance of the clan's most important ceremonies. Naduli, on the other hand, claimed Kiwawu as the place of origin and principal estate for the Oribi Antelope clan, but he failed to introduce a *mutaka* (caretaker) who looked after the estate. Furthermore, Kiwawu did not contain a memorial (*ekijjukizo*) indicating its significance for the clan. While Naduli stated in his testimony that the bodies of twelve previous heads of clan were buried at the estate, he could not show their burial sites and attributed this inability to the fact that no caretaker remained at the estate, a custom that deviated from common practice in other clans. The court also noted that unlike Sekamwa, Naduli failed to provide a reason for his predecessors' departure from the principal estate without leaving a caretaker behind and provided no proof that any of the clan ceremonies performed to respect the clan's ancestors were carried out at Kiwawu.

In the face of these disparities in evidence, the Lukiiko court felt obliged to side with "the person who speaks of a place with a caretaker [mutaka] rather than one who is his own forefather [oli ayejjajja yekka]." Zakayo Naduli, the court remarked, was "like a well or river without a source—the water flows but comes from nowhere." "What kind of river is that?" the court asked, and then it explained that Naduli's claim that Kiwawu served as the clan's place of origin appeared fraudulent because he possessed no forefather to support his claim. According to the court, Naduli found himself "without anybody to hold his hand," and since "in Ganda customs a person is understood by his ancestry," its members felt compelled to rule that the Oribi Antelope clan had originated from a common ancestor, Kiggye, rather than from an "empty place" as claimed by Naduli.[16]

The case of Eriya Sekamwa versus Zakayo Naduli concerning the origins of the Oribi Antelope clan illustrates the most common and public way in which the discourse and practices of clanship became embroiled in the social tensions that consumed Buganda during the first three decades of the twentieth century. Naduli's inability both to find a sufficiently large and influential network of clanmates to support his claims to the clan's headship and to prove his heritage through the display of ancestral burial sites was the principal reason for his defeat in the Lukiiko court. His failure to present a founding ancestor to claim him as a child rendered him, in the words of the court, "like a well or river without a source." The Lukiiko's explanation of its decision in favor of Sekamwa illustrates that genealogical reckoning and the display of burial sites became a compelling form of argumentation in the legal disputes between clanmates that engulfed colonial Buganda. During this period, genealogical reckoning became, at least in the courtroom setting, a mode of argumentation designed to achieve prominent positions within clan networks, to gain access to the freehold plots that accompanied such distinctions, and ultimately to reap the benefits derived from a more privatized form of land ownership. In their efforts to situate themselves favorably in the arguments over inheritance and succession, in other words, clan leaders sought to crystallize clan histories and practices into a corpus of knowledge that they could deploy in the legal arena. One consequence was that the dynamic capacities of clans and the more expansive ways of thinking about clanship—a topic explored throughout this book—narrowed significantly in these courtroom settings.

In some respects, the effects of the internal clan disputes that emerged in the 1920s continue to dominate many aspects of clan politics in contemporary Buganda. The coronation of Ronald Muwenda Mutebi as the thirty-sixth kabaka of Buganda on July 31, 1993, marked the official restoration of the monarchy following more than two decades of political instability in Uganda.[17] As part of his efforts to restore Buganda's institutions, Kabaka Mutebi reinstituted the Court of the Prime Minister of the Assembly, otherwise known as Kisekwa's court, which was responsible for hearing cases regarding disputes over clan leadership. In an announcement made at Sharing Hall, in Nsambya on June 25, 1992, Mutebi declared that while Kisekwa's court would once again hold hearings, cases previously ruled upon by his predecessors could not be brought forward again unless an appeal was still pending. The announcement resulted in the filing of a series of suits, many dating from the first part of the twentieth century. The records of these cases, heard almost eighty years after the members of the bataka movement began to agitate about lost clan lands in the 1920s, reveal that some of the broader social transformations initiated during the early colonial period have had enduring effects on the language and practices of clanship in Buganda. At the core of these cases lies the principle of hereditary rights and the burning issue of land ownership. When a group of elderly leaders in the Crow clan sought to dismiss the clan's young leader on account of his disrespectful and offensive behavior, for example, Kisekwa's court refused to acknowledge the leader's actions as grounds for dismissal, noting that "in Ganda clan traditions, the clan head is not chosen for his capabilities but rather according to his ancestry [obuzaale]."[18] In all of its rulings, the court's guiding principle was that "all appointments must follow the proper hereditary line of inheritance," and its members consistently stressed the significance of proving one's ancestry.

A thorough account of the history of the clan concept in twentieth-century Buganda, however, must consider the different fate of clanship beyond these courts, and here I can offer only some tentative comments based on observations of contemporary clan practices. Ganda clans have been reinvigorated by their king's return from exile. The restoration of the Ganda kingdom has led to a renewed interest in clanship and the capacity of clan networks to contribute to the collective well-being of Buganda's citizens. Most clans hold regular meetings—usually once a month—at schoolhouses, churches, shops, *butaka* estates, and other venues scattered throughout Kampala and beyond. I attended many such gatherings, during which attendees discussed matters related to inheritance, organized last funeral-rites ceremonies, devised campaigns for raising funds for educational scholarships, formulated plans for developing clan lands, and organized public events such as formal introductions to the *kabaka* and the annual coronation celebration.[19]

In some respects these efforts resemble those of early clan leaders as recorded in Ganda clan histories. The leaders of clans and subsections of clans are people who possess specific and valuable sorts of knowledge, and the participation of these leaders and their followers in collective endeavors renders clanship a potentially effective means of promoting collective well-being, or in language perhaps more suited to policy concerns in contemporary Africa, "development." For instance, the current minister of health for Buganda, Nelson Kawalya, explained to me that he ran a vaccination campaign in Buganda through the clan leadership and clan networks. The inclusion of clan heads and other clan leaders in this campaign helped ease suspicions about vaccination, which many Baganda associate with family planning.[20] The difference between these and earlier efforts, of course, lies in the types of knowledge that have become highly valued. Many clan leaders in contemporary Buganda are well-educated, successful men who hold degrees in higher education obtained either in Uganda or abroad. Priests, bishops, and well-off Muslims who have made the pilgrimage to Mecca also hold clan leadership positions. These people possess the skills required to prosper in contemporary Uganda, and clanship serves as a way to organize and deploy these various skills for the collective good of clan members. In other words, while the types of knowledge marshaled through clan networks have changed dramatically over the past hundred years, these new forms of knowledge are employed as part of a compositional, community-building process with roots in the distant Ganda past.

How are we to understand these developments? What sorts of broader historical narratives should we draw upon in our efforts to interpret these transformations in Ganda practices of clanship over the course of the twentieth century? Viewed from the perspective of the long-standing connection between clanship and public healing presented in this study, these transformations might be regarded as part of the considerably deeper history of collective well-being in the region. In this formulation, the histories of Christianity, commodification, and development would be interwoven into broader historical narratives whose trajectory begins in the Great Lakes region. Such an analysis would offer a solution to the problem of representation in African history identified by Steven Feierman. In an important article about the incommensurability of African and European historical narratives, Feierman noted that while historians can situate twentieth-century studies about the spread of Christianity or the incorporation of a certain type commodity within broader narratives about the multiple varieties of Christianity or the longer history of commodities, we cannot place them within narratives grounded in Africa. The solution to this problem, Feierman argued, is to situate the currently disconnected stories about the experiences of African communities during the colonial period in historical narratives grounded in Africa.[21]

In composing the sorts of deep, Africa-based historical narratives suggested by Feierman, however, we must take care to avoid equating the need for such narratives with the ultimately futile quest for the ever-elusive "African voice."[22] Instead, these narratives should highlight the variety of discourses and practices that circulated in the distant African past and the shifting interactions between multiple forms of authority. In addition, rather than merely composing these narratives to counter European-centered macrohistories, we must recognize the possibility that the fundamental architecture of African historical narratives might differ from that of Europe-based narratives and that these differences have serious consequences for how we view Africa's pasts. Of perhaps equal importance, we must acknowledge the limitations that historians of the precolonial period face in producing narratives about the distant past. Because of the differences between the sorts of sources available to historians of modern Europe (or of colonial Africa, for that matter) and those available to historians of precolonial Africa, these narratives can never be entirely commensurate. The possibility of writing a historical ethnography of eighteenth-century Buganda, for example, simply does not present itself as a viable option given the sources at hand. As demonstrated in this book, however, we can produce historical narratives about the ideas and practices that informed broad transformations in the contours of African societies. And these deep, Africa-based historical narratives provide an appropriate platform for examining the reconfiguration of African societies that occurred in the twentieth century.[23]

GLOSSARY

butaka. Clan estate on which important ancestors were buried.

butaka bukulu. Principal clan estate.

cwezi (pl. *cwezi*). Spirit that could return from the underworld, where ancestral ghosts resided, even if it had no heir to look after in the world of the living.

cwezi kubándwa. Form of spirit possession involving cwezi.

ggulu. Sky.

jjajja. Grandparent; patriarch; ancestor; founder of a clan.

jjembe (pl. *mayembe*). Horned charm.

kabaka (pl. *bakabaka*). King.

kabbiro. Secondary totem.

kabona. Priest.

katikkiro. Prime minister.

kibuga. Capital.

kiggwa (pl. *biggwa*). Sacred site located on a clan estate; shrine found on principal clan estate; shrine of a lubaale.

kijja (pl. *bijja*). Burial ground.

kitongole (pl. *bitongole*). Chiefship created by the kabaka for a specific purpose.

kubándwa. To be possessed by a spirit.

kugema. To inoculate; immunize; ward off (disease, calamity).

kyoto (pl. *byoto*). Hearth.

lubaale (pl. *lubaale*). National spirit of Buganda; spirit whose efficacy reached beyond a particular locale.

lubiri. Palace.

lubuga. Queen sister.

lugero. Fable; story.

lukiiko. Gathering of chiefs in the courtyard of the king to discuss affairs; later, the parliament of the kingdom.

lunyiriri (pl. *nnyiriri*). Minor lineage within a clan; line; row.

magombe. Place of the dead; underworld.

mailo. Land controlled as private property, allotted in square miles.

matooke. Green banana eaten as a staple food.

mmándwa (pl. *bandwa*). Spirit medium; spirit that possesses a medium.

muganda (pl. *baganda*). Person of Buganda.

mulaguzi (pl. *balaguzi*). Diviner.

mulangira (pl. *balangira*). Prince.

mumbejja (pl. *bambejja*). Princess.

musambwa (pl. *misambwa*). Territorial spirit that usually appears in the form of a wild animal or resides in a feature of the natural environment.

musawo (pl. *basawo*). Healer; specialist in herbal treatments.

musiige (pl. *basiige*). Boy or girl serving as a page in the king's palace.

musujja. Fever.

mutaka (pl. *bataka*). Clan leader; guardian of a butaka.

mutuba (pl. *mituba*). Major lineage within a clan; fig tree.

muzimu (pl. *mizimu*). Ancestral ghost.

muziro (pl. *miziro*). Avoidance; totem.

mwoyo. Life force, soul.

nnamasole. Queen mother.

nsi. Earth; land.

ssabo (pl. *masabo*). Shrine.

ssaza (pl. *masaza*). Province.

ssiga (pl. *masiga*). Largest subdivision of a clan; maximal patrilineage; cooking stone.

notes

1. Public Healing, Political Complexity, and the Production of Knowledge

1. Ssalongo Benedicto Walusimbi, interview, 12 October 2001.
2. Ibid. Mulago hospital is the largest public hospital in Kampala.
3. George William Kalule, interviews, 29 September and 3 October 2001.
4. For an extremely useful introduction to the voluminous literature on Buganda, see Karlström, "Buganda." More recently published works on early Ganda history include Wrigley, *Kingship and State*; Richard Reid, *Political Power*; Hanson, *Landed Obligation*; and Médard, *Le royaume du Buganda*. For a historiographic review of the secondary literature, see Richard Reid, *Political Power*, 7–12.
5. Schoenbrun, "Past Whose Time Has Come."
6. For a discussion of how Ganda royal officials sought to fortify their positions of power during the early colonial period, see Kodesh, "Renovating Tradition." See also Twaddle, "On Ganda Historiography"; and Rowe, "Myth, Memoir, and Moral Admonition."
7. Like many early writers, Apolo Kaggwa tended to ignore the often significant distinction between doubled consonants, which carry a heavy sound in Luganda, and single consonants, which have a soft sound. Thus the prime minister spelled his name Kagwa, which I retain in citations and in the bibliographic entries, while using the now widely accepted form Kaggwa in the text.
8. See, e.g., Bikunya, *Ky'Abakama Ba Bunyoro*; K.W., "Kings of Bunyoro-Kitara," "The Kings of Bunyoro-Kitara. Part II," and "The Kings of Bunyoro-Kitara. Part III"; Nyakatura, *Abakama ba Bunyoro-Kitara (Anatomy of an African Kingdom)*; Lubogo, *History of Busoga*; and Katate and Kamugungunu, *Abagabe b'Ankole*.
9. Southwold, *Bureaucracy and Chiefship*; Kiwanuka, *History of Buganda* (quotation on iii); Wrigley, "Changing Economic Structure" and *Kingship and State*.
10. This continuity stems in part from the fact that much of this scholarship relied for sources on the works of earlier Ganda intellectuals. In his fascinating study of Buganda's early history, for example, Christopher Wrigley comments that his work "is in the main an extended commentary on Kagwa's *Kings*." Wrigley, *Kingship and State*, 7. Despite being published in 1996, Wrigley's book was the culmination of several decades of research in the region. In an effort to bring evidence other than oral traditions to the question of Buganda's early history, Benjamin Ray skillfully analyzes Ganda royal rituals to shed light on the kingdom's origins. Yet in so doing Ray accepts the orthodox accounts of dynastic traditions and presents a rather static account of the kingdom's development that does not allow for change until foreign influence. Ray, *Myth, Ritual, and Kingship*.
11. Richard Reid, *Political Power*; Hanson, *Landed Obligation*, ch. 3; Médard, *Le royaume du Buganda*.

12. McIntosh, "Pathways to Complexity," 4.

13. See, e.g., Guyer and Belinga, "Wealth in People"; Hanson, *Landed Obligation*; Apter, *Black Kings and Critics*; Packard, *Chiefship and Cosmology*; Feierman, *Peasant Intellectuals*; Newbury, *Kings and Clans*; McIntosh, *Beyond Chiefdoms*; and MacGaffey, *Religion and Society in Central Africa*.

14. Arens and Karp, introduction.

15. Kuper, "Lineage Theory," 92. Despite this pronouncement, Kuper explained that he did not expect the lineage model to be abandoned completely because it "suit[ed] modern notions of how primitive societies were organized" (92).

16. MacGaffey, "Changing Representations," 189, 198, 197. MacGaffey focuses in particular on Europeans' fascination with matriliny, but his comments apply more broadly to a preoccupation with lineality in general.

17. Ibid., 207.

18. Guyer and Belinga, "Wealth in People," quotation on 118.

19. Vansina, *Paths in the Rainforests*, 258. MacGaffey recognizes as much, noting that Kongo "have a clear idea of a corporate matrilineal clan subdivided into matrilineages, and think of their society as organized by a repetitive series of them." MacGaffey, "Changing Representations," 197. Justin Willis makes a similar point in his examination of clanship in western Uganda. Willis, "Clan and History in Western Uganda," 583–84.

20. Willis, "Clan and History in Western Uganda," 583. For examples of pioneering works on East Africa that drew upon the clan as a unit of analysis, although not always explicitly, see Ogot, *History of the Southern Luo*; Muriuki, *History of the Kikuyu*; and Katoke, *Karagwe Kingdom*.

21. Willis, "Clan and History in Western Uganda," 584–85. As Willis notes, this undertaking was embraced with particular enthusiasm by historians of Uganda, where the recurrence of clan names and totemic avoidances over a wide area hinted at the prospect of writing about the deep past as a "history of the clans" (584). For examples of Great Lakes histories that draw connections between clans in various parts of the region, see Buchanan, "Kitara Complex" and "Perceptions of Ethnic Interaction"; Cohen, *Historical Tradition of Busoga*; Hartwig, *Art of Survival in East Africa*; Rennie, "Precolonial Kingdom of Rwanda"; and d'Hertefelt, *Les clans du Rwanda ancien*.

22. Willis, "Clan and History in Western Uganda," 587.

23. The use of the kinship idiom as part of the language of clanship in many African communities, along with the fact that the terms designating "clan" in many African languages represent metaphorical extensions of meaning from "residence" or "home," reinforces this widespread conception.

24. Newbury, "Clans of Rwanda," 392.

25. Chrétien, *Great Lakes of Africa*, 88.

26. Ibid., 89; Newbury, "Clans of Rwanda," 391; d'Hertefelt, *Les clans du Rwanda ancien*, 391.

27. The number of clans in Buganda varies depending on whom one asks. These variations reflect ongoing disputes concerning whether some social groupings constitute separate clans or branches within a clan.

28. For the structure of Soga clans, see Cohen, *Historical Tradition of Busoga*, 6–12.

29. While no two clans share a secondary totem, a clan's secondary totem may serve as the primary totem for another clan.

30. The fieldwork that informs this book could not have been undertaken without the support of these assistants, a term that does not fully convey their contribution to this project. I am particularly indebted to Musa Lwanga Mayanja.

31. On 24 May 1966 the Ugandan army staged a bloody attack on the palace of the *kabaka* of Buganda, Frederick Walugembe Muteesa II. Under the command of Colonel Idi Amin and on orders from Prime Minister Milton Obote, troops set the palace ablaze, arrested many royalists, and killed thousands of unarmed civilians in other areas of Buganda. With no army to resist Obote's actions, Kabaka Muteesa II fled to London, where he died three years later under suspicious circumstances. His son and heir, Ronald Muwenda Mutebi, lived in exile in London until 1986, when he returned to Uganda following the overthrow of Obote's government by Yoweri Museveni's National Resistance Movement. For an insightful analysis of Buganda's restoration, see Karlström, "Cultural Kingdom in Uganda."

32. For one of the earliest and clearest statements of this premise, see Feierman, "Struggles for Control." See also Prins, "But What Was the Disease?"; Feierman and Janzen, *Social Basis of Health and Healing*, 1–23; and Vaughan, "Healing and Curing."

33. See, e.g., Livingstone, *Debility and the Moral Imagination*; Hunt, *Colonial Lexicon*; White, "They Could Make Their Victims Dull"; Landau, "Explaining Surgical Evangelism"; and Burke, *Lifebuoy Men, Lux Women*.

34. For noteworthy examples of how a focus on public healing illuminates our understanding of social and political dynamics prior to the twentieth century, see Janzen, *Lemba*; and Schoffeleers, *River of Blood*.

35. Feierman, "Colonizers, Colonized," 203.

36. Livingstone, *Debility and the Moral Imagination*, 16–21, quotation on 16.

37. Schoenbrun, *A Green Place, A Good Place*, 12–13.

38. Klieman, *"The Pygmies Were Our Compass."*

39. Quoted in Tucker, *Eighteen Years in Uganda*, 85.

40. Hattersley, *Uganda by Pen and Camera*, 48. In discussing the views of the early Pan-Africanist activists and missionaries Alexander Crummell and Edward Blyden, Anthony Appiah similarly noted that what these two men "stressed, time and

time again, was the openness of Africans, once properly instructed, to monotheism; what impressed them both, despite the horrors of African paganism, was Africans' natural religiosity." Appiah, *In My Father's House*, 23.

41. For example, Alfred Bishop Tucker commented that "there are features in [lubaale], dim and misty, it is true, but which nevertheless at times lead one to suppose that it was once—possibly ages ago—in contact with Christianity." Tucker, *Eighteen Years in Uganda*, 84–85. Similarly, the Church Missionary Society missionary Philip O'Flaherty described *lubaale* as "a mixture of Alexandrian Gnosticism and ancient Egyptianism in which Lubare [*sic*] incarnate takes the place of Christ and the whole system the place of a corrupted Christianity." Quoted in ibid., 85.

42. See Miti, "Short History," 11–14; Mair, *African People*, 223–65; and Hattersley, *Uganda by Pen and Camera*, 41–59, respectively. These represent but a handful of a large number of similar examples.

43. For an examination of the relationship between Kaggwa, Roscoe, and Roscoe's Cambridge mentor Sir James G. Frazer, see Ray, *Myth, Ritual, and Kingship*, 22–53.

44. See, e.g., Welbourn, "Some Aspects of Kiganda Religion"; Hansen, "Colonial Control of Spirit Cults"; and more recently, Médard, "Croissance et crises," specifically the chapters "La religion méconnue du Buganda" and "Royauté et religion: Complémentarités et concurrences."

45. Remarking on how the process of finding the appropriate Setswana words for Christian concepts constituted a critical aspect of the missionary endeavor and the colonizing process, Landau writes that "the 'high God' is the questioner's God, the '[Holy] Spirit' the questioner's Spirit: they are ready-made decisions of translation, not evidence." Landau, *Realm of the Word*, xx. See also Landau, " 'Religion' and Christian Conversion "; Shaw, "Invention of 'African Traditional Religion' "; and Peterson and Walhof, "Rethinking Religion."

46. Appiah, *In My Father's House*, 108.

47. On the implications of analyzing African responses to misfortune in terms of medical anthropology rather than religion, see Whyte, "Anthropological Approaches to African Misfortune."

48. Feierman, "Colonizers, Colonized," 202–3.

49. Schoenbrun, "Conjuring the Modern in Africa."

50. For a useful discussion on respecting disciplinary concerns in the service of interdisciplinary scholarship in the African context, see Stahl, *Making History in Banda*, ch. 1.

51. See Schoenbrun, *A Green Place, A Good Place* and *Historical Reconstruction*; Tantala, "Early History of Kitara"; Hanson, *Landed Obligation*; and, among Feierman's many works on health and healing, "Struggles for Control," "Colonizers, Colonized," and "Explanation and Uncertainty."

52. Hunt, *Colonial Lexicon*, 23.

53. See, e.g., Vail and White, *Power and the Praise Poem*; Barber, *I Could Speak until Tomorrow*; Bozzoli and Nkotsoe, *Women of Phokeng*; Hunt, *Colonial Lexicon*; White, *Speaking with Vampires*; Ibrahim, "Birth of the Interview"; Cooper, "Oral Sources"; and Giles-Vernick, *Cutting the Vines of the Past*.

54. Vansina first laid out his methodology for the collection and treatment of oral traditions in *De la tradition orale: Essai de la methode historique*, published in English as *Oral Tradition: A Study in Historical Methodology* (1965). He later revised his method in *Oral Tradition as History* (1985).

55. See Spear, "Oral Tradition"; Tantala, "Early History of Kitara"; and Cohen and Odhiambo, *Siaya*.

56. White, *Speaking with Vampires*, 53.

57. For vampire stories, see White, *Speaking with Vampires*; for an illuminating examination of the Congolese artist Tshibumba Kanda Matulu's painted narrative of Zaire, see Fabian, *Remembering the Present*; for life histories as a vantage point from which to approach larger historical issues, see, e.g., Marcia Wright, *Strategies of Slaves and Women*; Van Onselen, *The Seed Is Mine*; and Davison, *Voices from Mutira*.

58. Fabian, *Remembering the Present*, 297–98, my emphasis.

59. See, e.g., the contributions to White, Miescher, and Cohen, *African Words, African Voices*.

60. White, "True Stories," 281.

61. Vansina, *Children of Woot*.

62. White, "True Stories," 283.

63. Cohen, "Undefining of Oral Tradition."

2. Genre, Historical Imagination, and Early Ganda History

1. George William Kalule, interview, 29 September 2001.

2. Ssalongo Ssegujja Musisi, interview, 16 March 2002.

3. The following presentation of "Kintu and Bemba the Snake" draws on Kagwa, *Kings of Buganda*, 5–7; Cunningham, *Uganda and Its Peoples*, 170–78; Kagwa, *Ekitabo Kye Kika Kyenseenene*, 40–41; Hattersley, *English Boy's Life*, 72–74; Daudi Bakika and Jemusi Bwagu, "The Balangira (Princes) Clan in Buganda," in Source Materials in Uganda History, Volume 3; John Bapere, "Kintu and the People With Him on Masaba Hill," in Source Material in Uganda History, Volume 3; Ludoviko Kibato, "The Harp of the King of Buganda," in Translations from *Munno* and Other Periodicals; Nsimbi, *Amannya Amaganda N'Ennono Zaago*, 183–85; and Kakoma, Ntate, and Serukaga, *Ekitabo Eky'Abakyanjove Ab'e Mmamba Mu Ssiga Lya Nankere e Bukerekere*, 3–4. I thank John Rowe for providing me with a copy of Translations from *Munno* and Other Periodicals.

4. Bemba often appears specifically as a python (ttimba).

5. In some versions the Mukiibi character appears as Ndugwa, the name used for the head of the Pangolin clan.

6. In some versions Kigave appears as Lugave, the Luganda word for "pangolin." The word *kigave*, however, carries the same meaning.

7. No references to tortoises or groups associated with tortoises appear in any other Ganda sources. Nsimbi, however, relates that the tortoise was originally the Pangolin clan's secondary totem and therefore could represent a group of people who, unlike those associated with the Pangolin, were not successful in parlaying their prominence in local healing complexes into clan stature. Nsimbi, *Amannya Amaganda N'Ennono Zaago*, 185.

8. The details of this part of the narrative differ in some versions, but the result is always the same: Nfudu and Kigave trick Bemba into having his head chopped off.

9. Ogot, "Construction of Luo Identity," 42.

10. The phrase "colonial clutter" is from Wrigley, *Kingship and State*, 110.

11. Kagwa, *Bakabaka b'e Buganda*, 3–4; Cunningham, *Uganda and Its Peoples*, 170–78. The Church Missionary Society missionary C. W. Hattersley published a version of the narrative as part of his account of his son's childhood in Uganda. See Hattersley, *English Boy's Life*, 72–74.

12. "Kintu Ne Bemba" (Kintu and Bemba), in Source Materials in Uganda History, Volume 3; Bakika and Bwagu, "Ekika Kye Balangira Mu Buganda," 73; Lawi Wakibi Sekiti, "The Baganda of Mbale," in Translations from *Munno* and Other Periodicals; Kibato, "Harp of the King of Buganda."

13. Buligwanga, *Ekitabo Ekitegeza Ekika Kye Mamba*, 14–17; Kakoma, Ntate, and Serukaga, *Ekitabo Eky'Abakyanjove*, 3–4.

14. Miti, "Short History," 15–17; Nsimbi, *Amannya Amaganda N'Ennono Zaago*, 184–85; Kaguba, "Genealogy of Kabaka Kintu," 207–8.

15. Twaddle, "On Ganda Historiography," 86, 97–98.

16. Kagwa, *Kings of Buganda*, 5.

17. As Michael Twaddle has pointed out, the specific location of Podi in a known geographical locale (Bunyoro) only appeared in the second edition of *Bakabaka b'e Buganda*, published in 1912. See Twaddle, "On Ganda Historiography," 87.

18. Kagwa, *Kings of Buganda*, 1–6.

19. Roscoe, *Baganda*, 136–37.

20. Quoted in Médard, "Syncretic Changes," 8.

21. Stanley, *Through the Dark Continent*, 345.

22. Médard, "Syncretic Changes," 10–12.

23. Wrigley, *Kingship and State*, 111–13.

24. For example, see Daudi Musoke, "The Origins of the Baganda," in Source Material in Uganda History, Volume 3; "Even Wise Men Can Be Mistaken," in ibid.; and J. T. K. Gomotoka, "Kintu in Bukedi and Kami," in ibid. Not all Baganda agreed with the interpretation that Kintu had traveled through eastern Uganda to reach Buganda or that the languages and cultures of those areas were similar to

that of Buganda. The interpretation of Kintu's advent from the east, however, seemed to dominate elite Ganda intellectual circles in the early colonial period. For dissenting arguments, see "Even Wise Men Can Be Mistaken"; and Andereya Batulabudde, "Ngora Bukedi," in Source Materials in Uganda History, Volume 3.

25. Twaddle, "On Ganda Historiography," 94–96.
26. J. T. K. Gomotoka, "How Ssekabaka Kintu Came," in Source Materials in Ugandan History, Volume 3. Benjamin Ray has demonstrated that these debates formed part of the controversy about whether Kintu had been indigenous to Buganda or an immigrant with outside origins, a discussion that revolved around the competing interests of kings (and by implication chiefs) and clans in colonial Buganda. Ray, *Myth, Ritual, and Kingship,* 99–103. See also Kiwanuka, *History of Buganda,* 94–95.
27. Gomotoka, "How Ssekabaka Kintu Came."
28. In one article, Gomotoka responded to some of his colleagues' fears that the idea of Kintu as a foreigner (and thus of the Baganda as not the indigenous people of the area) might provide a precedent for European settlement by arguing that European state formation in many ways resembled that of Buganda. He pointed to the example of medieval Germany, where, after a series of invasions and population movements, "those who rule those lands [today] were not the original people there since the beginning of the world." Ibid.
29. For a detailed historiographic overview of "Kintu and Bemba the Snake," see Kodesh, "Beyond the Royal Gaze," 37–56.
30. Gray, "Early History of Buganda"; Oliver, "Traditional Histories," 112 (quotation); Kiwanuka, *History of Buganda,* 32–35; Cohen, *Historical Tradition of Busoga,* 84–123. For an interpretation of "Kintu and Bemba the Snake" that examines the narrative in light of the royal rituals established at Buddo Hill in the mideighteenth century, see Ray, *Myth, Ritual, and Kingship,* 74–86.
31. See Wrigley, *Kingship and State,* 106–10; and Atkinson, "Traditions of the Early Kings."
32. For a related discussion of the various ways the Kintu figure was understood in the region, see Wrigley, *Kingship and State,* 118–19.
33. Cohen, *Historical Tradition of Busoga,* 19–21, 44–45.
34. Ibid., 20–21.
35. Soga clan histories suggest a possible connection between the Kintu figure and the leopard totem. All the groups of people who adopted the leopard as their totem in southern Busoga traced their ancestry to Kintu, which indicates that the *musambwa* may once have functioned as the *nkuni* spirit for these communities. However, it is also quite likely that the connection between the leopard totem and Kintu in southern Busoga occurred after the rise to prominence of Kintu the conqueror-king in Buganda, where the Leopard clan provides the priest for Kintu's royal tomb at Magonga. For the connection between Kintu and the leopard totem in southern Busoga, see ibid., 89, 119.

36. On the integrative capacity of the ritual center devoted to Kintu at Magonga, see Hanson, *Landed Obligation*, 40–41.

37. The Leopard, Lion, Frog, Pangolin, Grey Monkey, Grasshopper, Colobus Monkey, Otter, Elephant, Oribi Antelope, Bird, Bead, Yam, and Buffalo clans all held estates near Magonga that served as the permanent residences for their representatives at Kintu's shrine at Nnono. Kagwa, *Customs of the Baganda*, 10–11; Wrigley, *Kingship and State*, 118–19.

38. Kakoma, Ntate, and Serukaga, *Ekitabo Eky'Abakyanjove*, 2, 14, 21, 37–38.

39. For Leopard clan histories that detail how Mwanje acquired this position, see Nsimbi, *Amannya Amaganda N'Ennono Zaago*, 207–10; Kagwa, *Clans of Buganda*, 61–63; Council of the Ssiga of Mwanje, "Essiga Lya Mwanje e Nnono Magonga"; and Council of the Leopard Clan, "Olukiko Lw'Akasolya Mu Kika Ky'Engo."

40. On the "Lion-Leopard complex" in Busoga and Buganda, see Cohen, *Historical Tradition of Busoga*, 86–89.

41. For a more detailed discussion of shifts in the deeply rooted traditions of health and healing in the region, see Schoenbrun, *A Green Place, A Good Place*, 197–203.

42. Roscoe, "Python Worship in Uganda," 89–90.

43. In addition to being the head of the estate, the shrine's priest also served as the medium's interpreter. See Roscoe's account of the same event in Roscoe, *Baganda*, 322.

44. The verb *okukuma* also means "to keep up a fire," perhaps hinting at Lukumirizi's responsibility for maintaining the slow fires that burn continuously inside shrines.

45. While Roscoe did not provide any information concerning whether there were any tensions between the medium and the priest at Sserwanga's shrine, it is possible that mediums and priests might have represented different interests. In his testimony at the Enquiry into Native Land Tenure in the Uganda Protectorate in 1906, Kaggwa stated that in the past when people had gathered together to build a shrine, any possible objections voiced by the senior member of the clan who controlled the land had been met with threats from the medium leading the delegation. See Roscoe and Kagwa, "Enquiry into Native Land Tenure," 4–5.

46. Unexpected challenges, such those faced by ancestral ghosts (*mizimu*) following the development of novel types of spiritual entities, helped guide such transformations by opening up new opportunities for innovation and critiquing older notions.

47. On the importance of reciprocal obligation, both between chiefs and their followers and between ancestral spirits and their earthly descendants, in the knitting together of the early Ganda polity, see Hanson, *Landed Obligation*, ch. 2.

48. Tantala, "Early History of Kitara," 613.

49. Schoenbrun, *A Green Place, A Good Place*, 199–200. Noting the possible connection between the image of a python coiling itself around its prey, the twisting of metal

to make arm and neck rings, and the importance of these rings as regalia for mediums and rainmakers in the Great Lakes region, Renee Tantala suggests that Great Lakes historical actors may have drawn this analogy during the Iron Age, or perhaps even earlier if rings made of fiber preceded those forged from iron. See Tantala, "Early History of Kitara," 613–15.

50. For the derivation of *musambwa*, see Schoenbrun, *A Green Place, A Good Place*, 200.

51. Tantala, "Early History of Kitara," 601–3; Kenny, "Powers of Lake Victoria," 722–23; Shadle, "Patronage, Millenialism," 47.

52. F. Lukyn Williams, "Myth, Legend, and Lore," 68.

53. J. T. K. Gomotoka, "The Going of the Messengers of H. H. the Kabaka Daudi Cwa II on Inspections of Buganda," in Translations from *Munno* and Other Periodicals; Nnalongo Nakasi, interview, 9 February 2002.

54. For a more extensive discussion of this ontological transformation, see Schoenbrun, *A Green Place, A Good Place*, 197–98.

55. For the western Ugandan conceptions, see Tantala, "Early History of Kitara," 262–63, 365–66, 607–8; for the Buganda formulations, see Roscoe, *Baganda*, 285–86. Some aggrieved ghosts also stayed in the middle world and could be pernicious. For a discussion of the similar yet distinct ontological transformation involving ancestral ghosts in Bunyole, in eastern Uganda, see Heald, *Controlling Anger*, 204–5.

56. In certain localities surrounding Lake Victoria, but particularly in areas beyond the well-watered lakeshores, the connection between pythons, *mizimu*, and bodies of water formed part of an even broader association between pythons and rainmaking. As Tantala has noted, this widespread connection possibly developed from pythons' habit of residing in water during the heat of the day and their visibility during the rainy season as they sought refuge on higher ground and in trees. Tantala, "Early History of Kitara," 644n28.

57. On the waters of Lake Victoria as a vehicle for ontological transformation, see Kenny, "Stranger from the Lake."

58. Nsimbi, *Amannya Amaganda N'Ennono Zaago*, 211; Kubi Kiviri Muyondo, interview, 31 October 2001.

59. Richard Reid, *Political Power*, 244.

60. Kubi Kiviri Muyondo, interview, 31 October 2001.

61. Hajji Blukhan Kasumba Kabulidde, interview, 3 November 2001.

62. Miti, "Short History," 1606.

63. The communities living along the lake's eastern shores preserved the keel once a canoe fell into a state of disrepair. Kenny, "Powers of Lake Victoria," 725–27. Significantly, the canoe paddle was the principal emblem for Mukasa, the most revered spiritual force associated with Lake Victoria. Each mainland shrine dedicated to Mukasa in Buganda housed a paddle that had been blessed by the shrine's priest, and the association of the canoe paddle with python centers

considerably further west of Lake Victoria could possibly represent priestly attempts at linking their authority to Mukasa's powers. Roscoe, *Baganda*, 290; Tantala, "Early History of Kitara," 612–13.

64. C. W. Hattersley described Buddo Hill as a place where many snakes dwelt because the area's inhabitants feared killing them. Hattersley, *English Boy's Life*, 74.

65. Hajji Kawooya Ssemandwa Bakazirwendo, interview, 4 October 2001; Committee of the Lungfish Clan, "Ekitabo Ky'Ekika Ky'Emmbama," 2; Nsubuga, "Abazzukulu Ba Kkerebwe E Lukumba, Bwerenga Mu Ssiga Lya Kirulu E Bwenga Mu Kika Ky'Emmamba," 9. Lungfish clan history constitutes a matter of considerable debate, and not all versions claim Bemba as an ancestor.

66. Richard Reid, *Political Power*, 227–50; Kenny, "Stranger from the Lake," 16–20.

67. For the clan's activities in the Buvuma archipelago, see Jensen, "Die Erweiterung des Lungenfisch-Clans in Buganda durch den Anschluss von Bavuma-Gruppen." I thank Henri Médard for providing me with a French translation of this article.

68. On canoe construction in Buganda, see Roscoe, *Baganda*, 383–90; and Richard Reid, *Political Power*, 228–31.

69. See, e.g., Roscoe, *Baganda*, 383.

70. Kagwa, *Customs of the Baganda*, 114–15; Roscoe, *Baganda*, 290–94; Nsimbi, *Amannya Amaganda N'Ennono Zaago*, 127.

71. Kenny, "Mutesa's Crime," 610n52.

72. For an analysis of the ritual symbolism of the Buddo rites, see Ray, *Myth, Ritual, and Kingship*, 78–86. For descriptions of the rites, see Kagwa, *Customs of the Baganda*, 11–13; Roscoe, *Baganda*, 190–96; Ashe, *Chronicles of Uganda*, 111–13; and Nsimbi, *Amannya Amaganda N'Ennono Zaago*, 154.

73. Lush, "Kiganda Drums," 9; Jjumba and Council of the Ssiga of Jjumba, *Ekitabo Eky'essiga Lya Jjumba*, 10; Kakoma, Ntate, and Serukaga, *Ekitabo Eky'Abakyanjove*, 46; Kenny, "Powers of Lake Victoria," 728; Tantala, "Early History of Kitara," 611, 646n35; "The Ancient Things Do Not Cease," in Translations from *Munno* and Other Periodicals.

74. Schoenbrun, *A Green Place, A Good Place*, 202–6. I further discuss the evidence supporting this claim in chapter 3.

75. Ssalongo Lukoda Wamala Kaggwa, interview, 4 February 2002; Ssalongo Ssegujja Musisi, interview, 16 March, 2002; Simon Mwebe, interview, 5 May 2002.

76. Connections between the pangolin's unusual physical characteristics and its metaphorical significance stretch well beyond Buganda and are particularly prevalent in central Africa. See Roberts, *Animals in African Art*, 83; Douglas, "Animals in Lele Religious Symbolism"; Kodesh, "Beyond the Royal Gaze," 94–97; and F. Lukyn Williams, "Myth, Legend, and Lore," 69–70.

77. This conclusion accords with the extremely precise and calculated decisions made by diviners and mediums in many parts of Africa with respect to the

creatures employed in their respective activities. See Peek, "African Divination Systems," 198–99.

78. I discuss the types of networks forged by itinerant mediums in chapter 3.

79. The rich ethnographic record in the Great Lakes region consistently describes the state of possession as having one's head seized by an overpowering force.

80. The following presentation of "Kintu and Nambi" draws on several published versions of the narrative in both English and Luganda: Le Veux, *Manuel de langue luganda*, 449–58; Kagwa, *Engero Za Baganda*, 1–8; Johnston, *Uganda Protectorate*, 700–705; Roscoe, *Baganda*, 460–64; Hattersley, *Uganda by Pen and Camera*, 41–42; and Alice Werner, "African Mythology," 172–74.

81. In some versions it is Kintu who returns to fetch the grain.

82. Le Veux, *Premier essai*, 449–58; Wilson and Felkin, *Uganda and the Egyptian Sudan*, 220–21.

83. See Roscoe, "Notes on the Manners and Customs," 124–25, "Further Notes on the Manners and Customs," 26, and *Baganda*, 460–64.

84. Kagwa, *Engero Za Baganda*, 1–8; Johnston, *Uganda Protectorate*, 700–705.

85. Miti, "Short History," 1–9; Zimbe, *Buganda Ne Kabaka*, 6.

86. Kagwa, *Engero Za Baganda*, 115, quoted in Ray, *Myth, Ritual, and Kingship*, 60.

87. Miti, "Short History," 1–9.

88. Le Veux, *Manuel de langue luganda*, 449n1. Wrigley argues that Kaggwa derived his version of the narrative from Le Veux's, a claim that, if correct, would illustrate the influence of early missionary teachings on the interpretations presented by Baganda converts. See Wrigley, *Kingship and State*, 90.

89. Ray, *Myth, Ritual, and Kingship*, 60–61.

90. Kagwa, *Customs of the Baganda*, 161; Roscoe, *Baganda*, 136.

91. Hattersley, *Uganda by Pen and Camera*, 43.

92. Quoted in Ray, *Myth, Ritual, and Kingship*, 61.

93. See, e.g., Wrigley, *Kingship and State*, 89–98; Ray, *Myth, Ritual, and Kingship*, 56–58, 68–72; and Cohen, *Historical Tradition of Busoga*, 84–85. For a detailed historiographic overview, see Kodesh, "Beyond the Royal Gaze," 106–12.

94. Roscoe, *Baganda*, 285–89; Mair, *African People*, 224–25.

95. Lanning, "Shafts in Buganda and Toro." For the use of kaolin in possession ceremonies, see Tantala, "Early History of Kitara," 725; and Roscoe, "Python Worship in Uganda."

96. Tantala, "Early History of Kitara," 450n37. In his description of initiation ceremonies for *cwezi* mediums in Bunyoro, Nyakatura noted that *cwezi* spirits would "split open the ground" to make their appearance when induced by the rhythmic beating of the *ntimbo* drums. Nyakatura, *Aspects of Bunyoro Customs*, 60. Ttanda might also derive from *-tánd, "to begin," which occurs in Luganda, Runyoro, and Runyankore and may be translated as the "place of beginnings," a possible

reference to the place where ancestors dwell. Lutanda could also be a class-5, mass plural form of *eitanda* (*ttanda* by gemination), reflecting the long, narrow character of the shafts it names. I thank Jan Vansina and David Schoenbrun, respectively, for pointing out these possibilities.

97. George William Kalule, interview, 29 September 2001; Hajji Kawooya Ssemandwa Bakazirwendo, interview, 4 October 2001; Nsimbi, *Amannya Amaganda N'Ennono Zaago*, 137–38.

98. See, e.g., Tantala, "Early History of Kitara," 556; Morris, *Heroic Recitations*, 76; Lugira, *Ganda Art*, 97; Kagwa, *Customs of the Baganda*, 90, 120–21; and Heald, *Controlling Anger*, 63.

99. This is a common association throughout much of Bantu-speaking Africa. Jacobsen-Widding, *Red-White-Black*.

100. Beattie, "Initiation," 156, and "Spirit Mediumship in Bunyoro," 160–61; Tantala, "Early History of Kitara," 261, 268–69, 388–91; Heald, *Controlling Anger*, 204–5.

101. Bena Namyalo, interview, 22 September 2001. In the Cwezi traditions of western Uganda, images of a domain covered in black, sooty ashes dominate descriptions of the underworld. See Tantala, "Early History of Kitara," 388–91, 578.

102. According to dynastic traditions in western Uganda, the Tembuzi preceded the Cwezi as rulers of a large kingdom covering much of the region.

103. John Beattie noted that spirit mediums in Bunyoro wore headdresses decorated with cowrie shells and the black and white fur of the colobus monkey. In addition, prayers recited at the conclusion of *cwezi* possession ceremonies in Bunyoro included the lines "You decorated like the colobus monkey" and "You are as beautiful as the colobus monkey." See Beattie, "Initiation," 152; Byaruhanga-Akiiki, *Religion in Bunyoro*, 46; and Nyakatura, *Aspects of Bunyoro Customs*, 75.

104. Tantala, "Early History of Kitara," 556–60.

105. Kagwa, *Clans of Buganda*, 2–5; Roscoe, *Baganda*, 142; Kagwa, *Customs of the Baganda*, 10; Nsimbi, *Amannya Amaganda N'Ennono Zaago*, 190–94.

106. Wrigley, *Kingship and State*, 94.

107. Cohen, *Historical Tradition of Busoga*, 90.

108. Murphy, *Luganda-English Dictionary*, 601; Snoxall, *Luganda-English Dictionary*, 340.

109. Baganda often refer to the process of placating ancestral ghosts as "calming" or "cooling down" the spirits.

110. The noun *mmandwa* derives from the Proto–Great Lakes Bantu root **kubándwa*, "to be consecrated to a spirit." See Schoenbrun, *Historical Reconstruction*, 178.

111. Welbourn, "Some Aspects of Kiganda Religion," 181n17; Cohen, *Historical Tradition of Busoga*, 90.

112. Berger, *Religion and Resistance*, 69–70, and "Fertility as Power," 73.

113. In Bunyoro, for example, senior mediums in the *cwezi kubándwa* cults asked the initiate's relatives for a payment, referred to as the *mbandwa*'s bridewealth, and a new *mbandwa* remained in seclusion for four days, a practice that mimicked a wife's four-day seclusion in her husband's home after marriage. At equivalent ceremonies in Buganda and Nkore, participants partook of a feast that resembled a wedding banquet, and upon returning from the bush, novices sang songs appropriate for a bride's wedding party. Nyakatura, *Aspects of Bunyoro Customs*, 58, 62; Byaruhanga-Akiiki, *Religion in Bunyoro*, 53.

114. Beattie, "Initiation," 155–59; Berger, *Religion and Resistance*, 20–21; Tantala, "Early History of Kitara," 286; Kaggwa and Welbourn, "*Lubaale* Initiation," 219.

115. Roscoe, *Baganda*, 275, and "Python Worship," 90.

116. Ali Ssalongo Kiwanda, interview, 10 April 2002. See also Roscoe, *Baganda*, 283.

117. Mubinge Zabeti, interview, 13 December 2001.

118. The following presentation of "Kintu and Kisolo" draws upon Kagwa, *Kings of Buganda*, 6–7, and *Clans of Buganda*, 7; Nsimbi, *Amannya Amaganda N'Ennono Zaago*, 222–23; Roscoe, "Further Notes on the Manners and Customs"; Kato Peter Lukoma and Namasole Baagalayaze, interview, 18 December 2001; and Kato Benedict Kimbowa Ssemwanga, interview, 4 February 2002.

119. Some versions remark that Kintu left Magonga on a long hunting expedition.

120. Atkinson, "Traditions of the Early Kings," 21, 26–27; Ray, *Myth, Ritual, and Kingship*, 166–67; Wrigley, *Kingship and State*, 99–105. For a historiographic overview, see Kodesh, "Beyond the Royal Gaze," 126–28.

121. In the Cwezi narratives focusing on the Kisengwe area near Mubende Hill, for instance, the usurper king Bukuku, who represented a line of priests who controlled a local node of authority centered around the area's python god, belonged to a clan (Ranzi) that claimed the otter as their totem. Similarly, the ubiquitous *cwezi* mediums, who eventually supplanted Bukuku's line of priests, also drew on the otter's metaphorical associations by adorning the animal's skin as part of their ritual regalia. Tantala, "Early History of Kitara," 600–601; Schweinfurth et al., *Emin Pasha*, 265.

122. Kato Peter Lukoma and Namasole Baagayalaze, interview, 18 December 2001; Kato Peter Lukoma, interview, 21 December 2001; Lameka Sonko Ssenkungu, interview, 27 December 2001.

123. Kato Benedict Kimbowa Ssemwanga, interview, 4 February 2002.

124. Roscoe, *Baganda*, 143.

125. For an insightful account of some of the transformations in the Kintu figure from the mid-nineteenth century on, see Médard, "Syncretic Changes."

126. Yoder, "Quest for Kintu."

127. Ray, *Myth, Ritual, and Kingship*, 99–103.

128. Hanks, *Language and Communicative Practices*, 274.

3. Clanship and the Pursuit of Collective Well-Being

1. For Buganda, see M. S. M. Kiwanuka's introduction to Kagwa, *Kings of Buganda*, xxix; and Kiwanuka, *History of Buganda*, 31. For Busoga, see Cohen, *Historical Tradition of Busoga*. And for western Uganda, see Buchanan, "Kitara Complex."

2. For notable exceptions, see Willis, "Clan and History in Western Uganda"; and Newbury, *Kings and Clans* and "Clans of Rwanda." While Newbury's analysis of clanship on Ijwi Island is notable for its efforts to treat clans in a historical manner, it is concerned more with the "external components of clan identity"—the relationships both between clans and between clans and royalty—than with the "internal components of clan identity," which Newbury determined were both less important and "impossible to ascertain with any precision" for the nineteenth century (6).

3. George William Kalule, interview, 3 October 2001.

4. Yoweri Museveni's guerrilla movement to defeat then president Milton Obote. Museveni's movement began in the early 1980s.

5. Omutaka Mbajja, interview, 8 December 2001.

6. Charles Alex Nsejere, Mugwanya Mugema, Sserwanga Ndawula Katumba Balamaga, and Michael Mugadya Selubidde, interview, 26 October 2001; Hassan Sserwadda, interview, 21 December 2001; Ssalongo Ssegujja Musisi, interview, 16 March 2002; Yozefu Sserwaji and Mbuga Atanansio, interview, 28 March 2002.

7. The derivation may also refer to the process by which old bodies become exhausted and die, with their spirits remaining around their burial sites, located on *biggwa*. I thank David Schoenbrun for this suggestion.

8. Charles Alex Nsejere, Sserwanga Ndawula Katumba Balamaga, and Michael Mugadya Selubidde, interview, 26 October 2001.

9. Ssalongo Benedicto Walusimbi, interview, 12 October 2001; Charles Alex Nsejere, Sserwanga Ndawula Katumba Balamaga, and Michael Mugadya Selubidde, interview, 26 October 2001; members of the Kasimba clan members, interview, 31 October 2001; Ssalongo Ssegujja Musisi, interview, 16 March 2002; Yozefu Sserwaji and Mbuga Atanansio, interview, 28 March 2002; Omutaka Kibondwe, interview, 7 April 2002.

10. Ssalongo George Mulumba, interview, 5 March 2002; Omutaka Kibondwe, interview, 7 April 2002; Ssenyoga Kalika, interview, 13 June 2002.

11. Members of clans that claim indigenous status in Buganda are known as *bannansangwa*, which translates literally as "those who were found [on the land]."

12. Kagwa, *Clans of Buganda*, 7.

13. In the transformed dynastic version of this narrative, Kintu appears as the first king of Buganda, Kisolo as his prime minister (*kattikiro*), and Lutaya as Kintu's head of servants (*ssabaddu*). See Kagwa, *Clans of Buganda*, 7, and *Customs of the Baganda*, 10; Roscoe, *Baganda*, 143; and Nsimbi, *Amannya Amaganda N'Ennono Zaago*, 222.

14. Falasiko Bali Muttajjo, interview, 12 December 2001; Kato Peter Lukoma, interview, 21 December 2001; Lameka Sonko Ssenkungu, interview, 27 December 2001.

15. The name Muganga derives from the verb *okuganga*, "to heal, cure."

16. Kato Benedict Kimbowa Ssemwanga, interview, 4 February 2002.

17. Roscoe, *Baganda*, 143.

18. Kato Benedict Kimbowa Ssemwanga, interview, 4 February 2002.

19. In addition to the talented doctor Muganga and the priest Ssemwanga, Ssenkungu also produced the person credited with the discovery of bark cloth in Buganda, and the bark-cloth-rich Mawokota region in which he lived constituted an early center for bark-cloth production in Buganda. Another son, Sonko, rose to prominence as a respected diviner. See Kagwa, *Clans of Buganda*, 8–10; Kato Peter Lukoma, interview, 21 December 2001; Lameka Sonko Ssenkungu, interview, 27 December 2001; and Nsimbi, *Amannya Amaganda N'Ennono Zaago*, 224. On the history of the bark-cloth industry in Buganda, see Richard Reid, *Political Power*, 70–76.

20. The *jjembe* Nantaba eventually occupied a prominent position at the royal enclosure and was presented to the newly crowned king in an elaborate ceremony headed by its caretaker, Nakatanza, who slowly carried the horn to the king "like a pregnant woman near the time of her delivery." See Roscoe, *Baganda*, 325–27.

21. The descendants of the renowned drummer Kawuula Lukungo capitalized on their inherited talents to achieve the position of chief royal drummer.

22. Ssalongo Semakula Mukasa, interview, 4 December 2001; Zaidi Ssemakula Kitagana, interview, 9 April 2002; Ali Ssalongo Kiwanda, interview, 10 April 2002; Roscoe, *Baganda*, 153, 315, 325–27; Kagwa, *Customs of the Baganda*, 122; Mair, *African People*, 121; Y. Kikulwe, "The Ancient Acts of the Rulers of Bulemezi," in *Translations from Munno and Other Periodicals*; Nsimbi, *Amannya Amaganda N'Ennono Zaago*, 136–37, 143, 183–88, 249.

23. Kato Benedict Kimbowa Ssemwanga, interview, 4 February 2002; Kiwanuka, *History of Buganda*, 84; Nsimbi, *Amannya Amaganda N'Ennono Zaago*, 224.

24. The following discussion of innovations in spirit mediumship in the Great Lakes region relies upon Schoenbrun, *A Green Place, A Good Place*, 202–6, 265–69.

25. Based on glottochronology, Schoenbrun points to 500 BC as the time when Great Lakes Bantu began to diverge from its linguistic parent, Mashariki Bantu. Ibid., 46.

26. Ibid., 266–67. The form of spirit possession practiced in Buganda shared the most general characteristics of the practice as recorded in the ethnographic record for other parts of the Great Lakes region. Trained mediums called upon one of a variety of spirits, which seized the medium's head (*kukwata ku mutwe*) and spoke to the audience through the possessed individual. Overwhelmed by the power of the possessing spirit, the medium in a sense became the spirit, embodying a previously formless force.

27. I point to the early second millennium AD as the earliest possible period because the historical actors who spoke the dialects that composed the Rutara subgroup were in regular contact until the middle of the second millennium.

28. Schoenbrun, *A Green Place, A Good Place*, 267–68.

29. Ibid., 202–6.

30. Tantala, "Early History of Kitara," 257–357.

31. Berger, *Religion and Resistance*, 17, and "Rebels or Status Seekers?" 158.

32. For the emergence of pastoralism in the region, see D. A. M. Reid, "Role of Cattle"; Schoenbrun, "Cattle Herds and Banana Gardens"; and Robertshaw and Taylor, "Climate Change."

33. *Ensete* spp. (*Musaceae*), a close relative of *Musa* spp., occurs wild in many parts of Africa (as well as in Asia) and has been domesticated in southwestern Ethiopia. Unlike *Musa*, however, wild banana fruits are almost inedible because they contain little pulp and many seeds.

34. According to Gerda Rossel, the first *Musa* cultivar to become established in East Africa was the French Medium Green plantain, which was introduced to the northern Swahili coast and took off as a food crop beginning in the eighth century. This was followed by the introduction of other plantain cultivars as well as the arrival of the East African Highland banana. Rossel, *Taxonomic-Linguistic Study*, 221.

35. The following discussion relies upon Schoenbrun, "Cattle Herds and Banana Gardens."

36. As Schoenbrun has noted, independent innovations for cooking and beer varieties in both Forest and Rwenzori, sibling speech communities of West Highlands, indicate three separate courses of development for banana cultivation in this part of the Great Lakes region. Evidence for areal contacts, however, suggests continued exchanges of knowledge between these communities, and in the case of West Highlands it clearly indicates that West Highlanders developed their expertise in banana farming through contacts with Forest peoples and Rutarans.

37. Based on new phytolith evidence obtained from their excavations at Munsa, in western Uganda, B. Julius Lejju, Peter Robertshaw, and David Taylor have recently proposed the presence of bananas in the region during the fourth millennium BC. While this date is significantly earlier than that proposed by Schoenbrun based on historical linguistic evidence and glottochronological reckoning, it does not necessarily call into question the timing and nature of the social processes accompanying the shift to intensive banana cultivation in the northern Great Lakes region. Lejju, Robertshaw, and Taylor, "Africa's earliest bananas?"

38. Schoenbrun, "Cattle Herds and Banana Gardens." Wrigley made a similar argument using different sources and analytical units. See Wrigley, "Bananas in Buganda." Based on new linguistic evidence for the North Nyanza part of this story, Rhiannon Stephens argues that the initial shift to more intensive banana farming

occurred in the final centuries of the first millennium. See Stephens, "History of Motherhood," 137–53.

39. Rossel, Taxonomic-Linguistic Study, 101–2.

40. Schoenbrun, A Green Place, A Good Place, 82.

41. The following discussion relies on Hanson, Landed Obligation, 28–38; and Schoenbrun, "Cattle Herds and Banana Gardens." For the history of farming and herding practices prior to this period, see Schoenbrun, "We Are What We Eat."

42. Hanson, Landed Obligation, 37–38; Wrigley, "Bananas in Buganda."

43. Situated on the shorelines to the south of Buganda's heartland, Buhaya had rainfall amounts similar to Buganda's. Differing soil qualities, however, prevented the same type of intensive cultivation as in Buganda. Banana production in Buyaha could be sustained only with the help of mulches brought in from outside, with the result that there developed "islands of [fertile banana groves] surrounded by depleted grasslands that could support only rare annual crops." Wrigley, "Bananas in Buganda," 66–67.

44. Hanson, Landed Obligation, 28–29. See also Schoenbrun, "Cattle Herds and Banana Gardens," 40–42; and Kottak, "Ecological Variables," 355.

45. Hanson, Landed Obligation, 28–29. See also Wrigley, Kingship and State, 234–36; and Kottak, "Ecological Variables."

46. Due to (female) sterility, most banana cultivars produce no seeds, making sexual propagation impossible. Banana plants therefore have to be propagated vegetatively and cannot maintain themselves in the wild. See Rossel, Taxonomic-Linguistic Study, 12.

47. Hanson, Landed Obligation, 30–31; Schoenbrun, "Cattle Herds and Banana Gardens."

48. Hanson, Landed Obligation, 37–38; Kottak, "Ecological Variables," 367.

49. Hanson notes that the consistent rainfall required for banana plants to bear fruit year-round meant that the hills closest to the lake, which offered the best conditions for growing bananas, attracted the greatest attention from communities transitioning from a mixed-farming system to a banana-based productive economy. These areas witnessed the most extensive cultivation of banana varieties and contained the highest population densities. However, considerable local variation in the amount of rainfall prevailed even in areas with the heaviest rainfall, resulting in differing qualities in banana lands in a given area. As Hanson observes, the soil structure of the region's characteristic hills also determined the varying suitability of land for intensive banana cultivation. The thin soils found on hilltops grew short grass and were well suited for grazing livestock but not for raising crops. The middle and upper slopes, on the other hand, were covered with the rich loams in which banana gardens thrived. Finally, neither the lower slopes nor the valley floors had productive soils capable of raising and sustaining banana trees. In addition to the varying soil qualities found on each hill, the

hillsides in certain areas—southern Buganda, for instance—contained a higher percentage of loams and were therefore better suited for growing bananas. Hanson, *Landed Obligation*, 38–39. See also Kottak, "Ecological Variables."

50. The simultaneous development of terminologies for unilineal inheritance rules and for property characterized by the presence of perennial crops supports this claim. See Schoenbrun, *A Green Place, A Good Place*, 171–84.

51. Schoenbrun, "Cattle Herds and Banana Gardens," 53.

52. Schoenbrun, *A Green Place, A Good Place*, 172–75; Musisi, "Transformations of Baganda Women," 57–59; Kottak, "Ecological Variables," 357; Fallers, "Social Stratification," 72–73, 89–92.

53. Hanson, *Landed Obligation*, 31–33.

54. Ibid., 33.

55. Kottak, "Ecological Variables," 367. Kottak was not concerned, however, with the ideological roots of these transformations in the relationship between the living and the ancestors.

56. Feierman, "Colonizers, Colonized," 202.

57. Wrigley, *Kingship and State*, 84.

58. For a notable exception, see Hanson, *Landed Obligation*, ch. 1.

4. Political Leaders as Public Healers

1. On public healing as social criticism, see Feierman, "Healing as Social Criticism." For examples of analyses of public healing as a form of rebellion or an alternate form of authority that lay beyond the purview of state institutions, see Berger, *Religion and Resistance*; Freedman, *Nyabingi*; des Forges, "The Drum is Greater Than the Shout"; Berger, "Fertility as Power"; and Feierman, "Colonizers, Colonized," 197–200.

2. Two classic examples are Alpers and Ehret, *Eastern Africa*; and Twaddle, "Toward an Early History."

3. The following presentation of the Kimera narrative draws upon Le Veux, *Manuel de langue luganda*, 262–70; Kagwa, *Kings of Buganda*, 10–16; Kagwa, *Clans of Buganda*, 15–18; Nsimbi, *Amannya Amaganda N'Ennono Zaago*, 38–43; Jjumba and Council of the Ssiga of Jjumba, *Ekitabo Eky'essiga Lya Jjumba*, 3–4; Mukasa, "Reason for the Post of Mugema"; and Stanley, *My Dark Companions*, 126–60.

4. As Kiwanuka points out in his translation of Kaggwa's *Kings of Buganda*, Bigo is a common name in Buganda and here refers to a village in Busiro rather than to the well-known Bigo earthworks in Bwera.

5. The reason for Kalemeera's departure for Bunyoro presented here draws on Kaggwa's version of the Kimera story in his dynastic history. Other versions of the narrative describe how Kalemeera traveled to Bunyoro to engage in trading activities. See Le Veux, *Manuel de langue luganda*, 262; Stanley, *My Dark Companions*,

121; and Nsimbi, *Amannya Amaganda N'Ennono Zaago*, 39. I discuss the relevance of this depiction of Kalemeera in the following sections.

6. Henry Morton Stanley's version of the narrative, in *My Dark Companions*, 122–25, reports that Kimera's dazzling flute playing induced a comalike state in Nakku, who then informed Kimera that she intended to have him replace Ssebwana as ruler of Buganda.

7. Gray, "Early History of Buganda," 266–67.

8. Comprising six counties, the disputed territories became known as the "lost counties," two of which contained important centers of Nyoro royal ritual as well as the sites of Nyoro royal tombs. These territories were originally associated with Bunyoro but fell under Ganda jurisdiction following the redefinition of territorial boundaries in the colonially inspired Uganda Agreement of 1900. The British colonial officer Henry Colville originally promised the counties to Buganda in 1894, prior to Bunyoro's incorporation into the Uganda Protectorate, but it was the Uganda Agreement of 1900, between the British and the Baganda, that cemented the transfer of authority over these counties to the Ganda kingdom.

9. K.W., "Kings of Bunyoro-Kitara"; "The Kings of Bunyoro-Kitara. Part II"; "The Kings of Bunyoro-Kitara. Part III."

10. Nyakatura's dynastic history was originally published in Runyoro as *Abakama ba Bunyoro-Kitara*. Winyi (K.W.) was one of the three informants Nyakatura mentioned by name. Like Winyi, he noted that "it was during the reign of [Mucwezi] Ndahura that the empire of [Bunyoro]-Kitara reached the summit of its expansion. He ruled an empire that extended as far as Kavirondo, Abyssinia, Congo, and parts of modern Tanzania. Those who may wish to dispute this fact must first of all explain why the Kitara language is spoken all over the areas mentioned." Nyakatura, *Anatomy of an African Kingdom*, 30.

11. Ibid., 50, 64, 210. Nyakatura's work was not the first to make this particular connection between Mpuga Rukidi and Kimera. Ruth Fisher, for example, had recorded a similar story several decades earlier. See Fisher, *Twilight Tales*, 121.

12. Crazzolara, "Lwoo People" and *Migrations*.

13. For a detailed historiography of the Kimera narrative, see Kodesh, "Beyond the Royal Gaze," 199–214.

14. For a structuralist interpretation, see Atkinson, "Traditions of the Early Kings," 30–35. For an interpretation of the narrative within the framework of comparative mythology, see Wrigley, "Kimera." While Wrigley initially dismissed the possibility that the Kimera narrative concealed the effects of a Nyoro incursion into Buganda, he later reversed this position, commenting that he could no longer ignore the account of Kimera's origins in Bunyoro. In his revised interpretation, Wrigley asserted that the story of Kalemeera's journey to Bunyoro and Kimera's triumphant return alluded to an act of homage paid by new kings of

Buganda to their Nyoro overlords. He concluded his analysis by remarking that "whereas the original pattern of the tale of Kimera comes from neolithic myth and ritual, its proximate source is to be found in local political relations of recent centuries." Wrigley, *Kingship and State*, 142–45, 194–97.

15. See Oliver, "Traditional Histories," "Royal Tombs," and "Discernible Developments"; Cohen, *Historical Tradition of Busoga*, 78–83, 109; Kiwanuka, *History of Buganda*, 40–41, 53–63; Ray, *Myth, Ritual, and Kingship*, 86–89, 95–99; and Wrigley, *Kingship and State*, 194–97.

16. In his analysis of the Kimera narrative, John Gray noted that the ancient Greeks told a similar story of the infant Perseus and his mother, Danae. Gray, "Early History of Buganda," 266. Similarly, Wrigley pointed out overlapping images in the Kimera narrative and the ancient Greek drama *Choephoroe of Aeschylus*. Wrigley, *Kingship and State*, 142–43.

17. Gray, "Early History of Buganda," 266; M. S. M. Kiwanuka, editorial note in Kagwa, *Kings of Buganda*, 11; Ray, *Myth, Ritual, and Kingship*, 87.

18. For Tantala's analysis of the different contexts of transmission for the Kitara epic and her description of the ideology of *cwezi kubándwa*, see Tantala, "Early History of Kitara," chs. 2 and 4.

19. The following paragraph draws upon ibid., 404–8.

20. Tantala, "Early History of Kitara," 407.

21. Berger, *Religion and Resistance*, 20–21. See also Beattie, "Initiation"; Nyakatura, *Aspects of Bunyoro Customs*, 61–62; and Byaruhanga-Akiiki, *Religion in Bunyoro*, 54–55. On *lubaale* initiation in Buganda, which closely corresponds to *emandwa* initiation in Bunyoro (especially in the use of kinship terminology) and Ankole, see Kaggwa and Welbourn, "*Lubaale* Initiation." On similar initiation practices among the Sumbwa in northwestern Tanzania, see Cory, "Buswezi."

22. Bamunoba and Welbourn, "Emandwa Initiation in Ankole," 17–19.

23. Tantala, "Early History of Kitara," 406.

24. Bamunoba and Welbourn, "Emandwa Initiation in Ankole," 17, 23.

25. On the use of pots in initiation ceremonies and funeral rites, see ibid., 17–18. Pots also figured in the capture of malevolent ancestral ghosts, which were imprisoned in pots and either buried in the bush or burned. See Beattie, "Spirit Mediumship in Bunyoro," 164–65.

26. See Stanley, *My Dark Companions*, 122–25.

27. For example, the regalia for Nakaima, the medium at Ndahura's shrine at Mubende, included leopard skins, cowrie shells, a wild pig's tooth, seed beads, and colobus monkey skins. See Lanning, "Surviving Regalia." In their description of *emandwa* initiation practices in Ankole, Bamunoba and Welbourn noted that a candidate's sponsor provided him or her with a bracelet of white beads prior to the ceremony. Bamunoba and Welbourn, "Emandwa Initiation in Ankole," 17.

28. See Speke, *Journal of the Discovery*, 205–6. Stanley described Kimera as "a king of

Uganda [Buganda], who by his exploits in hunting deserves to be called the Nimrod of that country." Stanley, *My Dark Companions*, 127.

29. For the relationship between the hunter cliché and *kubándwa* practices, see Tantala, "Early History of Kitara," 706–8.

30. Nyakatura, for example, described the Cwezi as excellent hunters and noted that Ndahura rested with his dogs at Butara upon his retreat to Rwagimba, near Lake Busongora. Nyakatura, *Anatomy of an African Kingdom*, 30, 47.

31. Hanson, *Landed Obligation*, 45; Nsimbi, *Amannya Amaganda N'Ennono Zaago*, 249.

32. Stanley, *My Dark Companions*, 146–47.

33. In West Highlands languages such as Rundi, the root **-seegu* yielded the term *ikisheegu* (pl. *ibisheegu*), meaning "initiate to the cult of Kiranga" or "senior initiators of Kiranga cult initiates." See Schoenbrun, *Historical Reconstruction*, 231, 233–34.

34. See, e.g., Nyakatura, *Aspects of Bunyoro Customs*, 60.

35. Ibid.; Beattie, "Initiation," 158.

36. On the notion of *mahano* in Bunyoro, see Tantala, "Early History of Kitara," 261–65.

37. Byaruhanga-Akiiki, *Religion in Bunyoro*, 54; Bamunoba and Welbourn, "Emandwa Initiation in Ankole," 18.

38. The Basonga of western Uganda, who figure prominently in the narratives describing the promotion of *cwezi kubándwa*, observe the grasshopper as their totem. Baganda, Banyoro, and Batoro recognize an affinity between members of the Ganda Grasshopper clan and Basonga groups throughout western Uganda. For the role of the Basonga in the inception of *cwezi kubándwa*, see Berger, "Deities, Dynasties, and Oral Tradition"; and Tantala, "Early History of Kitara," 771–72.

39. While Baganda trace their ancestry patrilineally, the absence of a royal clan in Buganda meant that Ganda kings belonged to their mothers' clans. Nakimera, "Mother of Kimera," is a favorite name among female members of the Grasshopper clan in Buganda.

40. Almost all Grasshopper clan histories label their ancestors "Bahima," a tag intended to mark the clan's connection with pastoralism. In his history of the Grasshopper clan, Kaggwa noted that Grasshopper clan members in Buganda are known as "Bahima who do not herd cattle," referring to their abandonment of their pastoralist occupation in favor of an agricultural lifestyle. Quoted in Kiwanuka, *History of Buganda*, 40.

41. Kagwa, *Clans of Buganda*, 11–15; translated excerpts from Kagwa, *Ekitabo Kye Kika Kyenseenene*, in Kiwanuka, *History of Buganda*, 39–40; Nsimbi, *Amannya Amaganda N'Ennono Zaago*, 278–81.

42. Lanning, "Excavations at Mubende Hill."

43. Nyakatura, *Anatomy of an African Kingdom*, 30; Tantala, "Early History of Kitara," 740–41.

44. For the early history of salt production at Katwe, in southwestern Uganda, see Barrett-Gaines, "Katwe Salt," chs. 2 and 3.

45. Roscoe, *Bakitara or Banyoro*, 234–35, and *Northern Bantu*, 76–77; Connah, *Kibiro*, 59.

46. Byaruhanga-Akiiki, *Religion in Bunyoro*, 45–46.

47. Ibid., 46.

48. This understanding of the cult of Ndahura's diffusion derives from Cwezi narratives recording Ndahura's return "home" to Lake Masyoro (Lake George) after he abdicated the throne to Wamara. Tantala, "Early History of Kitara," 742–43. For Ndahura's retreat "home," see Nyakatura, *Anatomy of an African Kingdom*, 30.

49. Tantala, "Early History of Kitara," 791n97.

50. Simon Mwebe, interview, 5 May 2002.

51. Kamuhangire, "Pre-Colonial Economic and Social History," 76.

52. Kagwa, *Clans of Buganda*, 13; Nsimbi, *Amannya Amaganda N'Ennono Zaago*, 280.

53. Tantala, "Early History of Kitara," 743.

54. Ibid., 388–91.

55. Fisher, *Twilight Tales*, 82–83.

56. See, e.g., Nyakatura, *Anatomy of an African Kingdom*, 31. On Isimbwa as the archetypical *cwezi* itinerant medium, see Tantala, "Early History of Kitara," 704.

57. I thank Ben Twagira for telling me of this use of the term.

58. Snoxall, *Luganda-English Dictionary*, 84; Le Veux, *Premier essai*, 170.

59. This practice is captured in a praise name for the female *cwezi* Rukoke, Nyakalika Irika engabu nk'abasaija (She who carried and brandished a shield like a man). Nyakatura, *Aspects of Bunyoro Customs*, 71.

60. Nyakatura, *Anatomy of an African Kingdom*, 60–62; Byaruhanga-Akiiki, *Religion in Bunyoro*, 53–54.

61. On the militant aspect of the spread of the cult of Ndahura, see Nyakatura, *Anatomy of an African Kingdom*, 22, 25–26; and Fisher, *Twilight Tales*, 93–95.

62. The title Mugema derives from the verb *okugema*, "to inoculate, immunize, ward off (disease, calamity)." This meaning derives from the older and more widespread meaning "to protect." For the history of the Grey Monkey clan, see Kagwa, *Clans of Buganda*, 15–19; Nsimbi, *Amannya Amaganda N'Ennono Zaago*, 273–78; Jjumba and Council of the Ssiga of Jjumba, *Ekitabo Eky'essiga Lya Jjumba*; Mukasa, "Reason for the Post of Mugema"; and Charles Alex Nsejere, Sserwanga Ndawula Katumba Balamaga, and Michael Mugadya Selubidde, interview, 26 October 2001.

63. George William Kalule, interview, 29 September 2001; Hajji Kawooya Ssemandwa Bakazirwendo, interview, 4 October 2001; Nsimbi, *Amannya Amaganda N'Ennono Zaago*, 190–94.

64. For the broader use of the term *mukongozzi* to mean "medium," see Nsimbi, *Amannya Amaganda N'Ennono Zaago*, 120; and Kaggwa and Welbourn, "Lubaale

Initiation," 218. The term was frequently used in this sense in conversations with mediums. To point to one example, an attendant at the shrine of the queen mother Kanyange, the mother of Kabaka Ssuuna, explained that the *mukongozzi* for Kanyange "is identified by [Kanyange's] spirit. She comes and speaks out and can say things about the dead Queen Mother's life, which makes people realize that she is a *mukongozzi*."

65. For *okuvuuvuuma*, see Le Veux, *Premier essai*, 974–75; and Murphy, *Luganda-English Dictionary*, 576. For the history of the Buffalo clan, see Nsimbi, *Amannya Amaganda N'Ennono Zaago*, 281–83; and Office of the Buffalo Clan, "History of the Buffalo Clan."

66. Significantly, Bakka and its surrounding localities later became the place where newly installed Ganda kings underwent an elaborate nine-day sequence of rituals known as *okukula*, which culminated in the recognition of the new king "as Kimera." For a description of the *okukula* rites, see Kagwa, *Customs of the Baganda*, 16–18; Roscoe, *Baganda*, 210–13; and Kakoma, Ntate, and Serukaga, *Ekitabo Eky'Abakyanjove*, 15–17. On Ndahura's campaigns, see Fisher, *Twilight Tales*, 89–95; and Nyakatura, *Anatomy of an African Kingdom*, 22, 25–26.

67. Fisher, *Twilight Tales*, 93–94; Nyakatura, *Anatomy of an African Kingdom*, 22; K.W., "Kings of Bunyoro-Kitara," 159.

68. Nyakatura, *Aspects of Bunyoro Customs*, 66. According to Nyakatura, *ekokoro* is a disease that attacks the nose and upper lips, disfiguring the face completely.

69. For example, the first reference to smallpox in Rwandan dynastic traditions appears in the mid-eighteenth century. See Vansina, *Antecedents to Modern Rwanda*, 127, 266n2.

70. The origins of smallpox remain unknown. The disease may have been endemic in the densely populated Nile and Ganges river valleys at the beginning of first millennium, from where it could have spread to southwestern Asia and Europe. Fenner et al., *Smallpox and Its Eradication*, 216–17.

71. The disease caused by *variola minor* and its spread was exactly like *variola major*. But whereas *variola major* killed more than 20 percent of its victims, *variola minor* killed at most 1 percent. The global eradication of smallpox was declared by the World Health Organization in 1980.

72. In his study of the relationship between disease and imperialism, Sheldon Watts notes that "epidemiological studies suggest that the form of smallpox found in principal catchment areas for slaves later sold in the New World was *variola intermedius*." Mortality rates for *variola intermedius* ranged from 2.8 percent to 10.9 percent, making this strain less lethal than *variola major* but somewhat more lethal than *variola minor*. Watts, *Epidemics and History*, 111. Not all scholars acknowledge the existence of *variola intermedius* or the utility of attempting to differentiate further between *variola major* and *variola minor*. See, for example, Fenner et al., *Smallpox and Its Eradication*, 4, 177–78.

73. Dawson, "Socioeconomic Change and Disease." Pointing to the studies identifying the presence of an intermediate strain of smallpox in Africa, Dawson comments that "if Africa had its own strain of smallpox found in all parts of the
continent, the smallpox virus could hardly have been introduced and spread or
have undergone the very same change throughout the continent in recent times."
For an overview of the evidence regarding inoculation in Africa, see Herbert,
"Smallpox Inoculation in Africa." Despite presenting evidence for widespread
inoculation, Herbert correctly concludes that the broader question of the origins
of the practice await further investigation.

74. Oral traditions and the observations of European explorers attribute the deaths of
several nineteenth-century Great Lakes kings to smallpox. In Buganda, for example, Kabaka Ssuuna died of smallpox brought by his army from Kiziba in October
1856 or 1857. This was the third outbreak of the disease during Ssuuna's reign.
Médard, "Croissance et crises," 78.

75. Yaws is an infectious and contagious disease related to syphilis and pinta. The
causative agent is *Treponema pallidum*. If left untreated, the disease can result in
severe skin ulcers and the destruction of bone and cartilage, leading to defor-
mities and disfiguration. Recent examinations of skeletal remains from Lake
Turkana, in Kenya, suggest that treponematosis (in the form of yaws) had its
origins in Africa during the Middle Pleistocene, 1.5 million years ago. Walker
and Hay, "Yaws"; Mafart, "Goundou"; Rothschild, Hershkovitz, and Rothschild,
"Origin of Yaws."

76. Nyakatura, *Anatomy of an African Kingdom*, 22; Fisher, *Twilight Tales*, 93–94. There
is also another possible interpretation of the skin diseases mentioned in oral
traditions describing the activities of Ndahura's armies. In many places in the
region, skin diseases were considered the result of moral indiscretions; therefore, their mention in oral traditions may refer to the prevalence of indecent
activities characterized by skin sores rather than to smallpox or yaws as biological entities. I thank one of the anonymous reviewers of the manuscript for this
possible interpretation.

77. Lanning, "Excavations at Mubende Hill," 154; Barrett-Gaines, "Katwe Salt," 55–
56.

78. Uzoigwe, "Precolonial Markets in Bunyoro-Kitara," 48; Barrett-Gaines, "Katwe
Salt," 76.

79. These efforts built upon much older struggles to control ironworking in which
political leaders in iron-producing areas sought to attract smiths and smelters
into their domains in order to co-opt the powerful symbolic association between
iron production, fecundity, and fertility. See Herbert, *Iron, Gender, and Power*.

80. Schoenbrun, *A Green Place, A Good Place*, 168–71; Richard Reid, *Political Power*, chs. 4
and 7; Tosh, "Northern Interlacustrine Region."

81. The Kiro persona in Cwezi narratives represented a cult closely aligned with that

of the *cwezi* Ndahura. An important secondary center for the cult of Ndahura existed in the heart of an iron-producing area at Butiiti, in Mwenge.

82. He is selling, Kagwagu ehe eee
     He is selling salt ehe nunu
     He is selling ehe eee nunu
     My man is selling.
     Byaruhanga-Akiiki, *Religion in Bunyoro*, 251.

83. Tantala, "Early History of Kitara," 829–38. The correspondence between the locations of the tombs of the kings of Bunyoro and major markets suggests that these leaders built upon the political strategy of their predecessors. See Uzoigwe, "Precolonial Markets in Bunyoro-Kitara," 39, 61–62.

84. The development of *omuranga*, armed bands of twenty or more traders led by an appointed leader, indicates the nature of these dangers. Uzoigwe, "Precolonial Markets in Bunyoro-Kitara," 48–49; Good, "Salt, Trade, and Disease," 559.

85. Traders also established blood-brother relationships (*omukago*) as a form of protection. Uzoigwe, "Precolonial Markets in Bunyoro-Kitara," 48–49, 53; Kamuhangire, "Pre-Colonial Economic and Social History," 80; Barrett-Gaines, "Katwe Salt," 64–65.

86. For an example of the importance of spiritual protection in facilitating regional trade in southwestern Africa, see Janzen, *Lemba*.

87. Richard Reid, *Political Power*, 135–48.

88. In her study of the Katwe salt industry in southwestern Uganda, Kathryn Barrett-Gaines noted that "salt-making clans" developed lake transport of salt along the shores of Lakes Edward and Albert and that "traders forged kin-like relationships with people at various points along trade routes so that they would have a safe place to stop, to sell, and to sleep when they were away from home." Barrett-Gaines, "Katwe Salt," 64–65, 76, 85.

89. The connection between violence, trade, and the spread of disease produced tragic consequences in the second half of the nineteenth century as contact with the coastal trade in slaves and ivory increased. Good, "Salt, Trade, and Disease." On the prevalence of epidemics in nineteenth-century Buganda, see Médard, "Croissance et crises," 73–79.

90. Le Veux, *Manuel de langue luganda*, 266–67; Stanley, *My Dark Companions*, 121; Nsimbi, *Amannya Amaganda N'Ennono Zaago*, 39, 41. Both Kaggwa and Roscoe also credited Kimera with the early influx of iron implements into Buganda, with Roscoe noting that Kimera sent hoes and weapons into the area after he had learned the craft of metalworking in Bunyoro. In addition, Nyakatura, in his history of Bunyoro-Kitara, also describes Kato Kimera and his companions as traveling from Bunyoro to Buganda with large amounts of salt. Roscoe, *Baganda*, 379; Kagwa, *Customs of the Baganda*, 20; Nyakatura, *Anatomy of an African Kingdom*, 64.

91. Gray and Birmingham, "Some Economic and Political Consequences"; Kamuhangire, "Pre-Colonial Economic and Social History"; Connah, Kibiro, 216.
92. Schweinfurth et al., Emin Pasha, 175–76, quoted in Connah, Kibiro, 18.
93. Thruston, African Incidents, 143, quoted in Connah, Kibiro, 24.
94. Good, "Salt, Trade, and Disease," 565.
95. Ibid., 557. See also Kamuhangire, "Pre-Colonial Economic and Social History," 80. Richard Reid has also pointed out that Lord Frederick Lugard, the well-known British explorer and colonial administrator, noted the existence of a salt trade between Buganda and Katwe. See Reid, Political Power, 141.
96. As a major distribution point, Mubende served as a point of convergence for trade routes that led to both Katwe and Kibiro. See Uzoigwe, "Precolonial Markets in Bunyoro-Kitara," 48. On the trade between Ankole and Katwe, see Good, "Salt, Trade, and Disease," 558–61.
97. Connah, Kibiro, chs. 5–8, 9.
98. Unlike ancestral ghosts (mizimu), cwezi could return from the underworld even if they had no heirs to look after in the world of the living. Cwezi kubándwa thus provided hope for kinless, heirless, and childless people who sought to overcome the social challenges accompanying their condition by becoming mediums for a cwezi. See Tantala, "Early History of Kitara," 257–357. Based on linguistic evidence that points to the invention of bucweke, the term for the condition of an adult dying with no heirs or children, prior to the invention of the term cwezi, Schoenbrun argues that the innovation of cwezi kubándwa seems to have responded to an increasing anxiety over fertility. Schoenbrun, A Green Place, A Good Place, 196–97, 238–40.
99. On the relationship between climate change and political complexity in western Uganda, see Robertshaw and Taylor, "Climate Change."
100. Schoenbrun, "Conjuring the Modern in Africa."

5. Clanship, State Formation, and the Shifting Contours of Public Healing

1. In her recent analysis of Buganda's early history, Holly Hanson describes how the Ganda polity developed from the complex knitting together of relationships of reciprocal obligation linking followers to chiefs (and other sorts of authority figures) and chiefs to the king, whose primary responsibilities initially revolved around mediating competition among chiefs for followers. Hanson, Landed Obligation, ch. 2.
2. Wrigley, Kingship and State, 172 (quotation); Cox, "Growth and Expansion of Buganda."
3. Hanson, Landed Obligation, 50, 78, 82; Kottak, "Ecological Variables," 374; Kiwanuka, History of Buganda, 68–70, 99–100; Wrigley, Kingship and State, 172–78.
4. Wrigley, Kingship and State, 174–80 (quotation on 174); Kiwanuka, History of Buganda, 69–70, 99–102.

5. Kiwanuka, *History of Buganda*, 115.

6. Richard Reid, *Political Power*, 232.

7. Kiwanuka, *History of Buganda*, 72–78, 114–15; Wrigley, *Kingship and State*, 207–9; Hanson, *Landed Obligation*, 81–84.

8. Richard Reid, *Political Power*, 74.

9. Médard, "Croissance et crises," 184.

10. While Kaggwa may have remembered Mwanga II's installation in 1884, it is possible that Barolomayo Zimbe's description of the Buddo rites may be the only account by an eyewitness of any coronation ceremony prior to that of Daudi Chwa, which took place in 1913 and bore the unmistakable imprint of British colonial and Christian missionary influence. The following description of the Buddo rites draws upon Kagwa, *Ekitabo Kye Mpisa za Baganda*, 4–14; Roscoe, *Baganda*, 191–96; Snoxall, "Coronation Ritual"; Zimbe, *Buganda Ne Kabaka*, 79–82; Richards, *Changing Structure of a Ganda Village*, 35–45.

11. Prominent figures in Buganda, particularly royalty, were said to have had a still-born twin at birth. The stumps of these figures' umbilical cords were preserved and placed in the cylindrical base of a vaselike object. These symbols of royal twins were cared for by the mothers of the princes and princesses and accompanied their human counterparts throughout their lives, as the health and welfare of the humans was thought to be bound up with them.

12. The two battling parties were evidently quite large. Zimbe, who witnessed Mwanga's installation, estimated that there were four thousand people in the *kabaka*'s entourage.

13. Snoxall, "Coronation Ritual," 280.

14. Wrigley, *Kingship and State*, 79. For descriptions of this ritual, see Kagwa, *Customs of the Baganda*, 16–18; Roscoe, *Baganda*, 210–13; and Kakoma, Ntate, and Serukaga, *Ekitabo Eky'Abakyanjove*, 15–17.

15. Ray, *Myth, Ritual, and Kingship*, 83–84; Wrigley, *Kingship and State*, 210, 229 (quotation); Médard, "Croissance et crises," 425. Besides the Civet Cat clan, three other clans—the Mushroom, Colobus Monkey, and Frog clans—had their principal estates in the area and played crucial roles in the royal ritual.

16. For the use of the distinction between creative and instrumental power as an analytical tool, see Schoenbrun, *A Green Place, A Good Place*, 12–15. For an extended discussion of the differences between these two types of authority, with particular reference to the narratives about Nyabingi in northern Rwanda and southwestern Uganda, see Feierman, "Colonizers, Colonized" and "Healing as Social Criticism."

17. Kagwa, *Kings of Buganda*, 71.

18. The forest grove next to Kintu's shrine at Nnono is referred to as Kintu's palace (*lubiri*) and is regarded as the dwelling place of his spirit.

19. Here and elsewhere in the narrative, "Kintu" most likely refers to the spirit

medium presiding at Kintu's shrine, who during acts of possession assumed the identity of his or her spiritual patron.

20. The figure Ssenkoma appears in Kaggwa's version of the narrative. A chief named Namutwe takes the place of Ssenkoma in Roscoe's version, while in Stanley's rendition it is Mawanda's prime minister who emerges in Kintu's shrine.

21. Benjamin Ray argues that the story of Kintu's conquest at Buddo Hill "originated in Namugala's reign as a justification for the new ceremonies he established there." Ray, *Myth, Ritual, and Kingship*, 78. My argument differs from Ray's in pointing out that "Kintu and Bemba the Snake" circulated in Buganda in a predynastic context and became harnessed to the Ganda state in the mid-eighteenth century.

22. As my interviews with healers discussed in chapter 2 make clear, the previous conception of Kintu as a *musambwa*-type spirit did not wholly disappear. Rather, the ritual activities directed toward the spirit Kintu became part of collective efforts to ensure the well-being of Buganda.

23. The name Naggalabi consists of the verb *okuggala*, "to shut out," and the adjectival suffix -*bi*, "evil, danger," thus yielding "the place where evil and danger are shut out." According to dynastic accounts, Namuggala chose Buddo (Naggalabi) Hill as the ceremonial site on account of a pronouncement he and his three brothers had received from a diviner named Buddo prior to embarking on their endeavor to overthrow their uncle Kabaka Mawanda. Buddo had given the four brothers a *jjembe* and told them that "if any of you becomes king and steps on the *jjembe* he will never be overthrown. But whoever fails to step on the *jjembe* will never become king of Buganda." Kagwa, *Kings of Buganda*, 75. The four brothers had buried the *jjembe* on Buddo Hill and then proceeded to defeat their uncle Mawanda, after which one of them, Mwanga, had succeeded to the throne. Namuggala had then assumed the kingship after Mwanga's assassination and proceeded to step on the *jjembe* given to him by Buddo. According to Kaggwa, Buddo had then explained to Namuggala that "it was upon Naggalabi hill that his ancestor Kintu had beaten Bemba, the snake who originally ruled Buganda." Kagwa, *Customs of Buganda*, 12. See also Wrigley, *Kingship and State*, 210; Kagwa, *Kings of Buganda*, 69–81, and *Ekitabo Kye Mpisa za Baganda*, 7–8.

24. Kiwanuka, *History of Buganda*, 99–100, 110, 114–15; Médard, "Croissance et crises," 425; Wrigley, *Kingship and State*, 207–9; Hanson, *Landed Obligation*, 81.

25. Kagwa, *Kings of Buganda*, 73.

26. Kawooya Ssemandwa is discussed in chapter 2, Kisolo Muwanga in chapter 3, and Kimera in chapter 4.

27. Here I follow Wrigley's suggestion that despite his appearance in the early sections of the Ganda king list as the eighth Ganda king, Nakibinge more properly belongs with the generation of eighteenth-century Ganda kings that includes Mawanda and Namuggala. Wrigley argues for Nakibinge's placement in this

portion of the Ganda dynastic narrative based on the striking overlaps between the details of his reign and those of Mawanda's. The narratives surrounding both of these rulers included royal figures named Juma and Luyenje, and as discussed in this section, both kings—and these kings only—sought to garner Kintu's support by seeking an audience with his shrine attendants at Magonga. According to the Ganda dynastic narrative, Mawanda's soldiers burned down Nakibinge's shrine at Bbumbu, in Kyaddondo, which also suggests a connection between the two kings. As Wrigley points out, however, perhaps the most significant indication that Nakibinge and Mawanda belonged to the same historical period is the critical roles played by members of the Lungfish, Sheep, Seed, and Leopard clans in the narratives describing the reigns both kings. Wrigley, *Kingship and State*, 210–12.

28. The following summary of the Kibuuka narrative relies on Kagwa, *Kings of Buganda*, 26–29; Le Veux, *Manuel de langue luganda*, 271–78; Kagwa, *Ekitabo Kye Mpisa za Baganda*, 33–35; Roscoe, "Kibuka" and *Baganda*, 301–3; Kagwa, *Clans of Buganda*, 66–71; Nsimbi, *Amannya Amaganda N'Ennono Zaago*, 128–30; and Gray, "Kibuka."

29. Here I follow Kaggwa's version of the narrative as presented in *Kings of Buganda*. According to Le Veux's version, Nakibinge feared that there were too many Banyoro living around him and asked the Lungfish clan member Gabunga to take him to a diviner for advice. Accompanied by Gabunga, the queen mother, a servant, and a dog, Nakibinge set out to see the diviner, who, as in Kaggwa's version, advised the king to journey to Ssese to seek Kibuuka's assistance.

30. The story of Muzingu appears in Kagwa, *Ekitabo Kye Mpisa za Baganda*, 218. In Nsimbi's version of these events, the leaders of Mbaale sent Kirimungo, of the Lungfish clan, to inform Wannema of Kibuuka's death.

31. Kituuma's name, which derives from the verb *okutuuma*, "to give a name to," developed as a result of his exclaiming "Kibuuka wuuno" (The flyer is up there) upon seeing Kyobe's body in the tree branches. Similarly, Nakatandagira's name, which derives from the verb *okutandagira*, "to hurl down," related to the manner in which he dropped Kyobe Kibuuka's body down from the *mvule* tree in which he had been killed. See Nsimbi, *Amannya Amaganda N'Ennono Zaago*, 294–95.

32. The most commonly found definition of *ssaabaganzi* is "maternal uncle of the kabaka"; the *ssaabaganzi* is one of only three notables allowed to greet the *kabaka* while standing. In the Kibuuka narrative, however, the title can be viewed as referring to its perhaps older meaning, "chief of the household."

33. In his early work on the history of Busoga, David Cohen suggested that Bumogera, which appears in several clan histories, was an area located on the eastern side of Lake Victoria. Nsimbi likewise noted that Bumogera was located near Kisumu, on the eastern shores of Lake Victoria in present-day western Kenya, an identification I heard in several of the interviews I conducted. Wrigley suggested

that the place name Bumogera, which translates as "Land of the Peepers" (from the verb *okumoga*, "to peep"), "probably originated from the sight of canoe-men's heads appearing over the gunwales." One of Cohen's informants from the abaiseNhikodo clan related that the name derived from the method of fighting employed by the area's inhabitants, who mastered the art of fighting from tree-tops. This explanation might provide a clue to the source of the initial success of the followers of Kibuuka, who, as discussed earlier, achieved prominence on the Ganda mainland by employing this very technique. Cohen, *Historical Tradition of Busoga*, 94–100; Nsimbi, *Amannya Amaganda N'Ennono Zaago*, 252; Wrigley, *Kingship and State*, 167.

34. Accounts of Wannema's history are far less detailed than those of his sons Mukasa and Kibuuka, but see Nsimbi, *Amannya Amaganda N'Ennono Zaago*, 125–27.

35. Ibid., 293–99; Kagwa, *Clans of Buganda*, 66–71; Committee of the Sheep Clan, in Buganda Clan Office, Mengo, Responses to survey sent out to heads of clans in Uganda by Akakiiko Ka Ssabasajja Kabaka Akakola Ku Nsonga Ze Bika, 4–9; Kubi Kiviri Muyondo, interview, 31 October 2001.

36. Kagwa, *Clans of Buganda*, 71; Committee of the Sheep Clan, in Responses to survey, 2.

37. Kibuuka's main shrine, which housed the hero's jawbone, stood on a hill bordered on three sides by a forest sacred to Kibuuka and on the fourth by a large open space. Next to this shrine stood the house Bagambamunyoro, literally "They speak like a Munyoro," which, according to Kaggwa, meant that Banyoro were forbidden from entering Mbaale. Adjacent to Bagambamunyoro stood a third house, Namirembe, which served as an audience chamber and also as a place of detention for prisoners. The following description of Kibuuka's shrine site and the officials who attended to the shrine draws upon Kagwa, *Ekitabo Kye Mpisa za Baganda*, 218–22; and Roscoe, "Kibuka" and *Baganda*, 303–8. Unfortunately, Kaggwa did not describe the ceremony itself. Both he and Roscoe did, however, provide descriptions of the types of rituals undertaken at Mbaale prior to the commencement of battle. I discuss the significance of these activities below.

38. For example, Kiguli guarded Kibuuka's second "twin" (*omulongo*), Sebawutu served as the main bark-cloth maker, Namunyi thatched the roof of Kibuuka's shrine, Nakabango carried Kibuuka's shields, and Nkunyi rubbed Kibuuka's skins when they became wet. For a complete list of these officials and their duties, see Kagwa, *Ekitabo Kye Mpisa za Baganda*, 220–21.

39. Roscoe recorded that Kibuuka's compound housed forty mediums. Kaggwa, however, noted that while many mediums worked with Kibuuka in other places, the fourteen who participated in the ceremonies at the new moon were the most important and operated only at Kibuuka's shrine at Mbaale.

40. Roscoe reported that prisoners sent to Kibuuka by the kabaka were paraded before the assembled officials, after which they were given a doctored beer designed to prevent their ancestral ghosts from injuring the king and then killed at nearby sacrificial grounds.

41. Roscoe, Baganda, 305–7, 248–49; Kagwa, Ekitabo kye Mpisa za Baganda, 219, 221; Lush, "Kiganda Drums," 14–15.

42. Although it is not explicitly stated, these references to Nende more than likely refer to his important relics, such as his jawbone and his umbilical cord. For a full description of Nende's compound and officials, see Kagwa, Ekitabo Kye Mpisa za Baganda, 222–25; and Roscoe, Baganda, 308.

43. For a useful extended discussion of the development of Ganda military power and weaponry with particular emphasis on the nineteenth century, see Richard Reid, Political Power, chs. 9–11, and "Mutesa and Mirambo."

44. For instance, Kibuuka's role in Nakibinge's campaigns and the development of his shrine complex at Mbaale, in Mawokota, a borderland area situated on the cusp of Ganda and Nyoro speech communities, gave rise to the well-known saying, "One who does not want to reside among the Banyoro should return to Mbaale, where the Baganda filter themselves" (Ggwe atayagala kutuula na Banyoro, dda e Mbaale eri Abaganda abesengejje). Two other well-known sayings associated with Mbaale convey a similar message: "Return to Mbaale, where the true Baganda reside" (Odda Mbaale, mu Baganda banno); and "I am a Muganda of Mbaale" (Nze ndi Muganda we Mbaale). Wrigley, Kingship and State, 214–15; Nsimbi, Amannya Amaganda N'Ennono Zaago, 298 (quotations); Kagwa, Ekitabo Kye Mpisa za Baganda, 219.

45. In his biography of the Ganda regent Stanislaus Mugwanya, J. S. Kasirye noted that Ganda kings pledged princesses to lubaale "because they wanted to spy on the bakungu or other people who went to consult the lubaale on behalf of the balangira [princes] who wanted to capture the Nnamulondo (royal throne) from the Kabaka, so spies could inform the Kabaka in time." Kasirye, "Obulamu Bwa Stanislaus Mugwanya," in Source Materials in Uganda History, Volume 3, 339.

46. Feierman, "Healing as Social Criticism," 79.

47. Richard Reid, Political Power, 116. The Church Missionary Society missionary R. W. Felkin noted that the performance of the last funeral rites, a ceremony that in Buganda reflected a person's standing in a recognized social group, was not undertaken in the case of a slave's death. Instead, his or her body was thrown into the forest. Felkin also observed that any offspring resulting from a slave's marriage belonged to the head of household. Another commonly cited distinction between free and nonfree people was that the former could not inherit property. Felkin, "Notes on the Waganda Tribe," 746, 759; Roscoe, Baganda, 14–15.

48. Schoenbrun, "Violence and Vulnerability"; Richard Reid, Political Power, 113–23; Hanson, Landed Obligation, ch. 3; and Twaddle, "Ending of Slavery in Buganda"

and "Slaves and Peasants in Buganda." The most recent and most comprehensive analysis of slavery in the Great Lakes region is Médard and Doyle, *Slavery in the Great Lakes Region*.

49. Richard Reid, *Political Power*, 116.

50. Hanson, *Landed Obligation*, 60–61.

51. Tantala, "Early History of Kitara," 396–97; Schoenbrun, *A Green Place, A Good Place*, 238.

52. James Magala Mutetwa, Augustine Kizito Mutumba Ssalongo, and Mayanja Sebuliba Nyamanka, 16 April 2002. Similarly, in a story related to me concerning the colonial period the county chief Kimbugwe Luwandaga ordered some of his representatives to raid the shrine of a prominent medium named Kyaggwire. They tied him up in ropes and took him to the governor's court. During his court appearance, however, Kyaggwire became possessed by the spirit Lubanga, and his stick started flying around the room, prompting the governor to set him free. Iriyamu Baluli, interview, 13 February 2002.

53. Ali Ssalongo Kiwanda, interview, 10 April 2002. Similarly, in showing me around his estate and explaining the significance of the shrine located on it, the head of the patrilineage of Mbajja in the Lungfish clan explained that the mediums who operated at the shrine could step into the continuously burning fire while fully clothed without suffering any burns. Omutaka Mbajja, interview, 8 December 2001.

54. Kagwa, *Kings of Buganda*, 118–19. In another example, Kabaka Tebandeke, who according to Ganda dynastic traditions reigned a generation before Mawanda, suffered a severe loss of authority at the hands of the *lubaale* Mukasa. Shortly after ordering the killing of a number of Mukasa's mediums and the sacking of their shrines, Tebandeke contracted a serious illness that made him delirious and ultimately sent him into hiding in the forest. Similarly, the capital of the late eighteenth-century king Kyabaggu was afflicted with a plague of deadly rats following a military expedition in which the king's forces plundered Mukasa's shrine on Bubembe Island and killed his principal medium, Gugu. In an effort to reconcile with Mukasa, Kyabaggu ordered the construction of a new shrine, presented a large number of offerings, and dedicated one of his daughters, Princess Nakayiza, to the *lubaale*. Kagwa, *Kings of Buganda*, 56–57, 82–84.

55. Feierman, "Colonizers, Colonized," 199.

56. Significantly, many of these sanctuaries were located in Ssingo and Bulemeezi, territories that formed the contentious and vulnerable borderland in the periodic military struggles between Buganda and Bunyoro. See, for example, the cases of Kagaba Hill, which housed a shrine for the python spirit Magobwe and served as a place of refuge for the area's residents when Ganda armies passed through their villages, and Wajala Hill, in Nakasongola, which housed a shrine for the

spirit Lubanga and therefore was not plundered by advancing Ganda war parties, in Gomotoka, "The Going of the Messengers of H. H. the Kabaka Daudi Cwa II on Inspections of Buganda," in Translations from *Munno* and Other Periodicals.

57. Roscoe recorded that Nende had six wives who were princesses, all of whom claimed seats in the shrine on either side of the platform on which the *lubaale* sat. Roscoe, *Baganda*, 308.

58. In perhaps an overstatement of the extent of the practice, the pioneering missionary Robert Ashe noted in the latter part of the nineteenth century that "every Mumbeja [princess] is supposed to be a . . . nominal wife of a Divinity." Ashe, *Chronicles of Uganda*, 105.

59. The gendering of princesses as males did not represent the only instance in which conventional gender identities were subverted in Buganda. As Sylvia Nannyonga-Tamusuza has recently argued, gender socialization within the palace assigned the female gender to all commoners (*bakopi*), both men and women, in order to emphasize their submissiveness to the royal complex. Nannyonga-Tamusuza, *Baakisimba*.

60. Musisi, "Transformations of Baganda Women," 78–86; Hanson, *Landed Obligation*, 74.

61. Many observers reported that princesses were barred from having children. Such accounts, however, are ideological statements rather than general ethnographic observations of the fact that princesses did not produce children. The case of Princess Nassolo, who was one of *lubaale* Mukasa's wives and also led the successful rebellion against Kabaka Kagulu Tebucwereke, provides an example of the potential threat posed by princesses. Kagwa, *Kings of Buganda*, 62–66; Ashe, *Chronicles of Uganda*, 105.

62. According to ethnographic accounts from Busoga, for example, all female mediums had their own seats—a noticeable practice in a culture where women were generally prohibited from sitting on stools—and enjoyed treatment as men during states of possession. Similarly, female mediums in Burundi wore men's ceremonial dress called *imbega* and were permitted to judge trials, a privilege ordinarily reserved for men. In Nkore (Ankole), meanwhile, certain female "witches" represented a noticeable exception to a generally accepted practice that restricted to men the right to own and inherit property. Finally, *kubándwa* ceremonies in Rwanda erased the distinction between male and female practitioners by attributing to all initiates the quality *umugabo* (manliness). Berger, *Religion and Resistance*, 23, and "Fertility as Power," 68.

63. Berger, *Religion and Resistance*, 69–70; Berger, "Fertility as Power," 73.

64. Roscoe, *Baganda*, 9.

65. For a contextualized illustration of these undertakings, see the story in which Kabaka Mutebi dedicated several princesses to a medium in the Oribi Antelope

clan in the hope that this would guarantee his recovery from an illness and a prosperous life. Kiggye, Sekamwa, and the members of the Mpewo clan, *Ekitabo Ky'Ekika Kye Mpewo*, 15–17, 23–27.

66. Wrigley, *Kingship and State*, 215; Ray, *Myth, Ritual, and Kingship*, 83.

67. Southwold, *Bureaucracy and Chiefship*; Kiwanuka, *History of Buganda*, chs. 4–6; Musisi, "Women, 'Elite Polygyny,' and Buganda"; Ray, *Myth, Ritual, and Kingship*, 3.

68. Richard Reid, *Political Power*; Hanson, *Landed Obligation*, ch. 3.

69. The literal translation of Butambala, "Land of the people who do not wear clothes," from the verb *okwambala*, "to put on clothes," hints at the types of cultural constructions involved in military conquests.

70. The name Kizunga derives from the verb *okuzunga*, "to stagger, reel about, shake (the head)," a possible reference to the area's leader's engaging in acts of possession involving the spirits residing in the caves in which he resided.

71. Sekiti, "The Baganda of Mbale," in Translations from *Munno* and Other Periodicals.

72. Testimonies of Stanislas Mugwanya, Zachariah Kisingiri, and Nuhu Mbogo in Roscoe and Kagwa, "Enquiry into Native Land Tenure," 7, 11, 15; Kagwa, *Customs of the Baganda*, 123; Roscoe, *Baganda*, 327.

73. Hanson, *Landed Obligation*, 40–41.

74. On *minkisi*, see MacGaffey, "Changing Representations," 204–6.

75. Roscoe, *Baganda*, 324.

76. For a description of the various royal *mayembe*, see ibid., 323–29.

77. Kititu Hill took the name Kiggwa Hill after it became the Dog clan's principal estate.

78. Njala, "Manya Ebyafaayo By'Ekika Ky'abaganda Abeddira Embwa"; Nsimbi, *Amannya Amaganda N'Ennono Zaago*, 220; Nnalongo Nakasi, interview, 9 February 2002.

79. Nsimbi, *Amannya Amaganda N'Ennono Zaago*, 242.

80. Kagwa, *Kings of Buganda*, 45; Wrigley, *Kingship and State*, 179–80.

81. Kiwanuka, *History of Buganda*, 102.

82. Ganda dynastic narratives provide further reasons for tempering claims regarding the rise of royal authority, since they relate that Mutebi's reign commenced with his unsuccessful attempt to dismiss the chiefs Mugema and Kaggo. Kagwa, *Kings of Buganda*, 44.

83. Kiggye, Sekamwa, and the members of the Mpewo clan, *Ekitabo Ky'Ekika Kye Mpewo*, 15–17, 23–27. The monster figure and related characters, such as children born with a full set of teeth or hairy bodies, appear repeatedly in narratives found in Buganda as well as elsewhere in the region and signify a person endowed with potentially dangerous capacities in the ritual arena. For examples from areas outside of Buganda, see Tantala, "Early History of Kitara," 714; and

Kenny, "Stranger from the Lake," 13. See also David Cohen's discussion of the *mukama* figure in *Womunafu's Bunafu.*
84. Silvestri Kiguli Nkeretanyi, "Times Are Joining to the Others," in Translations from *Munno* and Other Periodicals.
85. Nsimbi, *Amannya Amaganda N'Ennono Zaago*, 299–301; Kiggye, Sekamwa, and the members of the Mpewo clan, *Ekitabo Ky'Ekika Kye Mpewo.*
86. Kagwa, *Clans of Buganda*, 107; Nsimbi, *Amannya Amaganda N'Ennono Zaago*, 308–10; Kiwanuka, *History of Buganda*, 75–76.
87. For more on the development of Buganda's naval fleet, see Richard Reid, *Political Power*, 243–48.
88. Nsimbi, *Amannya Amaganda N'Ennono Zaago*, 205–6; Council of the Reedbuck Clan, "Ebyafayo Bye Kika Kyenjaza Ne Jjaja Wakyo"; Kagwa, *Clans of Buganda*, 92.
89. Nsimbi, *Amannya Amaganda N'Ennono Zaago*, 243–44; Council of the Bean Clan, "Ebyafaayo By'Ekika Ky'Empindi."
90. Nsimbi, *Amannya Amaganda N'Ennono Zaago*, 295–96.
91. A description of these ceremonies appeared in the Luganda-language newspaper *Munno* in the first part of the twentieth century. See Y. Kikulwe, "The Ancient Acts of the Rulers of Bulemezi," in Translations from *Munno* and Other Periodicals.
92. The name Bwamikitimba, literally "Chiefs of the net [*Kitimba*] used for trapping large animals," suggests that the *mutaka* may have presided over a shrine around which the area's inhabitants gathered prior to engaging in collective hunting endeavors.
93. Similar though less detailed examples appear scattered throughout the Ganda historical record. For instance, shortly after his appointment the chief of Buddu, the *ppookino*, presented a sheep to Kaliika, the head of the Lark clan, and he periodically visited a python spirit at Bulonge on behalf of the *kabaka* to ensure the king's continued prosperity. Ssenyoga Kalika, interview, 13 June 2002; Roscoe, "Python Worship," 90.
94. One of the ways that Ganda kings and their representatives sought to overcome this reliance on local authorities was the creation of *ebitongole*, groups of unfree people who performed particular productive activities on behalf of their royally appointed patrons. As Holly Hanson has recently noted, however, Ganda chiefs sometimes used war captives to create *ebitongole* of their own, a practice that further hindered royal control of outlying areas. Hanson, *Landed Obligation*, 60–61.
95. Kato Benedict Kimbowa Ssemwanga, interview, 4 February 2002; Kagwa, *Kings of Buganda*, 90.
96. Morris Ssekintu, interview, 13 March 2002; Nsimbi, *Amannya Amaganda N'Ennono Zaago*, 217–18.
97. Nsimbi, *Amannya Amaganda N'Ennono Zaago*, 268, 311–12; Patrick Mulika, interview, 19 October 2001; Philimon Namuyimba, interview, 19 October 2001; George Edward Musisi-Mazzi, interview, 24 June 2002.

98. Nsimbi, *Amannya Amaganda N'Ennono Zaago*, 272, 313; Patrick Mulika, interview, 19 October 2001; Omutaka Wasswa, interview, 2 June 2002.

99. Hanson, *Landed Obligation*, ch. 3.

Conclusion

1. Morris Ssekintu, interview, 17 January 2007. All quotations from Ssekintu below are from this interview.

2. For a recent discussion of the role of "middle figures" in colonial Africa, see Lawrance, Osborn, and Roberts, *Intermediaries, Interpreters, and Clerks*. For a related discussion of the role of African research assistants in the production of anthropological knowledge at the Rhodes-Livingstone Institute, in Northern Rhodesia, see Schumaker, *Africanizing Anthropology*, ch. 7.

3. Allen Nakayenga, interview, 6 February 2002.

4. M. S. M. Kiwanuka, preface to Kagwa, *Kings of Buganda*.

5. M. S. M. Kiwanuka, "Notes on Translation and Spelling," in ibid., x.

6. M. S. M. Kiwanuka, interview, 19 January 2007.

7. Klieman, *"The Pygmies Were Our Compass,"* 70, 151, 160.

8. See Schoffeleers, introduction to Schoffeleers, *Guardians of the Land*, 27; Linden, "Chisumphi Theology," in ibid., 196–99; and D. Werner, "Miao Spirit Shrines," in ibid.

9. Schoffeleers, introduction, 41–42.

10. McCaskie, "Empire State," 469.

11. McCaskie, "Denkyira in the Making of Asante," 25.

12. MacGaffey, "Changing Representations," 206.

13. The civil war and social disorder that convulsed Buganda in the latter part of the nineteenth century—the so-called Christian Revolution—has been the subject of an extensive body of literature. For one of the most recent and to my mind most revealing analyses of this period, see Hanson, *Landed Obligation*, ch. 4. See also Wrigley, "Christian Revolution in Buganda"; Rowe, "Purge of Christians" and "Baganda Revolutionaries"; Michael Wright, *Buganda in the Heroic Age*; and Twaddle, "Muslim Revolution in Buganda."

14. For an analysis of the processes for the allotment of mailo and their consequences, see Hanson, *Landed Obligation*, chs. 5 and 6.

15. Ibid., ch. 7, quotations on 204.

16. "Okusala Omusango Gwe Kika Kye Mpewo" (The ruling of the case involving the Oribi Antelope clan), in Kiggye, Sekamwa, and the members of the Mpewo Clan, *Ekitabo Ky'Ekika Kye Mpewo*, 3–9.

17. Following the overthrow of Milton Obote's government in 1985, Yoweri Museveni's National Resistance Movement restored the kingships of Uganda's several kingdoms, with the exception of Nkore. Museveni declared that returned kings were to act as "cultural leaders" rather than political figures. For an in-

sightful analysis of Buganda's restoration, see Karlström, "Cultural Kingdom in Uganda."

18. Proceedings of clan court cases in Olukiiko Lwa Katikkiro Weddiro, Case No. KD 13/97, James Kyajja Watuula versus John Kunsa, Patrick Muliika, Dan Muliika, and Noah Muule Kimbowa. Apparently, the young leader had appeared at his father's funeral-rites ceremony in a drunken state and taken for himself the customary condolence fees collected upon a family member's death.

19. The Kabaka Foundation recently received a grant from the Ford Foundation to implement the Community Philanthropy Project, a program designed to facilitate development efforts throughout the kingdom. Upon receiving the grant, the foundation's board members determined that the most effective means of implementing the Community Philanthropy Project was through the kingdom's existing clan networks.

20. Nelson Kawalya, interview, 20 January 2007.

21. Feierman, "Colonizers, Colonized."

22. For a critique of the notion of the African voice, see the introduction to White, Miescher, and Cohen, *African Words, African Voices.*

23. For attempts at such an analytical approach, see Kodesh, "Renovating Tradition"; Schoenbrun, "Conjuring the Modern in Africa"; and Hanson, *Landed Obligation.*

BIBLIOGRAPHY

PRIMARY SOURCES
Archival and Unpublished Material
Buganda Clan Office. Mengo. Responses to survey sent out to heads of clans in
  Buganda by Akakiiko Ka Ssabasajja Kabaka Akakola Ku Nsonga Ze Bika. N.d.
  Copy of document in the author's possession.
———. Proceedings of clan court cases in Olukiiko Lwa Katikkiro Weddiro, 1997–
  2002. Copy of document in the author's possession.
Committee of the Lungfish Clan. "Ekitabo Ky'Ekika Ky'Emmamba" [The Lungfish
  clan book]. N.d. Copy of document in the author's possession.
Council of the Bean Clan. "Ebyafaayo By'Ekika Ky'Empindi" [History of the Bean
  clan]. Copy of document in the author's possession.
Council of the Leopard Clan. "Olukiko Lw'Akasolya Mu Kika Ky'Engo" [Meeting of
  the council of the Leopard clan]. 11 December 2001. Copy of document in the
  author's possession.
Council of the Reedbuck Clan. "Ebyafayo Bye Kika Kyenjaza Ne Jjaja Wakyo"
  [History of the Reedbuck clan]. Copy of document in the author's possession.
Council of the Ssiga of Mwanje. "Essiga Lya Mwanje e Nnono Magonga" [The
  patrilineage of Mwanje at Nnono, Magonga]. 29 October 2001. Copy of
  document in the author's possession.
Miti, James. "A Short History of Buganda, Bunyoro, Busoga, Toro, and Ankole."
  Translated by G. K. Rock. Africana Collection. Makerere University Library,
  Kampala.
Njala, Musisi Luwalira. "Manya Ebyafaayo By'ekika Ky'abaganda Abeddira Embwa"
  [History of the Dog clan]. 1995. Copy of document in the author's possession.
Nsubuga, Dick Makande. "Abazzukulu Ba Kkerebwe E Lukumba, Bwerenga Mu
  Ssiga Lya Kirulu E Bwenga Mu Kika Ky'Emmamba" [The descendants of
  Kkerebwe at Lukumba, Bwerenga, in the patrilineage of Kirulu at Bwenga in the
  Lungfish clan]. Copy of document in the author's possession.
Office of the Buffalo Clan. "History of the Buffalo Clan." Copy of document in the
  author's possession.
Roscoe, John, and Apolo Kagwa. "Enquiry into Native Land Tenure in the Uganda
  Protectorate." 1906. Shelfmark MS Africa s 17. Rhodes House, Bodleian Library,
  Oxford.
Source Materials in Uganda History, Volume 3. Africana Collection. Makerere
  University Library, Kampala.
Translations from *Munno* and Other Periodicals: 1910s–1920s. By Sir John Gray.
  Royal Commonwealth Society Library, Cambridge University Library.
Uganda National Archives (UNA), Entebbe. A46 series.

Interviews

Unless otherwise noted, all interviews were conducted in Luganda by the author and a research assistant.

Bakazirwendo, Hajji Kawooya Ssemandwa. 4 and 9 October 2001.

Baluli, Iriyamu. 13 February 2002.

Battwe, Edward Musisi. 7 February 2002.

Bira, Christopher Lwanga. 26 March 2002.

Ggolobi, Mulangira. 10 April 2002.

Kabulidde, Hajji Blukhan Kasumba. 3 November 2001.

Kaddu, Hajji Mahamoud. 29 April 2002.

Kaggwa, Ssalongo Lukoda Wamala. 4 February 2002.

Kalika, Ssenyoga. 13 June 2002.

Kalule, George William. 29 September and 3 October 2001.

Kasimba clan members. 31 October 2001.

Katerega, Hajji Mohammed Namuguzi. 13 March 2002.

Kawalya, Nelson. 20 January 2007.

Kibirige, Everest. 2 October 2001.

Kibondwe, Omutaka. 7 April 2002.

Kibuuka, Emmanuel Nsubuga. 4 June 2002.

Kiggye, Omutaka. 1 May 2002.

Kigo, Livingstone. 18 December 2001, 25 March 2002, and 8 April 2006.

Kimaanya, Sulimanyi. 11 June 2002.

Kinalwa, George Nakininsa. 14 October 2001.

Kitagana, Zaidi Ssemakula. 9 April 2002.

Kiwanda, Ali Ssalongo. 10 April 2002.

Kiwanuka, M. S. M. 19 January 2007.

Kiwanuka, Musimba Posiano. 25 November 2001.

Kiwanuka, Peter. 23 August 2006.

Kizito, Daniel. 7 April 2002.

Lukoma, Kato Peter. 21 December 2001, 3 March and 9 April 2002.

Lukoma, Kato Peter, and Namasole Baagalayaze. 18 December 2001.

Lutwame, Stanley, and Israel Emmanuel Kyagoba Wamala. 6 March 2002.

Luzinda, Canon. 28 November 2001.

Magunda, Kawumba. 6 February 2002.

Masoke, Kayita. 6 March 2002.

Matovu, Kigoongo. 5 August 2002.

Mayengo, Paulo N. 19 April 2002.

Mbajja, Omutaka. 8 December 2001.

Mbowa, Edward. 1 November 2001.

Mukasa, Ssalongo Ssemakula. 4 December 2001.

Mulika, Patrick. 19 October 2001.

Mulumba, Ssalongo George. 5 March 2002.

Mulwadde, Karibu. 30 October 2001.

Musisi, Luwalira Njala. 26 November 2001.

Musisi, Ssalongo Ssegujja. 16 March 2002.

Musisi-Mazzi, George Edward. 24 June 2002.

Musoke, A. S. B. 11 December 2001.

Musoke, Francis Ssalongo. 3 September 2002.

Mutawe, Joseph. 13 October 2001.

Mutetwa, James Magala, Augustine Kizito Mutumba Ssalongo, and Mayanja Sebuliba Nyamanka. 16 April 2002.

Muttajjo, Falasiko Bali. 12 December 2001.

Muyondo, Kubi Kiviri. 31 October 2001.

Mwebe, Simon. 5 May 2002.

Nakabiri, Mumbejja. 14 March 2002.

Nakasi, Nnalongo. 9 February 2002.

Nakayenga, Allen. 6 February 2002.

Nampama, Daudi Mitti Kabazzi. 28 October 2001.

Nampeera, Mariam. 5 December 2001.

Namukadde, Philip Sseruwagi. 18 January 2007.

Namuyimba, Philimon. 19 October 2001.

Namyalo, Bena. 22 September 2001.

Nsejere, Charles Alex, Mugwanya Mugema, Sserwanga Ndawula Katumba Balamaga, and Michael Mugadya Selubidde. 26 October 2001.

Nsubuga, Dick Makande. 11 December 2001.

Nyabo, Nakati. 5 June 2002.

Nyanyoonjo, Faisa. 14 February 2002.

Ssabalangira, Haji Abdullah. 5 June 2002.

Ssekindi, David Ssekibobo. 8 April 2002.

Ssekintu, Morris. 13 March 2002 and 17 January 2007. In English.

Ssemwanga, Kato Benedict Kimbowa. 4 February 2002.

Ssenkungu, Lameka Sonko. 27 December 2001.

Sserwadda, Hassan. 21 December 2001 and 2 August 2006.

Sserwaji, Yozefu. 26 March 2002.

Sserwaji, Yozefu, and Mbuga Atanansio. 28 March 2002.

Walusimbi, Ssalongo Benedicto. 12 October 2001 and 11 August 2006.

Wamagezi, Yozefu Ssenyongole Kaddu. 3 March 2002.

Wasswa, Omutaka. 2 June 2002.

Zabeti, Mubinge. 13 December 2001.

SECONDARY SOURCES

Alpers, Edward A., and Christopher Ehret. *Eastern Africa*. Vol. 4 of *The Cambridge History of Africa*, edited by Richard Gray. Cambridge: Cambridge University Press, 1975.

Anderson, David, and Douglas H. Johnson, eds. *Revealing Prophets: Prophesy in Eastern African History*. Athens: Ohio University Press, 1995.

Appiah, Kwame Anthony. *In My Father's House: Africa in the Philosophy of Culture*. Oxford: Oxford University Press, 1992.

Apter, Andrew. *Black Kings and Critics: The Hermeneutics of Power in Yoruba Society*. Chicago: University of Chicago Press, 1992.

Arens, William, and Ivan Karp. Introduction to *Creativity of Power*, edited by William Arens and Ivan Karp, xi–xxix. Washington, DC: Smithsonian Institution Press, 1989.

Ashe, Robert Pickering. *Chronicles of Uganda*. New York: Randolf, 1895.

Atkinson, R. R. "The Traditions of the Early Kings of Buganda: Myth, History, and Structural Analysis." *History in Africa* 2 (1975): 17–57.

Bamunoba, Y. K., and F. B. Welbourn. "Emandwa Initiation in Ankole." *Uganda Journal* 29 (1965): 13–25.

Barber, Karin. *I Could Speak until Tomorrow: Oriki, Women, and the Past in a Yoruba Town*. Washington, DC: Smithsonian Institution Press, 1991.

Barrett-Gaines, Kathryn. "Katwe Salt in the African Great Lakes Regional Economy, 1750s–1950s." PhD diss., Stanford University, 2001.

Beattie, John. "Initiation into the Cwezi Spirit Possession Cult in Bunyoro." *African Studies* 16, no. 3 (1957): 150–61.

———. "Spirit Mediumship in Bunyoro." In *Spirit Mediumship and Society in Africa*, edited by John Beattie and John Middleton, 159–70. London: Routledge, 1969.

Berger, Iris. "Deities, Dynasties, and Oral Tradition." In Miller, *African Past Speaks*, 61–81.

———. "Fertility as Power: Spirit Mediums, Priestesses, and the Pre-Colonial State in Interlacustrine East Africa." In Anderson and Johnson, *Revealing Prophets*, 65–82.

———. "Rebels or Status Seekers? Women as Spirit Mediums in East Africa." In *Women in Africa: Studies in Social and Economic Change*, edited by Nancy Hafkin and Edna Bay, 157–81. Stanford, CA: Stanford University Press, 1976.

———. *Religion and Resistance: East African Kingdoms in the Precolonial Period*. Tervuren, Belgium: Musée Royal de l'Afrique Centrale, 1981.

Bessell, M. J. "Nyabingi." *Uganda Journal* 6 (1938): 73–86.

Bikunya, P. *Ky'Abakama Ba Bunyoro* [The kings of Bunyoro]. London: Sheldon, 1927.

Bozzoli, Belinda, and Mmantho Nkotsoe. *Women of Phokeng: Consciousness, Life Strategy, and Migrancy in South Africa*. Portsmouth, NH: Heinemann, 1991.

Buchanan, Carole A. "The Kitara Complex: The Historical Tradition of Western Uganda to the 16th Century." PhD diss., Indiana University, 1974.

——. "Perceptions of Ethnic Interaction in the East African Interior: The Kitara Complex." *International Journal of African Historical Studies* 11, no. 3 (1978): 410–28.

Buligwanga, Eriya M. *Ekitabo Ekitegeza Ekika Kye Mamba* [Book of the Lungfish clan]. Kampala: Uganda Publishing, 1916.

Burke, Timothy. *Lifebuoy Men, Lux Women: Commodification, Consumption, and Cleanliness in Modern Zimbabwe*. Durham, NC: Duke University Press, 1996.

Byaruhanga-Akiiki, A. B. T. *Religion in Bunyoro*. Nairobi: Kenya Literature Bureau, 1982.

Chrétien, Jean-Pierre. *The Great Lakes of Africa: Two Thousand Years of History*. Translated by Scott Strauss. New York: Zone Books, 2003.

Cohen, David William. *The Historical Tradition of Busoga: Mukama and Kintu*. Oxford: Clarendon, 1972.

——. "The Undefining of Oral Tradition." *Ethnohistory* 36, no. 1 (1989): 9–18.

——. *Womunafu's Bunafu: A Study of Authority in a Nineteenth Century African Community*. Princeton, NJ: Princeton University Press, 1977.

Cohen, David William, and E. S. Atieno Odhiambo. *Siaya: The Historical Anthropology of an African Landscape*. Athens: Ohio University Press, 1989.

Comaroff, Jean, and John Comaroff. *Of Revelation and Revolution: Christianity, Colonialism, and Consciousness in South Africa*. Vol. 1. Chicago: University of Chicago Press, 1991.

——. "Revelations upon Revelation: After Shocks, After Thoughts." *Interventions* 3, no. 1 (2001): 100–126.

Connah, Graham. *Kibiro: The Salt of Bunyoro, Past and Present*. London: British Institute in Eastern Africa, 1996.

Cooper, Barbara M. "Oral Sources and the Challenges of African History." In *Writing African History*, edited by John Edward Philips, 191–215. Rochester, NY: University of Rochester Press, 2005.

Cory, Hans. "The Buswezi." *American Anthropologist* 57 (1955): 923–52.

Cox, A. H. "The Growth and Expansion of Buganda." *Uganda Journal* 14 (1950): 153–59.

Crazzolara, J. P. "The Lwoo People." *Uganda Journal* 5 (1937): 1–21.

——. *Migrations*. Vol. 1 of *The Lwoo*. Verona, Italy: Instituto Missioni Africane, 1950.

Cunningham, J. F. *Uganda and Its Peoples*. London: Hutchinson, 1905.

Davison, Jean. *Voices from Mutira: Change in the Lives of Rural Gikuyu Women, 1910–1995*. Boulder, CO: Lynne Rienner, 1996.

Dawson, Marc H. "Socioeconomic Change and Disease: Smallpox in Colonial Kenya, 1880–1920." In Feierman and Janzen, *Social Basis of Health and Healing in Africa*, 90–103.

des Forges, Allison. " 'The Drum is Greater Than the Shout': The 1912 Rebellion in Northern Rwanda." In *Banditry, Rebellion, and Social Protest in Africa*, edited by Donald Crummey, 311–33. London: James Currey, 1986.

d'Hertefelt, Marcel. *Les clans du Rwanda ancien: Elements d'ethnosociologie et d'ethnohistoire*. Tervuren, Belgium: Musée Royal de l'Afrique Centrale, 1971.

Douglas, Mary. "Animals in Lele Religious Symbolism." *Africa* 27, no. 1 (1957): 46–58.

Fabian, Johannes. *Remembering the Present: Painting and Popular History in Zaire*. Berkeley and Los Angeles: University of California Press, 1996.

Fallers, L. A., ed. *The King's Men: Leadership and Status in Buganda on the Eve of Independence*. London: Oxford University Press, 1964.

——. "Social Stratification in Traditional Buganda." In Fallers, *King's Men*, 64–116.

Feierman, Steven. "Colonizers, Colonized, and the Creation of Invisible Histories." In *Beyond the Linguistic Turn: New Directions in the Study of Society and Culture*, edited by Victoria E. Bonnell and Lynn Hunt, 182–216. Berkeley and Los Angeles: University of California Press, 1999.

——. "Explanation and Uncertainty in the Medical World of Ghaambo." *Bulletin of the History of Medicine* 74, no. 2 (2000): 317–44.

——. "Healing as Social Criticism in the Time of Colonial Conquest." *African Studies* 54, no. 1 (1995): 73–88.

——. *Peasant Intellectuals: Anthropology and History in Tanzania*. Madison: University of Wisconsin Press, 1990.

——. "Struggles for Control: The Social Roots of Health and Healing in Modern Africa." *African Studies Review* 28, nos. 2–3 (June–September 1985): 73–147.

Feierman, Steven, and John M. Janzen, eds. *The Social Basis of Health and Healing in Africa*. Berkeley and Los Angeles: University of California Press, 1992.

Felkin, R. W. "Notes on the Waganda Tribe of Central Africa." *Proceedings of the Royal Society of Edinburgh* 13 (1885–86): 699–770.

Fenner, F., D. A. Henderson, I. Arita, Z. Jezek, and I. D. Ladnyi. *Smallpox and Its Eradication*. Geneva: World Health Organization, 1988.

Fisher, Ruth. *Twilight Tales of the Black Baganda: The Traditional History of Bunyoro-Kitara, a Former Uganda Kingdom*. 2nd ed. London: Frank Cass, 1970.

Frazer, J. G. "Questions on the Manners, Customs, Religion, Superstitions, &c. of Uncivilized or Semi-Civilized Peoples." *Journal of the Anthropological Institute of Great Britain and Ireland* 18 (1889): 431–40.

Freedman, Jim. *Nyabingi*. Butare, Rwanda: Institute National de Recherche Scientifique, 1984.

Giles-Vernick, Tamara. *Cutting the Vines of the Past: Environmental Histories of the Central African Rain Forest*. Charlottesville: University of Virginia Press, 2002.

Good, Charles M. "Salt, Trade, and Disease: Aspects of Development in Africa's Northern Great Lakes Region." *International Journal of African Historical Studies* 5, no. 4 (1972): 543–86.

Gray, John Milner. "Early History of Buganda." *Uganda Journal* 2 (1935): 259–71.

——. "Kibuka." *Uganda Journal* 20 (1956): 52–71.

Gray, Richard, and David Birmingham, eds. *Pre-Colonial African Trade: Essays on Trade in East and Central Africa before 1900*. London: Oxford University Press, 1970.

——. "Some Economic and Political Consequences of Trade in Central and Eastern Africa in the Pre-Colonial Period." In Gray and Birmingham, *Pre-Colonial African Trade*, 1–23.

Guyer, Jane, and Samuel E. Belinga. "Wealth in People as Wealth in Knowledge: Accumulation and Composition in Equatorial Africa." *Journal of African History* 36, no. 1 (1995): 91–120.

Hanks, William F. *Language and Communicative Practices*. Boulder, CO: Westview, 1996.

Hansen, Holger Bernt. "The Colonial Control of Spirit Cults in Uganda." In Anderson and Johnson, *Revealing Prophets*, 143–63.

Hanson, Holly Elisabeth. *Landed Obligation: The Practice of Power in Buganda*. Portsmouth, NH: Heinemann, 2003.

Harrison, Alexina Mackay. *The Story of the Life of Mackay of Uganda, Pioneer Missionary*. London: Hodder & Stoughton, 1891.

Hartwig, Gerald W. *The Art of Survival in East Africa: The Kerebe and Long Distance Trade*. New York: Africana, 1976.

Hattersley, C. W. *An English Boy's Life and Adventures in Uganda*. London: Religious Tract Society, 1913.

——. *Uganda by Pen and Camera*. London: Religious Tract Society, 1907.

Heald, Suzette. *Controlling Anger: The Sociology of Gisu Violence*. Manchester: Manchester University Press, 1989.

Herbert, Eugenia. *Iron, Gender, and Power: Rituals of Transformation in African Societies*. Bloomington: Indiana University Press, 1993.

——. "Smallpox Inoculation in Africa." *Journal of African History* 16, no. 4 (1975): 539–59.

Hunt, Nancy Rose. *A Colonial Lexicon of Birth Ritual, Medicalization, and Mobility in the Congo*. Durham, NC: Duke University Press, 1999.

Ibrahim, Abdullahi A. "The Birth of the Interview: The Thin and the Fat of It." In White, Miescher, and Cohen, *African Words, African Voices*, 103–24.

Jacobsen-Widding, Anita. *Red-White-Black as a Mode of Thought: A Study of Triadic Classification by Colours in the Ritual Symbolism and Cognitive Thought of the Peoples of the Lower Congo*. Uppsala, Sweden: Almqvist & Wiksell, 1979.

Janzen, John M. *Lemba, 1650–1930: A Drum of Affliction in Africa and the New World*. New York: Garland, 1982.

Jensen, Jürgen. "Die Erweiterung des Lungenfisch-Clans in Buganda durch den Anschluss von Bavuma-Gruppen." *Sociologus* 19, no. 2 (1969): 153–66.

Jjumba, Elisa Muwanga, and the Council of the Ssiga of Jjumba. *Ekitabo Eky'essiga Lya Jjumba* [Book of the Patrilineage of Jjumba]. Kampala: Makerere University College Library, 1964.

Johnston, H. H. *The Uganda Protectorate*. Vol. 2. London: Hutchinson, 1902.

Kaggwa, L. B., and F. B. Welbourn. "*Lubaale* Initiation in Buganda." *Uganda Journal* 28 (1964): 218–20.

Kaguba, Charles E. S. "The Genealogy of Kabaka Kintu and the Early Bakabaka of Buganda." *Uganda Journal* 27 (1963): 205–16.

Kagwa, Apolo. *Bakabaka b'e Buganda.* Kampala: Uganda Bookshop, 1901.

———. *The Clans of Buganda.* Translated by James D. Wamala. Kampala: Uganda Bookshop, 1972.

———. *The Customs of the Baganda.* Edited by May Mandelbaum. Translated by Ernest B. Kalibala. New York: Columbia University Press, 1934.

———. *Ekitabo Kye Kika Kyenseenene* [Book of the Grasshopper clan]. Mengo: privately printed, n.d.

———. *Ekitabo Kye Mpisa za Baganda.* Kampala: Uganda Printing and Publishing, 1918.

———. *Engero Za Baganda* [Folktales of the Baganda]. 1902. Reprint, London: Sheldon, 1951.

———. *The Kings of Buganda.* Translated and edited by M. S. M. Kiwanuka. Nairobi, Kenya: East African Publishing House, 1971.

Kakoma, S. K. L., A. M. Ntate, and M. Serukaga. *Ekitabo Eky'Abakyanjove Ab'e Mmamba Mu Ssiga Lya Nankere e Bukerekere* [Book of Kyanjove people of the patrilineage of Nankere at Bukerekere in the Lungfish clan]. Kampala: East African Institute for Social Research, 1959.

Kamuhangire, Ephraim R. "The Pre-Colonial Economic and Social History of East Africa with Special Reference to South-Western Uganda Salt Lakes Region." In Ogot, *Hadith* 5, 66–89.

Karlström, Mikael. "Buganda: A Select Bibliography with Bibliographic Essay." http://buganda.com/biblio.htm.

———. "The Cultural Kingdom in Uganda: Popular Royalism and the Restoration of the Buganda Kingship." PhD diss., University of Chicago, 1999.

Katate, A. G., and L. Kamugungunu. *Abagabe b'Ankole* [The kings of Ankole]. Kampala: East African Literature Bureau, 1955.

Katoke, Israel K. *The Karagwe Kingdom: A History of the Abanyambo of North-West Tanzania.* Nairobi, Kenya: East African Publishing House, 1975.

Kenny, Michael G. "Mutesa's Crime: Hubris and the Control of African Kings." *Comparative Studies in Society and History* 30, no. 4 (1988): 595–612.

———. "The Powers of Lake Victoria." *Anthropos* 72, nos. 5–6 (1977): 717–33.

———. "The Stranger from the Lake: A Theme in History of the Lake Victoria Shorelands." *Azania* 17 (1982): 1–26.

Kiggye, Omutaka, Mayungwe Sebale Sekamwa, and the members of the Mpewo clan. *Ekitabo Ky'Ekika Kye Mpewo* [Book of the Oribi Antelope clan]. Kampala: Baganda Cooperative Society, n.d.

Kiwanuka, M. S. M. *A History of Buganda: From the Foundation of the Kingdom to 1900.* London: Longman, 1971.

Klieman, Kairn. *"The Pygmies Were Our Compass": Bantu and Batwa in the History of West Central Africa, Early Times to c. 1900 C.E.* Portsmouth, NH: Heinemann, 2003.

Kodesh, Neil. "Beyond the Royal Gaze: Clanship and Collective Well-Being in Buganda." PhD diss., Northwestern University, 2004.

———. "History from the Healer's Shrine: Genre, Historical Imagination, and Early Ganda History." *Comparative Studies in Society and History* 49, no. 3 (2007): 527–552.

———. "Networks of Knowledge: Clanship and Collective Well-Being in Buganda." *Journal of African History* 49, no. 2 (2008): 197–216.

———. "Renovating Tradition: The Discourse of Succession in Colonial Buganda." *International Journal of African Historical Studies* 34, no. 3 (2001): 511–41.

Kottak, Conrad P. "Ecological Variables in the Origin and Evolution of African States: The Buganda Example." *Comparative Studies in Society and History* 14, no. 3 (1972): 351–80.

Kuper, Adam. "Lineage Theory: A Critical Retrospect." *Annual Review of Anthropology* 11 (1982): 71–95.

K.W. [Tito Gafabusa Winyi]. "The Kings of Bunyoro-Kitara." *Uganda Journal* 3 (1935): 155–60.

———. "The Kings of Bunyoro-Kitara. Part II." *Uganda Journal* 4 (1936): 75–83.

———. "The Kings of Bunyoro-Kitara. Part III." *Uganda Journal* 5 (1937): 288–89.

Lan, David. *Guns and Rain: Guerrillas and Spirit Mediums in Zimbabwe.* London: James Currey, 1985.

Landau, Paul Stuart. "Explaining Surgical Evangelism in Colonial Southern Africa: Teeth, Pain, and Faith." *Journal of African History* 37, no. 2 (1996): 261–81.

———. *The Realm of the Word: Language, Gender, and Christianity in a Southern African Kingdom.* Portsmouth, NH: Heinemann, 1995.

———. " 'Religion' and Christian Conversion in African History: A New Model." *Journal of Religious History* 23, no. 1 (1999): 8–30.

Lanning, E. C. "Excavations at Mubende Hill." *Uganda Journal* 30 (1966): 153–63.

———. "Shafts in Buganda and Toro." *Uganda Journal* 20 (1956): 216–17, 22 (1958): 188–89.

———. "The Surviving Regalia of the Nakaima, Mubende." *Uganda Journal* 31 (1967): 210–11.

Larson, Pier M. *History and Memory in the Age of Enslavement: Becoming Merina in Highland Madagascar, 1770–1822.* Portsmouth, NH: Heinemann, 2000.

Lawrance, Benjamin N., Emily Lynn Osborn, and Richard L. Roberts, eds. *Intermediaries, Interpreters, and Clerks: African Employees in the Making of Colonial Africa.* Madison: University of Wisconsin Press, 2006.

Lejju, B. Julius, Peter Robertshaw, and David Taylor. "Africa's earliest bananas?" *Journal of Archaeological Science* 33 (2006): 102–13.

Le Veux, R. P. *Manuel de langue luganda.* 2nd ed. Algiers: Maison-Carree, 1914.

——. *Premier essai de vocabulaire luganda-français d'après l'ordre étymologique*. Algiers: Imprimerie des Missionnaires d'Afrique, 1917.

Linden, I. "Chisumphi Theology in the Religion of Central Malawi." In Schoffeleers, *Guardians of the Land*, 187–208.

Livingstone, Julie. *Debility and the Moral Imagination in Botswana*. Bloomington: Indiana University Press, 2005.

Lonsdale, John. "The Moral Economy of Mau Mau." In *Unhappy Valley*, by John Lonsdale and Bruce Berman, 265–504. London: James Currey, 1992.

Lubogo, Y. K. *A History of Busoga*. Jinja, Uganda: East African Literature Bureau, 1960.

Lugira, A. M. *Ganda Art: A Study of the Ganda Mentality with Respect to Possibilities of Acculturation in Christian Art*. Kampala: Osasa, 1970.

Lush, Allan J. "Kiganda Drums." *Uganda Journal* 3 (1935): 8–25.

MacGaffey, Wyatt. "Changing Representations in Central African History." *Journal of African History* 46, no. 2 (2005): 189–207.

——. *Religion and Society in Central Africa: The BaKongo of Lower Zaire*. Chicago: University of Chicago Press, 1986.

Mafart, Bertrand. "Goundou: A Historical Form of Yaws." *Lancet* 360 (2002): 1168–70.

Mair, Lucy. *An African People in the Twentieth Century*. London: George Routledge & Sons, 1934.

McCaskie, T. C. "Denkyira in the Making of Asante, c. 1660–1720." *Journal of African History* 48, no. 1 (2007): 1–25.

——. "Empire State: Asante and the Historians." *Journal of African History* 33, no. 3 (1992): 467–76.

McIntosh, Susan Keech, ed. *Beyond Chiefdoms: Pathways to Complexity in Africa*. Cambridge: Cambridge University Press, 1999.

——. "Pathways to Complexity: An African Perspective." In McIntosh, *Beyond Chiefdoms*, 1–30.

Médard, Henri. "Croissance et crises de la royaute du Buganda au XIX siècle." PhD diss., Université Paris I—Pantheon Sorbonne, 2001.

——. *Le royaume du Buganda au XIXe siecle*. Paris: Karthala, 2007.

——. "The Syncretic Changes, from the XVIII to the XX Century, of the Life of Kintu, First King of Buganda." Paper presented at the Kingship in Uganda Conference, Makerere University, Kampala, 1997.

Médard, Henri, and Shane Doyle, eds. *Slavery in the Great Lakes Region of East Africa*. Athens: Ohio University Press, 2007.

Miller, Joseph C., ed. *The African Past Speaks: Essays on Oral Tradition and History*. Hamden, CT: Archon Books, 1980.

Morris, H. F. *The Heroic Recitations of the Bahima of Ankole*. Oxford: Clarendon, 1964.

Mukasa, E. W. S. "The Reason for the Post of Mugema in Buganda." *Uganda Journal* 10 (1946): 150.

Muriuki, Godfrey. *A History of the Kikuyu*. Nairobi: Oxford University Press, 1974.

Murphy, John D. *Luganda-English Dictionary*. Washington, DC: Catholic University Press of America, 1972.

Musisi, Nyakanyike B. "Transformations of Baganda Women: From the Earliest Times to the Demise of the Kingdom in 1966." PhD diss., University of Toronto, 1992.

———. "Women, 'Elite Polygyny,' and Buganda State Formation." *Signs* 16, no. 4 (1991): 757–86.

Nannyonga-Tamusuza, Sylvia A. *Baakisimba: Gender in the Music and Dance of the Baganda People of Uganda*. New York: Routledge, 2005.

Newbury, David. "The Clans of Rwanda: An Historical Hypothesis." *Africa* 50, no. 4 (1980): 389–403.

———. *Kings and Clans: Ijwi Island and the Lake Kivu Rift, 1780–1840*. Madison: University of Wisconsin Press, 1991.

Newbury, David, and Catherine Newbury. "Bringing the Peasants Back In: Agrarian Themes in the Construction and Corrosion of Statist Historiography in Rwanda." *American Historical Review* 105, no. 3 (2000): 832–77.

Nsimbi, M. B. *Amannya Amaganda N'Ennono Zaago* [Ganda names and their origins]. Kampala: East African Literature Bureau, 1956.

Nyakatura, John W. *Abakama ba Bunyoro-Kitara*. Quebec: St. Justin, 1947.

———. *Anatomy of an African Kingdom: A History of Bunyoro-Kitara*. Edited by Godfrey N. Uzoigwe. Translated by Teopista Muganwa. New York: Anchor/Doubleday, 1973.

———. *Aspects of Bunyoro Customs and Traditions*. Translated by Zebiya Kwamya Rigby. Kampala: East African Literature Bureau, 1970.

Ogot, Bethwell A. "The Construction of Luo Identity and History." In White, Miescher, and Cohen, *African Words, African Voices*, 31–52.

———, ed. *Hadith 5: Economic and Social History of East Africa; Proceedings of the 1972 Conference of the Historical Association of Kenya*. Nairobi, Kenya: East Africa Literature Bureau, 1975.

———. *History of the Southern Luo*. Nairobi, Kenya: East African Publishing House, 1967.

Oliver, Roland. "Discernible Developments in the Interior, c. 1500–1840." In *History of East Africa*, vol. 1, edited by Roland Oliver and Gervase Matthew, 169–211. Oxford: Oxford University Press, 1963.

———. "The Royal Tombs of Buganda." *Uganda Journal* 23 (1959): 124–33.

———. "The Traditional Histories of Buganda, Bunyoro, and Ankole." *Journal of the Royal Anthropological Institute* 85 (1955): 111–17.

Packard, Randall. *Chiefship and Cosmology: An Historical Study of Political Competition*. Bloomington: Indiana University Press, 1981.

Peek, Philip M. "African Divination Systems: Non-Normal Modes of Cognition." In *African Divination Systems: Ways of Knowing*, edited by Philip M. Peek, 193–212. Bloomington: Indiana University Press, 1991.

Peterson, Derek R., and Darren R. Walhof. "Rethinking Religion." In *The Invention of Religion: Rethinking Belief in Politics and History*, edited by Derek R. Peterson and Darren Walhof, 1–18. New Jersey: Rutgers University Press, 2002.

Prestholdt, Jeremy. "On the Global Repercussions of East African Consumerism." *American Historical Review* 109, no. 3 (2004): 755–81.

Prins, Gwyn. "But What Was the Disease? The Present State of Health and Healing in African Studies." *Past and Present* 124 (1989): 159–79.

Ray, Benjamin C. *Myth, Ritual, and Kingship in Buganda*. Oxford: Oxford University Press, 1991.

Reid, D. A. M. "The Role of Cattle in the Later Iron Age Communities of Southern Uganda." PhD thesis, University of Cambridge, 1991.

Reid, Richard. "Mutesa and Mirambo: Thoughts on East African Warfare and Diplomacy in the Nineteenth Century." *International Journal of African Historical Studies* 31, no. 1 (1998): 73–89.

———. *Political Power in Pre-Colonial Buganda*. Athens: Ohio University Press, 2002.

Rennie, J. K. "The Precolonial Kingdom of Rwanda: A Reinterpretation." *Transafrican Journal of History* 2, no. 2 (1972): 11–53.

Richards, A. I. *The Changing Structure of a Ganda Village: Kisozi, 1892–1952*. Nairobi, Kenya: East African Publishing House, 1966.

Roberts, Allen F. *Animals in African Art: From the Familiar to the Marvelous*. New York: Museum for African Art, 1995.

Robertshaw, Peter, and David Taylor. "Climate Change and the Rise of Political Complexity in Western Uganda." *Journal of African History* 41, no. 1 (2000): 1–28.

Roscoe, John. *The Baganda: An Account of Their Native Customs and Beliefs*. London: Macmillan, 1911.

———. *The Bakitara or Banyoro*. Cambridge: Cambridge University Press, 1923.

———. "Further Notes on the Manners and Customs of the Baganda." *Journal of the Royal Anthropological Institute* 32 (1902): 25–80.

———. "Kibuka, the War-God of the Baganda." *Man* 7 (1907): 161–66.

———. *The Northern Bantu*. Cambridge: Cambridge University Press, 1915.

———. "Notes on the Manners and Customs of the Baganda." *Journal of the Royal Anthropological Institute* 31 (1901): 117–30.

———. "Python Worship in Uganda." *Man* 9 (1909): 88–90.

Rossel, Gerda. *Taxonomic-Linguistic Study of Plantain in Africa*. Leiden: Research School CNWS, 1998.

Rothschild, Bruce M., Israel Hershkovitz, and Christine Rothschild. "Origin of Yaws in the Pleistocene." *Nature*, 23 November 1995, 343–44.

Rowe, John A. "The Baganda Revolutionaries." *Tarikh* 3, no. 2 (1970): 34–46.

———. "Myth, Memoir, and Moral Admonition: Luganda Historical Writing, 1893–1969." *Uganda Journal* 33 (1969): 17–40, 217–19.

——. "The Purge of Christians at Mwanga's Court." *Journal of African History* 5, no. 1 (1964): 55–71.

Schoenbrun, David L. "Cattle Herds and Banana Gardens: The Historical Geography of the Western Great Lakes Region, *ca* AD 800–1500." *African Archaeological Review* 11 (1993): 39–72.

——. "Conjuring the Modern in Africa: Durability and Rupture in Histories of Public Healing between the Great Lakes of East Africa." *American Historical Review* 3, no. 5 (2006): 1403–39.

——. *A Green Place, A Good Place: Agrarian Change, Gender, and Social Identity in the Great Lakes Region to the 15th Century.* Portsmouth, NH: Heinemann, 1998.

——. *The Historical Reconstruction of Great Lakes Bantu Cultural Vocabulary: Etymologies and Distributions.* Cologne: Rudiger Koppe Verlag, 1997.

——. "A Past Whose Time Has Come: Historical Context and History in Eastern Africa's Great Lakes Region." *History and Theory* 32, no. 4 (1993): 32–56.

——. "Violence and Vulnerability in East Africa before 1800 CE: An Agenda for Research." *History Compass* 4–5 (2006): 741–60.

——. "We Are What We Eat: Ancient Agriculture between the Great Lakes." *Journal of African History* 34, no. 1 (1993): 1–31.

Schoffeleers, J. Matthew, ed. *Guardians of the Land: Essays on Central African Territorial Cults.* Harare: Mambo, 1979.

——. Introduction to Schoffeleers, *Guardians of the Land*, 1–46.

——. *River of Blood: The Genesis of a Martyr Cult in Southern Malawi, c. A.D. 1600.* Madison: University of Wisconsin Press, 1992.

Schumaker, Lyn. *Africanizing Anthropology: Fieldwork, Networks, and the Making of Cultural Knowledge in Central Africa.* Durham, NC: Duke University Press, 2001.

Schweinfurth, G., E. Ratzel, R. W. Felkin, and G. Hartlaub. *Emin Pasha in Central Africa: Being a Collection of His Letters and Journals.* Translated by Mrs. R. W. Felkin. London: George Philip and Son, 1888.

Shadle, Brett L. "Patronage, Millennialism and the Serpent God Mumbo in South-West Kenya, 1912–34." *Africa* 72, no. 1 (2002): 29–54.

Shaw, Rosalind. "The Invention of 'African Traditional Religion.' " *Religion* 20 (1990): 339–53.

Snoxall, R. A. "The Coronation Ritual and Customs of the Baganda." *Uganda Journal* 4 (1937): 277–88.

——, ed. *Luganda-English Dictionary.* Oxford: Clarendon, 1967.

Southwold, Martin. *Bureaucracy and Chiefship in Buganda.* East African Studies, no. 14. Kampala: East African Institute of Social Research, 1961.

Spear, Thomas. "Oral Tradition: Whose History?" *History in Africa* 8 (1981): 132–48.

Speke, John Hanning. *Journal of the Discovery of the Source of the Nile.* New York: E. P. Dutton, 1863; London: J. M. Dent & Sons, 1969.

Stahl, Ann Brower. *Making History in Banda: Anthropological Visions of Africa's Past*. New York: Cambridge University Press, 2001.

Stanley, Henry Morton. *My Dark Companions and Their Strange Stories*. New York: Charles Scribner's Sons, 1893.

——. *Through the Dark Continent*. Vol. 1. New York: Harper & Brothers, 1878.

Stephens, Rhiannon. "A History of Motherhood, Food Procurement, and Politics in East-Central Uganda to the Nineteenth Century." PhD diss., Northwestern University, 2007.

Tantala, Renee Louise. "The Early History of Kitara in Western Uganda: Process Models of Religious and Political Change." PhD diss., University of Wisconsin at Madison, 1989.

Tosh, John. "The Northern Interlacustrine Region." In Gray and Birmingham, *Pre-Colonial African Trade*, 103–18.

Thruston, A. B. *African Incidents: Personal Experiences in Egypt and Unyoro*. London: John Murray, 1900.

Tucker, Alfred R. *Eighteen Years in Uganda and East Africa*. Vol. 1. London: Edward Arnold, 1908.

Twaddle, Michael. "The Ending of Slavery in Buganda." In *The End of Slavery in Africa*, edited by Richard Roberts and Suzanne Miers, 119–49. Madison: University of Wisconsin Press, 1988.

——. "Muslim Revolution in Buganda." *African Affairs* 71 (1972): 54–72.

——. "On Ganda Historiography." *History in Africa* 1 (1974): 85–99.

——. "Slaves and Peasants in Buganda." In *Slavery and Other Forms of Unfree Labor*, edited by Leonie J. Archer, 118–29. London: Routledge, 1988.

——. "Toward an Early History of the East African Interior." *History in Africa* 2 (1975): 147–84.

Uzoigwe, U. N. "Precolonial Markets in Bunyoro-Kitara." In Ogot, *Hadith* 5, 24–65.

Vail, Leroy, and Landeg White. *Power and the Praise Poem: Southern African Voices in History*. Charlottesville: University of Virginia Press, 1991.

Van Onselen, Charles. *The Seed Is Mine: The Life of Kas Maine, a South African Sharecropper, 1894–1985*. New York: Hill & Wang, 1996.

Vansina, Jan. *Antecedents to Modern Rwanda: The Nyiginya Kingdom*. Translated by the author. Madison: University of Wisconsin Press, 2004.

——. *The Children of Woot: A History of the Kuba Peoples*. Madison: University of Wisconsin Press, 1978.

——. *Oral Tradition: A Study in Historical Methodology*. Translated by H. M. Wright. London: Routledge & Kegan Paul, 1965.

——. *Oral Tradition as History*. Madison: University of Wisconsin Press, 1985.

——. *Paths in the Rainforests: Toward a History of Political Tradition in Equatorial Africa*. Madison: University of Wisconsin Press, 1990.

Vaughan, Megan. "Healing and Curing: Issues in the Social History and Anthropology of Medicine in Africa." *Social History of Medicine* 7, no. 2 (1994): 283–95.

Walker, Stephen L., and Roderick J. Hay. "Yaws—a Review of the Last 50 Years." *International Journal of Dermatology* 39 (2000): 258–60.

Watts, Sheldon. *Epidemics and History: Disease, Power, and Imperialism*. New Haven, CT: Yale University Press, 1997.

Welbourn, F. B. "Some Aspects of Kiganda Religion." *Uganda Journal* 26 (1962): 171–82.

Werner, Alice. "African Mythology." In *The Mythology of All Races*, edited by John Arnott MacCulloch, 7:105–360. Boston: Marshall Jones, 1925.

Werner, D. "*Miao* Spirit Shrines in the Religious History of the Southern Lake Tanganyika Region." In Schoffeleers, *Guardians of the Land*, 89–130.

White, Luise. *Speaking with Vampires: Rumor and History in Colonial Africa*. Berkeley and Los Angeles: University of California Press, 2000.

——. "They Could Make Their Victims Dull: Genders and Genres, Fantasies and Cures in Colonial Southern Uganda." *American Historical Review* 100, no. 5 (1995): 1379–1402.

——. "True Stories: Narrative, Event, History, and Blood in the Lake Victoria Basin." In White, Miescher, and Cohen, *African Words, African Voices*, 281–304.

White, Luise, Stephan Miescher, and David William Cohen, eds. *African Words, African Voices: Critical Practices in Oral History*. Bloomington: Indiana University Press, 2001.

Whyte, Susan Reynolds. "Anthropological Approaches to African Misfortune: From Religion to Medicine." In *Culture, Experience and Pluralism: Essays on African Ideas of Illness and Health*, edited by Anita Jacobsen-Widding and David Westerlund, 289–302. Stockholm: Wiksell, 1989.

Williams, F. Lukyn. "Myth, Legend, and Lore in Uganda." *Uganda Journal* 10 (1946): 64–75.

Willis, Justin. "Clan and History in Western Uganda: A New Perspective on the Origins of Pastoral Dominance." *International Journal of African Historical Studies* 30, no. 3 (1997): 583–600.

Wilson, C. T., and R. W. Felkin. *Uganda and the Egyptian Sudan*. Vol. 1. London: Sampson Low, Martson, Searle & Rivington, 1882.

Wright, Marcia. *Strategies of Slaves and Women: Life-Stories from East/Central Africa*. New York: L. Barber, 1993.

Wright, Michael. *Buganda in the Heroic Age*. Oxford: Oxford University Press, 1971.

Wrigley, Christopher. "Bananas in Buganda." *Azania* 24 (1989): 64–70.

——. "The Changing Economic Structure." In Fallers, *King's Men*, 17–63.

——. "The Christian Revolution in Buganda." *Comparative Studies in Society and History* 2, no. 1 (1959): 33–48.

———. "Kimera." *Uganda Journal* 23 (1959): 38–43.

———. *Kingship and State: The Buganda Dynasty.* Cambridge: Cambridge University Press, 1996.

Yoder, John. "The Quest for Kintu and the Search for Peace: Mythology and Morality in Nineteenth-Century Buganda." *History in Africa* 15 (1988): 363–76.

Zimbe, Barolomayo M. *Buganda Ne Kabaka.* Kampala: Gambuze, 1939.

Index

Italicized page numbers refer to illustrations.

Buganda (*cont.*)

7; Bunyoro's possible conquest of, 102–5, 215–16n14; civil war in (19th century), 187, 232n13; cosmology of, 55; earliest documented description of, 20; flag of, 176; gender relations in, 156–57, 229n59; introductions and genealogies in, 12–13; "lost counties" (disputed territories) of, 215n8; maps of, 4, 28, 72, 74, 84, 114, 134; original nucleus of, 137; restoration of kingdom, 12, 191, 199n31; social hierarchy in, 135, 152–54; territorial expansion of, 131–35, 159–73. *See also* banana cultivation; clans and clanship; kings and kingship; oral histories/traditions; political complexity; public healing; royalty and royal officials; salt trade; state development and power; trade networks

Bunyoro: clans in, 10; dynastic narratives of, 106–7; initiation ceremonies in, 207–8n96, 208n103; marriage metaphor in, 209n113; Podi located in, 33, 202n17; possible conquest by, 102–5, 215–16n14. *See also* Kimera narrative

Burundi: clans in, 10; female mediums in, 229n62

Bushbuck clan, 161

Busoga. *See* Soga states

butaka. See clan estates (*butaka*)

Butambala: annexation and chief of, 160–61; meaning of word, 230n69

canoes, 44–46, 165, 205–6n63

centralization narrative, 3, 5, 7–9, 66, 137–38, 181–82

Chrétien, Jean-Pierre, 10

Christianity, 34, 54, 200n41. *See also*

biblical interpretations; missionaries and missionary attitudes

Christian Revolution, 232n13

Chwa, Daudi, 187

Civet Cat clan, 1–2, 100, 137, 223n15

clan estates (*butaka*): court cases concerning, 188–91, 233n18; maps of, 72, 74; near Magonga, 38, 204n37; shrines and sacred spaces (*biggwa*) on, 1–2, 13, 14, 68, 70–71, 73, 75; subdivisions associated with, 11; tours of, 13–14. *See also* shrines

clan formation: alliances vs. descent in, 113, 115, 147; clan narratives in process of, 79–81; composition of knowledge and, 68–69, 75–81; in context of state formation, 158–73; historical context of, 6; Kibuuka and, 146–49; *nkuni* spirits in, 36–37; transition to intensive banana cultivation and, 92–96; web of therapeutic networks in, 69–75

clans and clanship: alternative ways of thinking about, 5–7, 14, 25–26; assumptions in earlier depictions of, 9–10; collective well-being and knowledge linked in histories of, 68–69, 75–81; current practices of, 191–93; development funding distributed through, 233n19; geographic recurrence of names of, 198n21; indigenous status (*bannansangwa*) of, 76–77, 210n11; Kintu and Kisolo's altercation viewed from, 61–64; Kintu and Nambi's marriage viewed from, 55–59; leaders of, 12, 121, 158–70; list and distribution of, 72; matrilineal, 9, 198n19; number and size of, 10–11, 13, 199n27; patrilineal, 9; public healing, political violence, and, 112–

21; roles in installation rites, 136–
37, 223n15; royal power juxtaposed
to development of, 158–73; social
tensions in early 20th century, 190–
91; state-formation role of, 131–35;
terminology of, 9–10, 198n23;
therapeutic network formation and,
68, 69–75. *See also* clan estates
(*butaka*); clan formation; shrines;
totems; trade networks
clanship/collective well-being/political
complexity relationship: approach
to, 2–3, 6–7, 14–15; banana
cultivation and, 67–69; Kimera
narrative as lens on, 98–99; Kintu
narratives as encapsulating, 64–66;
possibilities opened by, 184–85;
spiritual and social reconfigurations
in context of, 65–66, 68–69, 93–94,
182–83; state development in, 183–
84. *See also* clans and clanship;
collective well-being; oral
histories/traditions; political
complexity
Cohen, David, 37, 225–26n33
collective well-being: clan contributions
in promoting, 2; of clans and
kingdom, 131–32; clanship and
knowledge linked with, 68–69, 75–
81; concept of, 15; personal well-
being linked to, 70–71, 73; political
development in context of, 6–7;
rituals concerning, 39–48, 73, 75;
trade networks and, 129–30;
violence to ensure, 99, 119. *See also*
public healing; spirit mediums and
public healers
colobus monkey as totem, 56–57,
208n103
Colobus Monkey clan: Bussi shrine of,
70–71; clan estates of, 204n37,

223n15; in Kimera narrative, 119,
120–21; Kintu and Nambi in context
of, 56–59; territorial spirit
protecting, 2
colonialism: Buganda and Bunyoro
territorial struggles in, 103–4;
practices targeted for eradication in,
22; royal officials and indirect rule
of, 3. *See also* intellectual history
Colville, Henry, 127, 215n8
communities: access to productive land,
129–30; banana cultivation's effects
on, 90–94, 213–14n49; clan concept
and, 68–69; development funding
for, 233n19; moral economy and,
16; processes for creating, 6–7, 79–
81, 161–62; ritual practices for
prosperity of, 39–48, 231n93;
violence for benefit of, 99, 119. *See
also* collective well-being; public
healing
Connah, Graham, 128
Crazzolara, J. P., 104
Crow clan, 126, 171, 191
Crummell, Alexander, 199–200n40
Cunningham, J. F., 32
cwezi (mediums): as hunters, 110;
initiation ceremonies in, 207–8n96;
as traders, 125–26; violence and,
118–19, 122, 125. *See also* Ndahura
cwezi (spirits): as new category of spirits,
85, 118, 222n98; spirit possession
(*kubándwa*) for, 85–86, 108, 128–29.
See also Ndahura
Cwezi traditions: Kimera narrative and,
103–4, 105; origins of people, 113,
115; otter totem in, 209n121; spirit
possession (*kubándwa*) in, 108, 117–
19, 217n38; Tembuzi leader Isaza in,
56–57, 208n102; underworld images
in, 117, 208n101. *See also* Ndahura

89–91, 92–93, 213–14n49; on
ebitongole, 231n94; as influence, 21–
22; on *mailo* estates, 188–89; on
reciprocal obligation, 204n47,
222n1; on royal medicines, 161;
on territorial expansion and
destabilization, 159, 172
Hattersley, C. W., 54, 206n64
Heart clan, 171
Herbert, Eugenia, 220n73
Hippopotamus clan, 11, 167
historical linguistics: bananas and
banana cultivation evidenced in, 87–
88, 89, 212n37, 212–13n38; benefits
and limits of, 21; glottochronology
in, 211n25; Great Lakes Bantu
classification in, 82, 211n25; Great
Lakes geography in, 84; as key to
temporal framework for *kubándwa,*
81, 83–86. *See also* Great Lakes Bantu
languages; Luganda (language)
historical narratives: of clans, 7–11, 69–
70; different ways of thinking about,
25–27; historical vs. mythical in, 5,
102–5; incommensurability of, 193;
kinship in, 8–9; of Kintu Episode,
35–36; of precolonial vs. recent past,
23–24; repositories for, 14; of royal
dynasties, 3; sources of, 18–21;
subjects appropriate for, 31, 32. *See
also* biblical interpretations;
historical linguistics; intellectual
history; oral histories/traditions
hunters and hunting, 110, 166, 217n30,
231n92

Ijwi Island clanship, 210n2
inheritance and succession, 68, 91–92,
214n50. *See also* fertility concerns;
land tenure (land-use rights)
initiation ceremonies: at Bakka, 137,

219n66; individual's social standing
evidenced by, 227n47; pots used in,
109, 216n25; rite of (birth) passage
in, 108–10; for spirit mediums, 63–
64, 207–8n96, 208n103; violent
elements of, 118. *See also* spirit
possession (*kubándwa*)
intellectual history: of colonial
Buganda, 31–35, 175–78, 187–88; of
colonial Bunyoro, 102–4; on Kintu,
29, 31–36, 202–3n24, 203n26,
203n28
ironworkers and iron trade, 124–25,
128, 171, 220n79, 221n90
Isaza (Tembuzi leader), 56–57, 208n102
ivory trade, 221n89

jjembe (sing.; charm), 38, 79, 137, 160–
63
Jjunju (*kabaka*), 80, 135, 170–71
Johnston, Harry, 52, 54

kabaka. See kings and kingship
Kabaka Foundation, 233n19
Kabazzi (title), 44–45
Kaggwa (Kagwa), Apolo: on Ganda
spirits and practices, 18; on
Grasshopper clan, 217n40; on
Kibuuka, 148, 149, 151, 225n29,
226nn37–38; on Kimera, 102–3,
221n90; on Kintu, 32–33, 35; on
Kintu and Kisolo's altercation, 61;
on Kintu and Nambi, 52, 53–54;
Kiwanuka's translation of, 179–81;
on Nende, 150, 227n42; political
authority and perspective of, 3, 187–
88, 207n88; on royal installation
rites, 136, 224n23; on shrine
building, 204n45; spelling of name,
197n7
Kalule, George William, 2, 27

Kasirye, J. S., 227n45

Kasujja (ancestor of Colobus Monkey
clan), 2, 120, 122

Kasujju, Kalali, 80

Kateregga (kabaka), 132, 159–60, 162–
63

Katwe salt deposits, 125, 127, 128,
221n88, 222n95

Kawalya, Nelson, 192

Kenny, Michael G., 45, 205–6n63

Kibiro: praise ritual at, 115; salt deposits
of, 125, 127–29

Kibuuka (lubaale): origins of, 143–44,
177; shrine and officials of, 145–50,
151–54, 156, 226nn37–39

Kiganda, Kajabaga, 80, 171

Kigave (Pangolin), 30–31, 49–50

kiggwa (pl. biggwa), 1–2, 13, 14, 73, 75.
See also shrines

Kimera (kabaka): assent to throne, 98;
Mawanda's power compared with,
142–43; Rukidi linked to, 103,
215n11; as spirit medium, 108–11,
121, 126, 130; as trader, 126–27, 130,
221n90. See also Kimera narrative

Kimera narrative: alternative
understandings of, 108–11;
approach to, 98–99; companions'
contributions in, 112–21; details of,
99–102; historical framework of,
127–28; historiography of, 102–5,
215n6, 215–16n14, 216–17n28;
kubándwa networks, trade, and
disease in, 126–30; Ndahura's story
juxtaposed to, 106–8, 113, 115–17,
122–24, 217n30, 218n48

kings and kingship: afflictions of, 164;
alternative focus away from, 186–87;
carriers of (mukongozzi), 120; clanless
nature of, 46; critical shift in
authority of, 142–43, 184; as

"cultural leaders," 232–33n17;
death and marriage of, 59; deaths
due to smallpox, 220n74; focus on
political role of, 3, 5, 197n10;
generations of, 224–25n27; healers'
conflicts with, 154–58, 228nn52–54;
installation rites for, 39, 47–48, 102;
institutionalization of divide with
healers, 6–7, 142–43; instrumental
power of, 138–43; list of, 133;
military counsel of, 143–54; okukula
kwa kabaka (ceremony) of, 137. See
also Buddo (Naggalabi) Hill

kinship: hierarchy in, 147;
interpretation of clan histories and,
69; in language of clanship, 198n23;
primacy of, 8–10

Kintu (founder of Buganda): derivation
of name, 36; as dynasty founder and
as kabaka, 64; historiography of, 29,
31–36, 203n26, 203n28; leopard
totem linked to, 203n35; as migrant
and portable spirit, 34–36, 138–39,
141–42, 202–3n24, 203n26, 203n28;
spirit medium assuming identity of,
223–24n19. See also Kintu narratives

Kintu narratives: altercation with Kisolo
in, 27, 60–64; alternative
conceptions of, 27, 29–30, 67;
Bemba defeated in, 27, 30–31,
39, 48, 50, 140; creative and
instrumental power in, 138–43;
dwelling place of spirit in, 223n18;
historical categorization and
transformation of, 31–36, 39;
historiography of, 31–36, 52–54,
60–61, 65–66, 202–3n24, 207n88;
Kasujja's initial encounter in, 2;
Kimera narrative juxtaposed to, 102;
Kintu and Nambi's marriage in, 50–
60; Magonga ritual site in, 36–39,

48, 76, 100; Mubiibi's role in, 30, 48–50; settings of, 64–66; temporal framework for, 81, 83–86
Kisingiri, Zakaria, 187
Kisolo. *See* Ssebyoto, Kisolo Muwanga
Kitara epic, 21, 107–8
Kiwanuka, M. S. M., 164, 179–81, 214n4
Klieman, Kairn, 16–17, 184–85
knowledge: circumstances and sites underlying production of, 20–26, 175–80; clans and collective health linked with, 68–69, 75–81, 183–84; colonial control of, 3; social organization of, 96
Kottak, Conrad P., 94, 214n55
kubándwa. *See* spirit possession (kubándwa)
kulanya (activity of introduction), 12–13
Kuper, Adam, 7–8, 198n15

Lake Victoria: banana cultivation along, 89–96, 213n43, 213–14n49; powers associated with, 45–46; pythons and ritual practices for prosperity of communities along, 39–48, 231n93; spirit associated with, 38. *See also* Great Lakes region
Landau, Paul, 19, 200n45
land tenure (land-use rights): ancestral spirits and control of, 93–96; intensive banana cultivation and, 90–92, 213–14n49; mailo estates and redistribution of, 188–91. *See also* inheritance and succession; lineage theory
Lanning, E. C., 216n27
Lark clan, 231n93
Lejju, B. Julius, 212n37
leopard as totem, 38, 203n35
Leopard clan, 38–39, 49–50, 204n37

Le Veux, R. P., 52, 53, 54, 126–27, 225n29
lineage theory: continued use of, 198n15; critiques of, 7–10; matrilineal societies in, 8, 198n16, 198n19; patrilineal societies in, 8, 92–93
lineality: banana cultivation and, 91–92; firstcomer status in, 40
Lion clan, 171, 204n37
literacy, 31, 32
Livingston, Julie, 15
lubaale (national spirits): composition of, 143–49; firstcomer status and, 161; gods distinguished from, 177–78; translation of term, 180. *See also* Kibuuka (lubaale); Mukasa (lubaale)
Luganda (language): emergence of, 84; kika in, 10; Kintu Episode written in, 32; kuwooya in, 57–58; mmandwa in, 57–58, 208n110; okugalula in, 118; "pangolin" in, 202n6; "python" in, 47–48; terms for bananas in, 88; "to begin" in, 207–8n96; training in, 11; translations of, 179–80
Lugard, Frederick, 187, 222n95
Lukiiko (parliament), 12, 188, 189–91
Lukumirizi (honorific designation), 42, 204n44
Lukungo, Kawuula, 211n21
lungfish as totem, 47
Lungfish clan: alliances of, 160; ancestral ghosts (mizimu) of, 71; history debated among, 206n65; principal estates of, 74; python center of, 39, 46–48; role in royal installation rite, 136–37; shrine and mediums of, 228n53
Lwo migrations, 104

MacGaffey, Wyatt, 8, 161, 187, 198n16, 198n19

Magobwe (python spirit), 44, 228–29n56

Magonga ritual site: clans contributing to, 38–39, 203n35, 204n37; as Kintu's "home," 37–39, 48, 76, 100, 143; Mawanda's visit to, 139–43

marriage as metaphor, 58–59, 63–64, 209n113. See also spirit possession (kubándwa)

Marsh Antelope clan, 167

Mawanda (kabaka): historical context of, 224–25n27; Kintu courted by, 139–43; territorial expansion under, 132–33, 135, 142, 165–69

Mawokota: aphorisms linked to, 227n44; Kibuuka's shrine in, 146–48; Otter clan's origins and territorial spirits in, 60, 62–64, 76

Mayanja, Musa Lwanga, 199n30

mayembe (pl. for jjembe; charms), 38, 79, 137, 160–63

McCaskie, T. C., 186

Médard, Henri, 34

mediums. See spirit mediums and public healers

methodology, 20–26. See also oral histories/traditions

misambwa spirits: acts of sacrifice and dedication to, 40–44, 45–46; alliances between, 62–64; concept of, 2, 37, 42; firstcomer status and, 161; in legitimation of rule, 168–70; pythons and water linked to, 185. See also ancestral ghosts (mizimu); Bemba the Snake; Kintu (founder of Buganda); spirit portability

missionaries and missionary attitudes, 34, 54, 200n41. See also biblical interpretations

Miti, James, 52, 53

mizimu. See ancestral ghosts (mizimu)

Mugalala/Mugarra (ancestor of Grasshopper clan), 113, 117–18

Muganga, Katwere, 60, 76

Mugwanya, Stanislas, 187

Mukasa (lubaale), 43, 47, 56, 79, 164, 205–6n63

Mukiibi. See Ndugwa, Mukiibi

Munno (newspaper), 32, 35, 52, 54

musambwa. See misambwa spirits

Musa spp., 87–88, 212nn33–34, 212nn36–37, 212–13n38. See also banana cultivation

Museveni, Yoweri, 71, 199n31, 210n4, 232–33n17

Mushroom clan, 150–51, 223n15

music and musicians, 110–11, 112

Mutebi (kabaka), 80, 132, 163–65, 229–30n65, 230n82

Mutebi, Ronald Muwenda, 191, 199n31

Muteesa (kabaka), 32, 33–34

Muteesa, Frederick Walugembe, II, 199n31

Muwanga (spirit), 62–64, 76–78. See also Ssebyoto, Kisolo Muwanga

Muwanga, Kisolo, 142

Mwanga (kabaka), 187

Mwanga II (kabaka), 223n10, 223n12

Naduli, Zakayo, 189–90

Nakabaale (priest), 56, 57, 146–47

Nakibinge, 44–45, 143–45, 224–25n27, 225n29

Nambi (Kintu's wife), 50–60, 63–64

Namuggala (kabaka): historical context of, 224–25n27; installation and rites of, 135–37, 138, 140–41, 224n23; political strategy of, 157–58

Nannyonga-Tamusuza, Sylvia, 229n59

National Resistance Movement, 199n31, 232–33n17

Ndahura: as cwezi medium, 109; as cwezi

political complexity (*cont.*)
  Kisolo's altercation viewed in, 61–
  64; public healing entwined with, 6–
  7, 14, 16–20, 98–99, 161–62; wider
  view of, 186–87
Porch Water clan, 171
power, creative and instrumental, 16–
  17, 137, 138–43. *See also* state
  development and power
priests: interests of mediums vs.,
  204n45; ritual practices for
  prosperity performed by, 40–44;
  roles of, 38, 47, 203n35, 204n43. *See
  also* spirit mediums and public
  healers
princesses: gender relations, authority,
  and, 156–57, 229n59; seats of,
  229n62; as spirit wives (and spies),
  63–64, 151–52, 227n45, 228n54,
  229nn57–58, 229–30n65; as threat,
  229n61
prosperity: guarantors of, 68–69; of
  intensive banana cultivation, 95–96;
  rituals for, 39–48, 231n93; trade and
  public healing linked to, 125–26. *See
  also* collective well-being; public
  healing
public healers. *See* priests; spirit
  mediums and public healers
public healing: clanship, political
  violence, and, 112–21; concept of, 15,
  20, 95; control of fertile lands in
  context of, 93–96; de-territorialized,
  88–89; disease spread, violence,
  and trade in context of, 122–30;
  documentary record of, 18–19; as
  form of practical reason, 19, 78, 95,
  178; gatherings around *kiggwa* for,
  73, 75; kings' and healers' conflicts
  and, 154–58, 228nn52–54; ordinary
  individuals' participation in, 151–

54; political activities entwined with,
  6–7, 14, 16–20, 98–99, 161–62;
  political violence and, 149–54;
  reconfigured boundaries of, 65–66,
  68–69, 93–94, 182–83; religion used
  to describe and interpret, 17–19,
  177–78, 199–200n40, 200n41;
  therapeutic networks formed in, 68,
  69–75; wider history of, 185–87. *See
  also* collective well-being; prosperity;
  public healing complexes; spirit
  mediums and public healers
public healing complexes: competition
  among, 61–62; Otter clan's role in,
  62–64; regional nature of, 49–50. *See
  also* collective well-being; public
  healing; shrines; spirit mediums and
  public healers
public health (Western concept), 15
pythons: arm and neck rings styled as,
  204–5n49; name of, 201n4; ritual
  practices linked to, 39–48, 231n93;
  territorial spirits and water linked to,
  44, 45–46, 185, 205n56. *See also*
  Bemba the Snake

rainmakers and rainmaking, 185, 204–
  5n49, 205n56
Ray, Benjamin C., 197n10, 203n26,
  224n21
reciprocal obligation, 43, 93–94, 161,
  204n47, 222n1
Reedbuck clan, 166–67
Reid, Richard, 133, 152, 159, 222n95
religion: African "natural religiosity"
  and, 199–200n40; dichotomy of
  state and, 180; as term, 19, 200n45.
  See also biblical interpretations
rituals: history of royal, 197n10; for
  kangawo, 168–70; pots used in, 109,
  216n25; for prosperity, 39–48,

231n93; related to new moon, 37–38, 41, 115–16, 148–49; whiteness/blackness distinction in, 56–57. *See also* Buddo (Naggalabi) Hill; drums; initiation ceremonies; spirit possession (*kubándwa*)

Robertshaw, Peter, 212n37

Roscoe, John: on Kibuuka, 149, 151, 226n37, 226n39, 227n40; on Kimera, 221n90; on Kintu, 33, 52, 54; on *mayembe*, 161–62; on spirits and ritual practices, 18, 40, 41–42, 43, 44, 48, 157, 229n57

Rossel, Gerda, 88, 212n34

royal and dynastic sources: attempts to shape historical discourse, 105; on Bemba, 35, 46; on Buganda's past, 3, 5, 197n10; on Kimera, 100–102, 104–5; on Ndahura, 106–8. *See also* intellectual history; Kaggwa (Kagwa), Apolo

royalty and royal officials: absence of royal clan and, 217n39; centralization of, 5; clan development juxtaposed to, 158–73; historicized perspective on, 98–99; ideology of, 131–32; indirect rule of, 3; narratives recited for, 112; royal children's caretakers and, 164–65; symbols of, 38, 185, 223n11. *See also* Buddo (Naggalabi) Hill; Kimera narrative; kings and kingship; Kintu (founder of Buganda); political authority and leadership; princesses

Rukidi, Isingoma Mpuga, 103, 215n11

Rwanda: clanship in, 10; mediums in, 229n62; smallpox in, 219n69

salt trade: deposits and production, 125, 127–29, 221n88; items exchanged in, 124–25; in Kimera narrative, 101–2,

126–27; political control of, 125, 129–30; praise rituals and, 115–16

Schoenbrun, David: on banana cultivation, 87–88, 212nn36–37; on creative and instrumental power, 16; on glottochronology and Great Lakes Bantu, 211n25; as influence, 21; on spirit possession, 67–68, 81, 83–85, 222n98

Schoffeleers, Matthew, 185–86

Seed clan, 161

Sekamwa, Eriya, 189–90

Sheep clan, 11, 146–49, 158, 160, 167

shrines: acts of sacrifice and dedication at, 40–44; creative power of, 138–43; different interests in, 204n45; fields of efficacy for particular, 85; fires within, 204n44; *kiggwa* compared with, 1–2; networks forged by webs of, 69, 75, 95–96; preserving materials of, 176–78; as refuges, 155, 228–29n56; repairs to, 47; as repositories and settings for narratives, 14, 64–66; ritual and political power fused in, 30

slavery: Ganda practice of, 135, 152–53, 231n94; trade of, 219n72, 221n89

snakes, 40, 44. *See also* Bemba the Snake; pythons

social evolutionist scholarship, 7–10

social health. *See* public healing

Soga states: Bumogera in, 225–26n33; female mediums in, 229n62; Kintu character in histories of, 36–38, 203n35; limits of exogamy and clan name as defined in, 11; raids into, 166, 167

Speke, John Hanning, 20, 110, 112, 132

spirit mediums and public healers: creative power of, 138–43; diversity of, 16; firstcomer lineages as

Stanley, Henry Morton, 34, 109–11, 126, 215n6, 216–17n28
state development and power: alternative explanations of, 7–9; Buddo rites and, 137–38; centralization narratives in, 3, 5, 7–9, 66, 181–82; clan development juxtaposed to, 158–73; clanship and public healing in context of, 183–84; clans' role in, 131–35; Germany and Buganda compared, 203n28; limits on, 96–97; organized violence linked to, 99; triumphalist version of, 159
Stephens, Rhiannon, 212–13n38

Tantala, Renee: on ancestral ghosts, 56–57, 117; on arm and neck rings, 204–5n49; on *cwezi* spirits, 85, 108, 117; as influence, 21; on Ndahura, 108, 115–16; on pythons and rainmaking, 205n56
Taylor, David, 212n37
termite hills, 184–85
territorial spirits. *See* Bemba the Snake; Kintu (founder of Buganda); *misambwa* spirits
Thruston, Arthur, 127
tortoise as totem, 30–31, 49, 50, 202n7
totemic avoidances, 10–11, 198n21
totems: characteristics and significance of, 38, 49, 56–57, 61–62, 77, 78, 203n35, 206n76, 208n103, 209n121, 217n38; diviners' and mediums' choices of, 206–7n77; primary and secondary, 11, 199n29
trade networks: disease vectors along, 122, 123–30; literacy linked to, 32; monitoring of, 166–67; political control of, 99, 125–26, 129–30; relationships among traders along,

221nn84–85; song of, 125, 221n82; territorial expansion to control, 132–33, 135, 163, 170–71; tombs of kings and markets linked in, 221n83. *See also* banana cultivation; bark-cloth production; hunters and hunting; ironworkers and iron trade; salt trade
translation, 19, 177, 179–80, 200n45
truth regimes (concept), 23
Tucker, Alfred Bishop, 200n41
Twaddle, Michael, 35, 202n17
twin symbol, 185, 223n11

Uganda: clan names and totemic avoidances in, 198n21; political instability in, 12, 199n31
Uganda Agreement (1900), 187–88, 215n8
Uganda Journal, 103
Uganda Museum, 175–77
Uganda Protectorate, 65, 187, 215n8

Vansina, Jan, 9, 23, 24
Victoria, Lake. *See* Lake Victoria
violence, political and organized: clan and state development linked in, 158–73; disease spread linked to, 122–23; fighting forces involved in, 135, 151–54; king's control of, 142–43; as predating centralization, 99; public healing activities as rallies for, 151–54; public healing, clanship, and, 112–21; refuges from, 155, 228–29n56; territorial expansion and, 132–35

Walumbe (Nambi's brother), 51, 53, 54, 55–56, 59
Walusimbi, Ssalongo Benedicto, 1–2
Wampamba, Tobi Kizito, 35

Wannema (spirit), 44–45, 146

water, bodies of: in ceremonies for kangawo, 169; praise rituals and, 115–16; territorial spirits and pythons linked to, 39–48, 185, 205n56. See also canoes; rainmakers and rainmaking; salt trade

Watts, Sheldon, 219n72

wealth in people (concept), 9

Welbourn, F. B., 216n27

White, Luise, 24

whiteness/blackness distinction, 56–57, 117

Willis, Justin, 9, 198n19, 198n21

Wilson, Charles Thomas, 52

Winy, Tito Gafabusa (pseud. K. W.), 103–4, 215n10

Wright, H., 33–34

Wrigley, Christopher: on banana cultivation, 212–13n38; on Bumogera, 225–26n33; on Ganda kings, 224–25n27; on Ganda territorial nucleus, 137; on Kaggwa's sources, 207n88; on Kimera, 215–16n14, 216n16; on Kintu and Bemba, 36; on ritual forms of authority, 96; sources of, 197n10

Yam clan, 204n37

Yoder, John, 65

Zimbe, Bartolomayo, 52, 223n10, 223n12